HH

YOUR NEXT FIFTY YEARS

BY GINITA WALL

The Way to Save

The Way to Invest

BY VICTORIA F. COLLINS

Couples and Money
(with Suzanne Brown)

Divorce and Money
(with Violet Woodhouse and M. C. Blakeman)

BY GINITA WALL AND
VICTORIA F. COLLINS

Smart Ways to Save Money
During and After Divorce

Your Next Fifty Year$

. . . .

A COMPLETELY NEW WAY

TO LOOK AT HOW, WHEN,

AND *IF* YOU SHOULD RETIRE

Ginita Wall, CPA, CFP

Victoria F. Collins, Ph.D., CFP

An Owl Book

Henry Holt and Company | New York

Henry Holt and Company, Inc.
Publishers since 1866
115 West 18th Street
New York, New York 10011

Henry Holt® is a registered
trademark of Henry Holt and Company, Inc.

Published in Canada by Fitzhenry & Whiteside Ltd.,
195 Allstate Parkway, Markham, Ontario L3R 4T8.

Library of Congress Cataloging-in-Publication Data
Wall, Ginita.
Your next fifty years: a completely new way to look at how, when, and if you should retire / Ginita Wall, Victoria F. Collins.—1st ed.
p. cm.
"An owl book."
Includes index.
1. Retirement—United States—Planning. 2. Middle aged persons—Finance, Personal. 3. Retirement income—United States. I. Collins, Victoria F. (Victoria Felton), date. II. Title.
HQ1063.2.U6W349 1997 96-40390
646.7'9—dc21 CIP

ISBN 0-8050-4568-6

Henry Holt books are available for special promotions and premiums. For details contact: Director, Special Markets.

First Edition—1997

Designed by Victoria Hartman

Printed in the United States of America
All first editions are printed on acid-free paper. ∞

10 9 8 7 6 5 4 3 2 1

We dedicate this book to our clients,
colleagues, and friends who shared with us
their thoughts and dreams for their next fifty years.
This book is for all of you,
whether planning to retire or *never* to retire.

Contents

Acknowledgments

No book is ever the result of the authors' efforts alone. The many clients, friends, and financial professionals who shared information and insights have helped develop the theme of this book and we appreciate their openness and honesty.

Special thanks go to Laura Tarbox, CFP, one of the top advisers in the country on the subject of retirement planning. She provided invaluable assistance to this project at a time when we needed her most. We also appreciate the professional help and guidance of many, including Mary Claire Blakeman; Kathleen Hansen, CFP; Rick Keller, CFP; Candace Bahr; and David Collins.

Several people provided inspiration and perspectives pivotal to this book. As we read Gail Sheehy's book *New Passages,* we were impressed with her research, and we are pleased that our thoughts parallel her conclusions about how all of us will face the future. We give special thanks as well to Joe Dominguez and Vicki Robin for helping us grasp the powerful relationship between money and time, and for sharing their observations in their provocative book *Your Money or Your Life.*

Our agents, Michael Larsen and Elizabeth Pomada, deserve high praise for their efforts and helpful support in getting this book to you. Theresa Burns, our editor at Henry Holt, was outstanding. Her astute input, challenging questions, and wonderful support (including comments that were even readable) all went toward making this book the best it could be.

A Personal Introduction

Our stories are probably not that different from those of the many baby boomers we have as clients and friends. There are days we long to simply walk away from the stress, the intensity, the demands of our work lives. There are days when a run on the beach, a game of golf, a trip to a spa, or just the time to create a gourmet dinner at home seem more appealing than anything else we can think of. There are times when guilt sets in because we are too busy earning a living to spend the hours we'd like with children, grandchildren, parents, or friends. There are times when retiring seems like nirvana.

Then there is the other side—when work seems satisfying. When our colleagues, associates, coworkers, or clients praise the job we've done, we wonder how life would feel without the day-to-day stimulation, not to mention the month-to-month paycheck. Yes, part of what is good about working is the financial satisfaction of earning a living and supporting a lifestyle with which we feel more or less satisfied.

We have spent a lot of time thinking about work and nonwork alternatives, and probably you have too. Will retirement mean more choices or fewer choices for you? That's really the big question, isn't it? Will you be able to travel, play, enjoy, and renew, or will you be limited in what you can spend and where you can live? Will retirement be more satisfying for you, or will you become bored and miss the stimulation that you experience from your everyday existence in the workplace? Will you miss your coworkers and the feeling of community that you had as you banded together to accomplish the task at hand? Will you be able to find new friends in retirement with whom you have so much in common?

Don't Retire—
There Are Better Things in Life

Retirement doesn't have to be an either/or status. You don't have to abandon everything about work to embrace everything about play. You don't have to give up your roots to travel, or give up your work to cherish your family. There's a reason we call this book a completely new way to look at retirement. Retirement really does *complete* your life. The concept of retirement at age sixty-five was created to ease people's life a bit during the second half of their last decade—their sixties. But now that people are living into their eighties and beyond, the concept of retirement at sixty-five, or earlier, is a bit outmoded.

The average age of retirement is now fifty-seven, with nearly thirty years left to go. Why should you spend a full third of your life in idle days of golf and television? Do you really want to sacrifice now, working extra hard and cutting expenses to save, just so you can be idle later? Or do you want to begin now to enjoy leisure activities, to integrate retirement into your life now rather than delaying your current enjoyment until later retirement?

Fact of life: Six out of ten working Americans believe they will need to work at least part time during retirement.

Working gives our lives definition and a framework, as well as providing an income. When you reach retirement, you may want to work part time, do consulting, or even volunteer. You may want to learn new skills to help you expand your horizons—computer skills, music, hobbies.

The first third of your life was spent combining play with learning. The middle third is devoted to lots of work and some play. In the last third of life it is time to integrate all the aspects of your life, work and play and learning, into a grand finale—by learning new skills, creating new activities, exploring new careers, spending time with family, and making time for the pursuits that you have found exciting during the first two-thirds of your life.

That's why we say, Don't retire—there are better things in life. From our vantage point as financial advisers, we can tell you there may be alternatives to retiring that you've not yet thought of. Alternatives that may give you the best of both worlds—work and relaxation.

Retirement planning is not a sprint but a marathon. It is not about saving like crazy to retire in five years, but about planning your resources for a journey that will lead you through a number of paid and unpaid jobs, challenges, and tasks in the years ahead. How satisfying or unsatisfying that journey is depends on how well you invest and manage your financial resources so that you have choices. Whether you are thirty, forty, or fifty, you'll need to plan for your next fifty years. We feel so strongly about this that we've named this book just for your future: your next fifty years.

An Exercise to Get Started

Here's a little exercise you can do to get started completing your life. Make a list of the things you would like to do that you simply don't have the time, energy, or financial resources to accomplish right now. Our personal lists would include reading good books, honing our computer skills, playing tennis and golf, becoming proficient at the piano, spending time with family and friends, and of course travel, travel, travel.

Now list the reasons why you can't accomplish those goals—and don't merely say "lack of time" or "no money." Those aren't good enough reasons—you probably have as much money now as you ever will, and you certainly have available all of the time that is allotted to each of us every day. The question is, how are you spending it? What drains your time or money away from accomplishing your dreams, from completing your life? Are you spending too much time at work? Are you too busy providing for children and parents? Do you spend time and money on activities that are neither useful nor satisfying? Write these down on your list.

Now look at the list of things you want to accomplish in your life. Would you rather wait for retirement to do them or would you like to do them now, if possible? Of course you would like to get started now, you're probably thinking, but you haven't won the lottery, nor has a rich uncle died and left you a fortune. But it's not too late—you have a fortune right at your fingertips. All you have to do is salvage it, like a prospector panning for gold. Here's how to do it. Compare your list of things you want to do with the list of things that are draining your resources. Isn't there one thing that you could begin to accomplish now, by beginning to eliminate one element of your life that drains you?

For example, if you want to spend more time reading but your time is frittered away watching television, set yourself a goal to read one-half hour a night, and watch one-half hour less of television. You will be able to read a book or so a week, while still living your daily life. If reading was part of what you wanted to do in retirement, congratulations. You are beginning to integrate retirement into your life right now. You are easing your way into a complete life.

If travel is something you've wanted to do, but work is too pressing, perhaps you can negotiate with your boss for a short sabbatical in a year or two. Then begin to save the money you will need to fund that sabbatical. Take the time off, and then come back refreshed, your attitude transformed by your miniretirement, ready to plunge into a new phase of your complete life. That is what today's retirement is all about.

Some New Themes for Retirement

If you have thought about retiring, chances are you have already read several books, attended hours or even days of seminars, crunched numbers on your calculator or computer, and talked at length with your family, coworkers, friends, and maybe even financial advisers. In your thinking and planning, you must consider how some of the trends and themes that we see developing will impact you. These themes are part of why retirement planning today is very different from the way it was in our parents' time.

Social capital

Retirement planning is not about planning for a certain date but about planning for the rest of your life. It is about lifestyle planning, incorporating work and nonwork goals. And as you complete your life, you must integrate your finances into the rest of your life. As you consider the next fifty years, consider the concept of social capital—the concept of using financial resources and managing your time for positive results beyond your own well-being. For both of us, as financial advisers and authors, we are at a stage of life where we want to make a difference. We know we can do that by investing in or purchasing products from companies that have the same values we do. We can make a difference by using our time to reach a common good, through paid work or volunteerism. Take a few moments now to think about the social capital you can invest to make a difference in your world. What is important to you, and what can you do to help others? What would you like to be remembered for? Make a list of things you would like to accomplish in the years ahead, and as you proceed through this book, keep the list handy so you can add to it and make revisions.

User-friendly investing

As you integrate your finances to complete your life, consider the concept of user-friendly investing. More and more people are taking responsibility for their financial lives, using on-line investment services or discount brokers who go to great lengths to make investing appealing and accessible for everyone. We have also seen tremendous growth of investment clubs for both men and women. With responsibility for making appropriate retirement investments being shifted from the shoulders of employers to employees, these clubs provide a great way to combine socializing and access to investment know-how. For busy professional women with little time, investment clubs can take the place of the old coffee klatches. As their interests and responsibilities mature, today's women may have the *Wall Street Journal* on their laps rather than children.

Egonomics, a term coined by Faith Popcorn, is another interesting theme and is a response to the high-tech world we live in. It suggests we will value companies that personalize their products in this increasingly depersonalized world we live in. The implication for those considering retirement is that the program and the investments are not one size fits all but must reflect the personality and lifestyle of the individual.

Vacation Deficit Disorder

From time to time we have both suffered from "Vacation Deficit Disorder," brought on by too little time off, and chances are you have suffered from it too. Just think though of the options we have available today to combat this malaise. During the next fifty years, you can bet the trend will be toward more creative options and more use of those options. Sabbaticals to rejuvenate and retool might mean less need to retire and more productivity over time. As a way of reducing the stress of the rat race, many are turning to voluntary simplicity or cashing out. They are exploring ways to reduce expenses and therefore lower the need for income from high-powered, high-paying, but unsatisfying jobs.

Retirement role reversals

Role reversals for men and women are yet another very different factor that impacts retirement today but did not in the past. We're talking about the women who want to work and the men who want to retire. It works fine if they are not married to each other, but it can cause conflict if they are. This may well be one of the issues that you must face as you plan for your retirement.

Retirement Is a Process, Not an Age

Let's get up close and personal. If you stopped working now, would you have enough money to retire? Will retirement mean the freedom to do all you want to do but haven't yet had time to do? Or would it be a struggle to make ends meet on what you've saved or what you expect to receive from your company pension or retirement plan? Is your picture of retirement a scary thought or a pleasant daydream?

If you are like the seventy-seven million baby boomers, who began turning fifty in 1996, chances are you've given some thought to these questions, and many of the following may be true for you:

- You're fed up with the message that baby boomers aren't saving enough.
- You've been bombarded by financial advisers and stockbrokers offering seminars on retirement planning, only to find there is a hidden sales agenda.
- You've tried the retirement-planning software, run the what-ifs, and still can't get a clear picture of what you can expect financially.
- You wonder how life without work would be for you and your spouse.
- You wonder if you can retire.
- You wonder if you should retire.

If any of these ring true for you, read on. We've "been there" with hundreds of clients and thousands of others who are feeling the same way you do. We hope this book will transform the way you look at retirement and guide you through the decisions you'll be making this year, next year, and in the years ahead.

In the pages that follow, we will give you what you need to know about investing, using whatever retirement plans you have to your best advantage, protecting your assets, and much more. Fifty years is a long time, after all, and we know you want to make the best of it. We are confident that if you follow the steps that we suggest in each chapter, you not only will expand your options for thinking about retirement but can look forward to a great future with or without work.

But where do *you* come in? Only *you* can make the decision about whether and when you want to retire and what lifestyle you want to enjoy. There will be trade-offs for you to make. It's up to you to choose. We will give you all of the facts, figures, and information you need to know about retiring. Then we'll nudge you to go beyond that data and help you explore the deeper priorities and impact of your decisions.

The fact is, retirement is not what it was in our parents' age—we live longer and healthier, fewer of us have pensions, and we enjoy more options for our future today. Retirement, as we have known it, is an obsolete concept. We'll tell you what you can expect as well as how to make a plan for retirement that includes renewal, refocus, and recharge. Instead of a single date in time or an age marking the change in what you do with your daily life, you must learn to think of lifelong learning, lifelong working, lifelong experiencing. If you do that, we can almost guarantee that you'll have a longer life and that the quality of that longer life will be enhanced. This can happen by not retiring—not in the sense you're used to, anyway.

For you, as we have said before, the message may be, Don't retire—there are better things in life. If you do opt for full retirement, this book will help you gain a new perspective on what you expect, want, and need from the retirement you are planning.

What You'll Find in This Book

Throughout this book, we'll challenge you to rethink your retirement ideas. In part I, "Do You *Really* Want to Retire?" we look at commonly held myths and misconceptions about retirement. We also explore your attitudes toward retirement, what really goes on between the balance sheets, how men and women differ when it comes to earning, saving, spending, and yes, planning their retirement. You'll learn how to identify your individual differences and whether you and your spouse, if you are married, are aligned or apart in your financial life. We discuss how the "triple squeeze" may be pinching you, and give you some ideas on how to reduce the pressure by communicating more effectively with your partner, children, and parents about your financial goals and needs.

As you begin creating a plan to complete your life in retirement, you may be surprised to learn that investments favored for retirement may actually lose you money; that saving for your retirement versus your children's college may actually *pay* their tuition. In part II, "Getting Ready," we cover what you need to know about investing, how to get the maximum benefit from whatever plans you have, and why women need retirement planning more than men do. You'll learn that if you are off to a late start, there are twelve things you can do to catch up quickly.

What about the unexpected, unplanned, and nontraditional? Part III covers how to kiss the rat race good-bye through early retirement or combat Vacation Deficit Disorder by giving you options for combining part work with part retirement. We also look at what you need to know about early retirement and coping with changes such as divorce, death of a spouse, disability, or loss of your job.

Chapters 10, 11, and 12 in part IV show you how to make the most of retirement—lifestyle choices, where to live, how to invest, how to minimize taxes, and insurance and estate planning. We give some specific action steps to keep your nest egg growing. You'll also find a time line to make both your planning and your life easier.

Throughout the book you'll find solid, practical information in Smart Tips sections, which are highlighted. Additional resources—books, magazines, software, an asset location inventory—as well as a handy glossary of investment terms are in the back of the book.

We encourage you to use this book as a step-by-step guide for the important decisions you are making right now. As you work your way through the book, you will find your attitude toward retirement changing. In the end this book is likely to transform the way you think about retirement, and you will start integrating retirement into your daily routine as you begin the journey to complete your life in your next fifty years.

We wish you a happy, healthy, and prosperous retirement, *whenever* you choose it.

PART I

DO YOU *REALLY* WANT TO RETIRE?

1

Surprising Truths about Retirement

If you are one of the four million baby boomers who turned fifty in 1996 or the seventy-three million more who will turn fifty in the years to come, you've probably been a guest or the honoree at a surprise party celebrating "the big five-oh." The party may be a surprise, but that half-century mark certainly is not. We think about the birthday long in advance and long afterward as well. For some it's a time to vow, "I've worked for others for the first fifty years, the next fifty are for me." Some find that fifty is tinged with sadness—at fifty they aren't as successful as they had hoped, and there's no turning back the clock. Others say it's just another birthday.

In your quiet moments, you may think about what life will be like after work. But retirement as our parents knew it may no longer be relevant today. As a matter of fact, it may even be obsolete.

Redefining Retirement

In the past, when death came a few years after retirement, it made sense to retire so you could enjoy the few years you had left. Now, though, you may live thirty, forty, or even fifty years beyond the traditional retirement ages of fifty-five, sixty-two, or sixty-five. For some of us, the span of our retirement years may actually exceed our work years. To play golf, travel, or indulge that hobby you never had time for may be your dream as you accept the "gold watch." But watch out: the good life may get monotonous. William Hogarty, senior partner with a large national accounting firm, received golf lessons and a trip when the company threw a "going away" party for him. But after a few years, though he enjoyed the links and the respite, he came back as a part-time consultant and now works almost as much as he did previously.

Retirement may also be an obsolete concept because—here's the hard part—you may not have enough financial resources saved to support the lifestyle you would like to enjoy for the next thirty to fifty years. For future retirees, a retirement that works may well be a working retirement. Fortunately there are many options for supplementing retirement income and still enjoying leisure time, everything from part time to flex time, to telecommuting, to turning a hobby into a moneymaker. It's a matter of finding what works for you.

It may make more sense to incorporate what's good about retirement into your work life now. Take a moment or two to visualize what you would most enjoy doing if you were retired. For us, reading, listening to classical music, watching the ocean, and working at a less intense pace rank right up there. We've both found that we can incorporate more of these activities into our current work lives if we simply prioritize and plan. That's only part of it, though. It's important to know the facts of what life might be like ahead:

1. In 1978 only 4 percent of the population reached age sixty-five financially independent and able to support retirement. That percentage remains pretty much the same today.

2. One in three baby boomers will reach at least age eighty-five. Seven out of ten baby boomer women will outlive their husbands. And baby boomers now represent one-third of the U.S. population.

3. Boomers have unreasonably high expectations of their retirement. Their expectations are unrealistic because

• home equity will not represent as significant a percentage of retirement assets as it once did;

• medical costs will increase by 200 to 250 percent over their lifetime;

• local and state property taxes are increasing, thus threatening their retirement cash flow, and energy, food, and other costs will increase;

• plans are currently before the Senate and the House that would allow companies to tax the $100 billion surplus in 22,400 pension plans covering eleven million workers and two million retirees. Without the surpluses, there may be no cost-of-living raises for retirees; and

• companies might reduce future benefits to avoid making the huge contributions needed to keep pace with aging baby boomers in their work force.

Don't be a DUMP or a LIMP

The future isn't a pretty picture, says Craig Karpel, author of *The Retirement Myth* (HarperCollins, 1995). He suggests that in the year 2015 there may be homeless shelters set up to help DUMPs (destitute unprepared mature people). He predicts a world in which Social Security will be a thing of the past, pensions will be in jeopardy, and baby boomers will live longer and need more long-term care than we can imagine. Cuba and Mexico will become health-care resorts to which Americans, weary of the rationing of medical care, will flock in increasing numbers for treatment. Karpel also predicts worldwide economic collapse as boomers sell investments and homes to raise cash on which to live.

Other researchers suggest that Karpel may be way off the mark. Richard Easterlin and Christine Schaeffer of the University of Southern California and Diane Macunovich of Williams College say that studies of household income that indicate that people today aren't doing as well as their parents give an incomplete picture because they don't take into account family size or important lifestyle differences.

Think about it. You may have delayed marriage or not have married at all. You may have fewer kids than your parents, or you may have remained childless. If you are married, chances are both of you are working. To compare your parents' wealth to your own, these researchers considered "average income per adult equivalent," which takes into account the number of adults and children who share each household's income. Because today's households are smaller, in real terms, boomers today are about two-thirds *better off* than their parents were at the same age. You may not have the same home ownership wealth that your parents' generation did, but your income advantage may leave you better off, according to Easterlin, Schaeffer, and Macunovich. They figure the average net worth of baby boomers was $52,800 in 1989, while people born from 1918 to 1927 had a net worth of $24,636 in 1989 dollars at comparable ages.

But here is the catch: the lifestyle adjustments that give your generation a higher standard of living will also make for a lonelier retirement. Even if boomers get wise and avoid being DUMPs, they may still end up financially secure but lonely LIMPS (lonely, independent, mature people). The proportion who will not have married by age sixty-five is projected to be 50 percent larger than it was for your parents' age group. High divorce rates make it far less likely that the retired boomers will be living with spouses. Baby boomers comprised the first generation that did not replace itself. In most cases baby boomers had more siblings than children. Fewer children mean that boomers may not have as many grown children around in their sunset years.

All of these factors come together to yield new highs in the proportion likely to live alone in retirement, the researchers say. They estimate that more than one-third of the men and women born from 1946 to 1955 will be living alone when they enter retirement, compared with just over 20 percent in their parents' generation. That means they will have to fund their retirement alone. Granted, for those boomers who have fewer or no children, in theory they should have larger retirement funds. However, it seldom seems the case that lower education and child-rearing costs mean more dollars socked away. Other lifestyle expenses always seem to gobble up the difference.

Retirement-Planning Myths

Financial security and quality of life—that's the bottom line, isn't it? Have you put off saving for your retirement? There's never a good time to save, is there? Our clients share some pretty good rationalizations with us from time to time for putting off saving seriously now. "My benefits package will be all I need to retire." Or how about: "We'll probably inherit money from our parents," or, "Our kids will be on their own soon and we'll be able to save more." Here's a good one: "Our lifestyle is expensive but necessary now for our success—so it's okay that we're not saving much." Said an eternal optimist, "When we retire, it will cost us significantly less money to live." Do any of these sound familiar to you?

Much of what you have learned from TV and radio shows, brokerage houses and financial planners, is simply not true. The media, with facts, figures, and some falsehoods, has colored your thoughts regarding retirement. Not everything you've heard is wrong, of course, but there are a lot of myths regarding retirement planning and your financial present and future. Some of the myths are just plain misconceptions. Others once were true, but changes in the economy, society, and the demographics of our country have made them obsolete. Whether you are close to retirement or far away, following are some myths and misconceptions to avoid.

Myth Number One: Your Retirement Savings Should Last Fifteen Years

Not long ago, the average life span was seventy-seven years and the average retirement age was sixty-two. But today people are living longer, so the average life span is increasing. And the longer you live, the longer your projected life expectancy will be. Men now aged sixty-five can easily expect to see eighty, and women turning sixty-five now can expect to live to age eighty-eight. You can be sure that these numbers will increase, possibly dramatically, in the future.

Margaret, age fifty-five, who is planning to take an early retirement package from her company, which is downsizing, expressed the dilemma during one of our retirement-counseling meetings: "Jim's mom and dad are still alive and kicking. Longevity seems to run in his family and mine too. I'm afraid we're going to have to plan for at least forty years of being retired. And one of our biggest fears right now is running out of money before we run out of life."

The truth: These days, you must plan your resources to get you to at least age eighty-five. If you are between ages forty and fifty now, you'd better plan for age one hundred or more.

Myth Number Two: You'll Be in a Lower Tax Bracket When You Retire

Many of the tax-deferred advantages of IRAs, deferred annuities, and other retirement plans are based on the assumption that when you retire, you'll have less income and therefore will pay less in income taxes. If your salary is large just before you retire, it is possible you may drop into a lower tax bracket. But put aside tax brackets for the moment and think about the effective tax rate—that's the actual fraction of your income that the IRS takes. The effective tax rate has risen consistently ever since individual income taxes first came into being in 1913. As you lose deductions and exemptions, and as state and local taxes continue to climb, you may actually pay a greater percentage of your income for federal, state, and local taxes after retiring than you did while you were working.

> The whole point all these years of putting money aside in my retirement plan and IRAs was that I'd be in a lower tax bracket when I took it out. My accountant tells me that's not the case now at all. This tax thing is really confusing. I'm not sure I've done everything I could to minimize taxes over these last several years. And

> I'm not just talking income taxes, there's estate taxes too to consider. (Walter M., age sixty-one, ready to retire)

The truth: While you may pay less in taxes than when you were working, you'll probably pay a higher percentage *of your income to taxes after retirement than before.*

Myth Number Three: You'll Have More for Your Retirement by Staying with One Employer

In most retirement plans you must be employed by the company for a number of years before your retirement is fully vested. If you leave employment before you are vested, you forfeit your unvested benefits. So if you change jobs often, vesting requirements may prevent you from building up much money in pension plans. But you may still come out ahead by changing jobs. Why? Even with the maximum number of years of service, fixed pensions usually offer a retirement benefit of no more than about 59 percent of the highest salary you reach before retiring. So if you stay in a job for decades just to build your pension, but your salary is lower, your retirement benefit will be less than it could have been. If you can raise your salary by changing employers more often, you will boost your benefit from any pension plan that you are vested in. Chances are you'll also be able to contribute more to popular self-funded retirement plans, such as 401(k) plans. They often vest sooner than fixed plans, so you can take your money with you if you leave. If a new job pays 5 to 10 percent more and has good benefits, you're probably better off switching jobs—but be sure to put some of that extra income into a 401(k) plan or an IRA.

> I hated the job for years, but the retirement benefits were so good, I didn't feel I could walk away. Now that I've made the decision, actually I'll probably be better off because the new job I'm going to is putting a 401(k) in place and they'll even match our contributions. (Jason A., age forty-six)

The truth: You shouldn't stay in the wrong job for the right pension.

Myth Number Four: In Retirement, You Should Preserve Your Capital and Live Off Income

Think again. Your main goal should be to preserve your spending power. If you retire at fifty-five and live until ninety, your retirement will have lasted almost as long as your working years. Inflation can erode even a good-size nest egg. There are two things you can do in the early years of retirement that will help. First, consider continuing to build wealth by working part time. Second, be sure to include equities (stocks) for growth in your investment portfolio. If you put an extra $25,000 a year into your $500,000 retirement plan for the first ten years, you will probably outrun inflation forever and never use up your money. Later, when you stop working completely, you'll have more dollars to spend.

> We both retired four years ago. We thought we'd be able to live comfortably because we spend little and we've always been so conservative in our investments. But as inflation increases our expenses and the government increases taxes, it sure seems now that we're going to have to get better returns, or Jim will have to work part time. (Sandra J., age fifty-three)

The truth: It isn't wise to stop working completely or adding to your nest egg just because you are retired.

Myth Number Five: Most People Work to Live, Not Live to Work

We are about equally divided when it comes to deciding what is more important—work or leisure—according to a study done in forty countries by Internal Research Associates, coordinated by Roper-Starch Worldwide, a marketing, public opinion, and advertising research firm.

"Work is the important thing. The purpose of leisure time is to recharge people's batteries so they can do a better job," says Tom, a thirty-nine-year-old entrepreneur. The study shows that in the United States, 39 percent of the respondents agreed with him.

"No, leisure is more important. The reason we work is to make it possible to have the leisure time to enjoy life," says Rebecca, in her early forties. Thirty-seven percent of us agree with this statement. Another 20 percent of U.S. workers surveyed took the balanced approach, saying work and leisure are of equal importance.

The truth: Combining leisure and work produces the most satisfaction.

Myth Number Six: After Retirement, You Won't Work Again

According to a recent poll, about three-fifths of Americans believe they will have to work at least part time during retirement to maintain their standard of living. Kemper Financial and Roper-Starch Worldwide found that 71 percent of baby boomers (age thirty-three to fifty-one) and 81 percent of twenty-two- to thirty-two-year-olds believe Social Security payments will not be there when they retire.

Whether your retirement income is sufficient or not, there are some definite benefits to working after you retire. Staying mentally alert and challenged is important to improving quality of life and increasing longevity. Ken A. is a great example. Having retired and sold his business, he found that his expertise as a consultant was not only needed and valued but, as he says, "I have more energy and enthusiasm than I would if I had no meaningful work. I want to feel that I'm still able to make a contribution."

Retirement also affords you more options for part-time or flex-time involvement, so you can tailor a schedule to fit your needs and wants. "I have a sense of freedom that I didn't have when I was working for Pacific Bell," says young retiree Linda D. "I can plan my own schedule, and that sure means less stress."

Need another reason to continue working? Staying involved in the business world, even in a limited way, allows for easier reentry, should you desire to return. "I took this part-time position because you never know. I don't want to lose my edge, I need to stay current in medicine, just in case I do decide to go back someday," says Francine S., age fifty-one.

The truth: Before you retire, it is important to develop interests and hobbies that you might like to or need to call on later for income.

Myth Number Seven: Your Home Is Now Your Own

Just as retirement as we know it may be a concept of the past, so is the empty nest. Many people between the ages of forty and seventy have continued to support adult children in some way. Modern facts of life tell us that marriages fail, jobs are lost, financial ventures don't turn out, and adult children do return to the nest. This "boomerang baby" phenomenon has been well documented. "Since 1975, the number of young adults age 25–29 living with their parents has nearly doubled," says Sheldon Goldenberg, a sociologist at Canada's University of Calgary who studies the trend.

> I've always believed that the best thing we could give our kids was roots and wings. They seem to be well rooted here at home. They've gone to school, worked a bit, but now are back to save money—theirs. For sure not ours. (Gerald M., age fifty-two)

As a baby boomer, you are also part of the sandwich generation. Rather than having a home of your own, you may find it full of permanent guests, including adult children and elderly parents. Today an estimated 60 percent of the dependent elderly live with their adult children. As people live longer, more and more retirees will find themselves responsible for aging parents, many of whom need day-to-day care.

Even if no one actually moves in with you, your retirement planning may be affected by children and parents who still count on you for financial help, draining savings that had been earmarked for your retirement.

The truth: Unless you are a childless orphan, know you will face difficult decisions about what support you can give to the generations before and after you.

Myth Number Eight: Your Expenses Will Decrease When You Retire

Most people believe they will need only 60 to 75 percent of their current income to enjoy the same lifestyle because of reduced expenses. Generally costs of transportation, clothing, and a few other expenses decline when a person retires, but other expenses, such as dining out and vacations, often go up. Housing will probably remain your most costly expense. Even if you pay off a thirty-year mortgage by the time you retire, property taxes, insurance, maintenance, and other costs will continue to rise. People sixty-five and older spend a larger portion of their income on housing than those forty-five to sixty-four, according to the Bureau of Labor Statistics.

> When Janet's and my parents retired, I remember their living costs went way down. I just don't see ours doing that. (Mark, age fifty-six)

The truth: Even if some costs decline, chances are your expenses during retirement will be greater than you anticipate.

Myth Number Nine: Medicare and Employer Insurance Will Cover Your Medical Bills

Reality check: If you are now at a midcareer point, you may get no health insurance when you retire. Three developments make it increasingly unlikely that employers will offer future retirees anywhere near the kind of coverage that current retirees are now enjoying. First, the annual double-digit rise in insurance costs makes it difficult for employers to pay premiums. Second, federal accounting guidelines discourage companies from making generous promises of future support to retirees. These guidelines require that such obligations reduce the profit a company can show on its balance sheet today, thus cutting the all-important bottom line. And finally, ever-greater numbers of workers are employed by smaller companies, often resulting in fewer benefits. Recent surveys have shown that a significant number of corporations are planning to reduce health benefits for those retiring in the near future. Beyond that, things are even worse.

> There are rumors that if our company merges with SFT, the early retirement package that they're offering us now won't be available anymore. With Doris's health, it could be a real burden if we don't get health care coverage. (Ed S., age fifty-seven)

Don't rely on Medicare, either. Under current law, you cannot collect benefits until age sixty-five, even if you retire sooner, and you can count on that threshold age rising in the future. Today, on average, Medicare pays less than half of one's health-care bills.

The truth: Attention to health, fitness, and taking care of yourself will reduce health-care costs. You must build these costs into your budget and take the time to follow through on exercise and diet. Consider, but don't count on, an employer's coverage or Medicare.

Myth Number Ten: When You Reach a Certain Age, It's Time to Retire

In the past, target ages for retirement were important. There were benchmark years—fifty-five, sixty, sixty-two, sixty-five—nice round numbers ideal for retirement. But as more people continue to work later in life or in part-time positions, the line between work life and retired life will blur. And as corporations move to avoid "age discrimination," the benchmarks will lose their import and be replaced by individually set target dates.

The truth: In the future, the finish line for your working years will more likely be determined by your financial readiness rather than your age, and you'll likely go into and out of work several times during retirement.

Myth Number Eleven: Your Retirement Plan Investments Will Be There When You Need Them

Due to the sheer numbers of baby boomers, those retiring may trigger a massive sell-off of pension and retirement fund assets that could depress investment values. "It's a bit scary," says Stanford University economist John Shoven, coauthor with Sylvester Schieber of the recent study "The Retirement Security of the Baby Boom Generation." While he does not predict a sell-off such as happened in the 1930s, he notes, "I'm predicting [a situation as in] the 1970s, when assets were undervalued. Returns on stocks might be only three percent above inflation vs. the 10 percent we've experienced lately." Pension assets, which accounted for only 2 percent of the national wealth in 1950, have swelled to 25 percent, a whopping $4.5 trillion. This is equal to the value of *all* of the residential real estate in the United States.

Shoven and Schieber predict that liquidation of pension funds to pay off retiring boomers will begin in 2010. By 2024, pension funds will sell more assets than they buy for the first time in history. In this buyer's market, prices could fall while interest rates rise.

The truth: To survive, you must have a fall-back or contingency plan in case your retirement income is not what you expect it to be.

Myth Number Twelve: It's Smart to Take Your Retirement Benefits in a Lump Sum

As companies shift their retirement benefits from traditional pensions to savings plans controlled by employees, such as 401(k)s, more workers are taking benefits in a single check. In 1994, 51 percent of workers older than forty took a lump sum vs. 39 percent who took regular lifetime payments. And if we look at gender differences, 44 percent of male workers over forty took their retirement benefits as lump sums, while 63 percent of women did. This clearly shows that women, who often earn less and so save less, may be forced by economic circumstances to spend rather than reinvest those dollars, and so are at an added disadvantage. The percentage of people taking lump sums is growing: in 1989 only 40 percent of workers took a lump sum, while 52 percent took lifetime payments.

The scary part is that few workers older than forty use their lump-sum distributions for retirement income. Studies by the Labor Department, the Social Security Administration, and the Employee Benefit Research Institute show that 36 percent of lump-sum recipients spend their money—on cars or new homes, to pay bills, or to start a business—

and only 32 percent roll the lump-sum payout into another tax-deferred retirement savings plan. Fourteen percent do a combination, and another 14 percent add it to nonretirement savings.

For many people, spending their retirement rather than investing it is extremely costly. Tax penalties wipe out 10 percent of the lump-sum payment for those under fifty-nine and a half.

> It seemed so easy to use that money to pay off my debts and to buy a bigger home. I wanted more room for my grandchildren. Reducing debt was smart, but now I'm seeing that my investment income isn't what I thought it would be, and it's really tight. (Amanda V., age fifty-five)

The truth: While a lump sum may feel like a windfall, spending it can leave a gaping hole in your nest egg.

Are You Ready to Retire?

The options we have available today for our work and lifestyle are mind-boggling. You can retire now, retire later, or never retire. You can work full time, part time, flextime, on a project-only basis, or do job sharing. You may choose to work from home, an office, or on the road. Today we can telecommute, using fax, modem, Internet, and E-mail to communicate with customers and coworkers. We can incorporate work into our lives of leisure, or leisure into our lives of work.

Later in this book we look into what it takes financially to retire, but right now it is time to explore the psychological aspects of retirement. How do you feel about the prospect of giving up your career? Are you prepared emotionally for the challenge of this major life change?

The following quiz is designed to help you clarify your feelings about retirement. It may raise psychological issues that you may not have considered. No matter what your decision regarding retirement—and you can change that decision next week or next year—take a moment to answer these questions. To complete the quiz, choose the one response that most closely represents your true feelings—not the answer you think is "right."

Preretirement Quiz

1. When I'm on the job I
   a. get excited about new projects.
   b. feel fulfilled at the end of the day.
   c. count the hours until I can leave.
2. The best thing about my work is
   a. the variety of people I meet.
   b. the stimulation; the challenge of solving problems.
   c. the paycheck.
3. When it comes to my job I would
   a. take on more responsibility as long as I wasn't bored.
   b. do this work even if I weren't paid.
   c. quit if I could.
4. At work I
   a. see problems as a chance to try out new ideas.
   b. rally everyone to work together when there's a "disaster."
   c. get easily upset when my staff makes mistakes.
5. My associates and coworkers
   a. are my main social contacts.
   b. are nice people but not my closest friends.
   c. are people I would never see if I didn't have to work with them.
6. When I retire I will
   a. spend more time with my spouse and family.
   b. enjoy seeing my friends.
   c. be alone most of the time.
7. If I had a day off I would
   a. start the dance lessons I've been wanting to take.
   b. go golfing, go swimming, or play poker.
   c. sleep.
8. I'm looking forward to retirement because
   a. I'm ready for a new phase of life.
   b. I can do whatever I want, whenever I want.
   c. I deserve a break from this crummy job.
9. Retirement will give me time to
   a. travel and discover new facets of life.
   b. devote myself to the volunteer work I enjoy.
   c. sit and do nothing for a change.

Give yourself five points for every *a* or *b* answer, three points for every *c* answer. If you scored above thirty-five points, you will probably enjoy your retirement years and use them to the fullest; between thirty and thirty-five, you may have a few areas in which you need to make adjustments, but you should not have major problems in retiring; below thirty, you need to reexamine your attitudes about retirement.

Here's why: The nine questions above are divided into three sections representing the three major aspects of your life affected by retirement: (1) the actual work you do, (2) your relationships and support systems, and (3) managing your free time.

Questions 1–3: Your work life

Answering *a* on these questions shows that you like new challenges and flexibility. Your biggest task in retirement may be to keep yourself from getting bored—but that should not be difficult if you approach retirement with the same gusto that you bring to your work life. Choosing *b* indicates that your work is an important part of your life's purpose. You'll need to think about how you will continue to fulfill that purpose after you've stopped working. If you hold on to your work identity too tightly, you could miss new opportunities. If you chose *c* in this section, you seem to be unhappy in your job and you are in it only for the financial security. It may be easier for you to walk away from work and enter retirement, but if you hold on to negative attitudes and bitterness, you may not enjoy your leisure time anyway.

Questions 4–6: Your relationships and support systems

Being married, having a family, or enjoying good friends can not only improve the quality of your retirement years, these relationships can actually help you live longer. According to some studies, being lonely and unmarried or in a bad relationship can reduce a person's life expectancy more than smoking or obesity. On question 4, an *a* or *b* answer suggests that you have the people skills needed to handle problems as they arise. If you chose *c* on this question, you need to think about how you will react when your spouse or a family member does not behave exactly as you would like them to when you're spending more time together. You may have had a staff to do your bidding at work, but if you act like a boss toward your spouse, you could be in for problems during retirement. Answering *a* or *b* on questions 5 or 6 indicates that you have some kind of social network in place, while the person choosing *c* needs to look at ways to develop closer ties to people. If you've had trouble making friends elsewhere, think about joining a church group or civic organization.

Questions 7–10: Your leisure time
If you can't come up with any good ideas for what you'd do with an extra day off (question 7), what will you do with the great expanse of time that retirement represents? While it might be nice to think about sleeping in as much as you'd like or sitting and doing nothing (response *c* on questions 7 and 9), you will not likely be fulfilled for very long. You don't have to become a triathlete in retirement, but you should plan for a healthy balance of physical activities and mental stimulation to maintain your health and emotional well-being. If you gave an *a* or *b* response to questions in this section, you're probably ready for the rewards of retirement.

The next chapter explores some perspectives on money that may be affecting the way you plan for your future and eventual retirement.

2

• • • • • • • • •

If You Keep Doing What You're Doing, You'll Get More of What You've Got

Retirement planning isn't just about what you've earned, saved, and will spend. By understanding your hopes, dreams, and concerns, you'll increase your chances of getting what you most want from retirement.

When individuals or couples come to our offices, they bring with them two files. The tangible file contains their tax returns, bank statements, retirement accounts, brokerage statements, insurance policies—documents we can lay out on the table, peruse, and analyze. The other file is one we can't see, but it is nonetheless as real and important. This file contains their dreams, hopes, fears, and memories. Past investments, both the winners and the dogs, missed career opportunities, messy divorces, unfulfilled early retirement dreams, and yes, the disagreements over money—they're all there. This is the psychological portfolio. Unless you understand and integrate your financial and psychological portfolios, your retirement plans probably will not work.

Here are some common retirement laments:

- "He traveled a lot on business, and I thought our retirement would be a great chance to travel together. I was looking forward to that. But now I find out that all he wants to do is stay at home and garden."
- "Being single means I have to take care of my own retirement. I can't lean on anyone else for it."
- "Just as I'm thinking about retiring, her career is starting to take

off. I never thought when she took a part-time job, it would develop into something so exciting for her."

- "I married for love—but not for breakfast, lunch, and dinner. I still need some time to do my own thing. Having him home all the time is hard on us both."
- "My spouse is clueless about money and it's so hard to talk with her about it."
- "We're having a romantic candlelight dinner and suddenly it's ruined when he [she] brings up the subject of money."
- "He doesn't know beans about our finances, and that really worries me."
- "We have the same arguments about money over and over—we're barely making it now. I don't know what we'll do when he retires and there's only my income."

Gender stereotypes don't explain all of the differences between people when it comes to money management. There are many individual differences that have nothing to do with whether you are a man or a woman. In our combined thirty-five years of financial planning experience, we've seen changes as well as common threads. In the pages that follow we explore five different perspectives on money, so you can identify your money style. If you're married you can determine your partner's style as well, and gain some insights into how you and your partner are different or similar in five dimensions.

No matter how you've dealt with finances in the past, *if you keep doing what you're doing, you'll get more of what you've got.* Whether you ran up your credit cards, or always paid taxes late, or saved money like a miser, or spent like there's no tomorrow, if you continue that habit, you're doomed for more of whatever that action cost you. If you are married, no matter what roles you and your spouse have played, no matter who balanced the checkbook, saw the tax adviser, or made the investment decisions, no matter who might have gotten into debt and who bailed him or her out, the simple fact is, if you keep doing what you're doing, you'll get more of what you've got.

If your financial life is grand and you're happy with where you are, that's great—no changes are needed. But if there's anything that isn't working right now in your financial life or anything that doesn't feel good about how you manage money, for whatever reason, now is the time to change it. And to change something, you first need to understand it.

Let's look at some individual differences in how people handle money. If you are single, this exercise is valuable for gaining insights into how you manage money and if there is anything you might want to change. As you go along, you might see some clues about the money behaviors of others who are important to you—your boss, your parent, your ex-spouse, your current love. If you are married, you'll get a clear picture of some ways you and your partner differ. You might think you already have a pretty good idea, but you may be in for a surprise or two.

Each area, or dimension, of difference has its own dynamic. It's easier to see each dynamic by using continuums that show the kinds of behavior possible between two polar extremes. We find that all individuals and couples encounter these five dimensions of difference from time to time, and that they handle such encounters with varying degrees of harmony. As you review the dynamics demonstrated in these continuums, realize that no position is right or wrong. If you are a couple and you and your partner are in different places on the continuum, keep in mind that your position on each continuum indicates only that you differ from your partner, not that one of you is "wrong."

THE FIVE DIMENSIONS OF INDIVIDUAL DIFFERENCES

Spend/Save

Spender . . . . Saver

Organizational Style

Generalist . . . . Detailist

Risk Comfort Level

Risk affinitive . . . . Risk aversive

Decision-making Style

Impulsive . . . . Reflective

Flexibility

Change adaptive . . . . Change avoiding

Adapted from Victoria Felton-Collins with Suzanne Brown, *Couples and Money* (New York: Bantam, 1990).

Few of us are on the extreme right or left of these spectrums. You may find yourself operating somewhere in middle ground. Nor is your position on these lines fixed. At one stage in life you may be very dependent on your mate, growing more independent over time, or vice versa.

If you are married, where you think you are on a continuum isn't necessarily where your partner thinks you are. You may consider yourself a methodical spender and saver ruled by moderation, while your partner sees you as a shop-happy spender. For example, one person's perspective on spend-save habits may be:

Her • *Him* •

Spender . . . . Saver

while the other's viewpoint looks more like:

Her • *Him* •

Spender . . . . Saver

Let's review each of these continuums in detail to see how they affect your financial outlook as you prepare for retirement.

How Do You Spend?

These are the most important, yet volatile, questions you might have as you consider retirement:

- What will I [we] spend my [our] money on?
- How will I [we] save my [our] resources?
- Whose priorities are more important or more valid?
- When we spend, will it be for my dreams or his [hers]?
- How can we manage our money effectively when one of us saves or spends compulsively?

We all want to live "the good life," and we all have different definitions of what the good life means. For some, a comfortable house, a functional car, and a little extra cash stowed away for tomorrow will do nicely. Others won't be satisfied until they're sipping champagne in Europe.

> I can't tell you how many times we've had this same discussion about my spending. It never seems to end. Why do you think I've worked so hard all my life? It's so I can have the things I enjoy—a Porsche, a nice home, good stereo equipment, and all the things that make life worth living. OK, so I go a little overboard sometimes with things we might not need, but Janet should be happy I take good care of her and the kids. (Edwin L., age fifty-one)

How you spend and save reflects your deepest personal values, your dreams, and what you think is important. Some couples are perfectly in sync with each other's habits. Others have a harder time of it. Some marriages go awry when both partners overspend and have to keep bailing each other out. Or when one likes to spend and the other likes to save, they suffer from their differences. Trouble can surface when both agree that money needs to be saved but clash over how much and where to invest.

Some couples swear they never openly disagree about where their money will go, yet their answers to the following questions are telling. How would you and your partner answer these questions?

- Do we have enough money to support our current lifestyle?
- Are we increasing our wealth in a way that keeps up with inflation and moves us closer to our long-term goals?
- Do we have a consistent savings and investment strategy?
- Do we know where our money goes?
- Do we usually agree on how money should be spent and saved?

If you answered no to any of these questions, your spending and saving patterns beg for a change. Schedule some personal time to think about what you might do differently. The general rule for managing money well is deceptively simple: spend less than you earn, and wisely invest what's left over. We all know that sounds a lot easier than it is.

> We are really proud of ourselves because when we started planning for retirement, we didn't see that there was much we could

save. Through careful budgeting and monitoring expenses, we not only found a way to reduce our cost of living, but each month we had the discipline to funnel those left-over dollars into three different mutual funds we had chosen. Boy, has it made a difference in how much we're saving! What's also interesting is that some of the fights over money that we used to have we don't have anymore. (Margot P., age forty-nine)

The goal for most of us is financial independence: that point at which we have enough investments generating income so that we no longer work out of necessity, though we may do so by choice. To achieve that, you must take an active stance toward your finances rather than a reactive one.

To direct cash flow instead of being swept along in its currents, first determine if your finances are profit driven or expense driven. If your finances are profit driven, you plan ahead, save, and make sure your money is working for you. If expense driven, you live enslaved by your bills and use your energies to keep up with obligations rather than funding mutual dreams.

Partners with different psychological portfolios will manage their financial portfolios differently. They hold their own standards for what financial independence means, and travel divergent paths to get there. Take a moment now on the spend-save continuum. Each of you should independently place your initials and your partner's initials at the points at which you feel your behavior is best reflected. Discuss your answers. Any surprises?

Spend/Save

Spender. . . . . Saver

Profile of a Spender

Spenders feel power, self-determination, and excitement from spending money and accumulating goods. Shopping perks up their self-image and rewards them for work well done. Spending money on others is a gesture of love and acknowledgment.

Spending veers toward danger when spenders spend to overcome depression ("When the going gets tough, the tough go shopping") or to nurture themselves by using material goods as surrogates for a deeper sense of self-love and reward. Addictive spenders buy:

- what they don't need (or sometimes even want);
- when there is not enough money; and
- without sensitivity to the needs of their family, friends, or personal financial integrity.

Profile of a Saver

Savers exhibit self-determination by accumulating wealth and saying a self-disciplined no to life's extraneous luxuries. They prefer the slow building of financial clout and capital to the fleeting thrill of a spending spree.

Addictive saving, however, is as insidious and destructive as overspending. The miser squirrels pennies for the mere sake of watching them accumulate. Saving becomes an end in itself.

Money, to the chronic saver, is not an investment in future happiness. There is always another tomorrow when the money will be better spent. And even that tomorrow never comes. If you are an addictive saver, you save:

- while depriving yourself and your loved ones of the material pleasures—even necessities—your money was meant to buy;
- instead of translating financial riches into any other kind of assets or investments with growth potential;
- to fill an inner emotional bank account that is never full—security is always just out of reach.

How Do You Manage Information?

Paper, paper everywhere. Each month you have reams of paper to read, sort, and file. Even if you have put your records on computer, your life is still cluttered with bills, bank statements, tax returns, paystubs, and receipts.

Each area of personal and business finance creates a paper trail. If you keep yours well manicured and organized, your creditors will love you, the bank will applaud you, your less-gifted friends will wonder how you do it, and the IRS will stay off your back.

If your paper trail is a wild, overgrown, twisted path strewn with errors made, records lost, checks bounced, accounts not reconciled, and receipts left who knows where, there will be no end to your penance. It may be time for professional help. People fed up with trying to sort it all out and trying to make wise financial choices based on muddled information may need professional help to get them organized and on the right track.

How important is knowing where you stand financially? Some people actually cherish not knowing. Confusion can be a miraculous buffer between personal self-esteem and the hard, bottom-line reality of how much they are quantifiably worth. Others pursue neatness as a diversion from the pursuit of other, larger goals. Conflicts can arise when one partner is completely neat while the other savors total clutter.

The continuum of organizational style is banked by two extreme types: generalists and detailists. Each has very distinct characteristics. Where would you place you and your partner on this line?

Organizational Style

Generalist . . . . Detailist

Profile of the Generalist

A generalist views bookkeeping and accounting as the bane of an otherwise perfect universe. Financial life is understood in only the more general sense: how much comes in; how much goes out. Period. Ask them specifics about their finances and retirement plans and their minds wander to thoughts of sunny shores in southern climes.

"No one ever got rich from balancing their checkbook," a generalist friend once chided. While it's true you won't earn your first million by writing down every check, you won't keep your first million without doing it. Unfortunately, generalists often don't realize that, and may falter financially as a result. If you aren't meeting the most basic due-diligence tasks, you probably aren't sure how organization can help you reach your objectives.

Profile of the Detailist

Detailists thrive in the domain of detail. Astute and vigilant, they track each dollar as it marches through their checkbooks or across their computer screens. Their records are immaculate. Their accounts are never a nickel off. They can tell you how much they spent this month compared to last month, or even last year. Desktops are empty. Files are neat. Their financial life runs with Swiss-watch accuracy.

If you've ever been audited by the IRS, you know that today's institutionalized society was made by and for detailists.

How Do You Feel about Risk?

Risk. It's there every time you step into your car, buy a stock, open your own business, or consider retiring. But what we think of as risky may be dramatically different from what our neighbor, parent, associate, or spouse might think of as risky. "Fool's gold" to one person might be a "sure thing" to the other. If you and your partner have unresolved differences in risk tolerance, committing mutually owned dollars can become an investment in disaster.

Fortunately though, many relationships have their own silent systems of checks and balances that keep risk within manageable limits, with one partner playing "gambler" to the other's "cautionary counselor." Those roles aren't always visible to outsiders. Many financial planners have had the unfortunate experience of concluding a plan of action based on the more vocal partner's approval of it, only to have it fall through because the silent spouse registered opposition once out of the office.

Janet and Eric came into our office for some financial advice on retirement. To our surprise, they were both pretty open about the fact that Eric loves to explore new business ideas and had suffered several business failures over the years. He was now in the initial stages of a newsletter publishing company that he had started about eight months earlier. When Janet left the room momentarily, Eric leaned over and confided in us that he had really taken more out of their retirement savings than he had let on to Janet, and things weren't going as well as he'd like. We encouraged him to reveal this to Janet, and with our help, they agreed on austerity cuts to their household budget that would be earmarked to replenish the retirement accounts. They also agreed that any future cash infusions to the business would have to come from bank loans or from selling part of the business rather than from personal assets.

The goal in financial planning is to use risk intelligently, for profit. In money, as in exercise, there's no gain without a little pain. Generally, the higher the risk, the higher the potential reward, and conversely, the lower the risk, the less money you stand to make. There are no risk-free investments; even the safety of your bank account depends on the solvency of the bank and the federal deposit insurance that protects you in case your bank fails.

Every financial portfolio is a reflection, in dollars, of the investors' psychological portfolio—the money messages and memories, gender differences, power dynamics, and money styles that create risk behavior. Economic partnerships (also known as "marriages") that work always honor the risk threshold of each partner. Between unbridled financial recklessness and utter financial stagnation is a level of risk that's right for both.

Most investment behavior falls in the middle range between conservative and aggressive. Look for a moment at these extremes on the continuum and note where you and your partner are. Interestingly, you may have changed positions over the years. You'll find that as you close in on retirement, you may change even more.

Risk Comfort Level

Risk affinitive . . . . Risk aversive

Profile of the Risk Affinitive

Those who have a high risk comfort level are robust investors. "No guts, no glory" is their motto. They're aggressive, dynamic, and action oriented, happiest when living on the edge. Driven by the promise of big returns, they take on financial life as they do any other game with a big jackpot.

Money is perceived as a "flow," a renewable resource that will come, go, and come again many times in their lives. Unlike the risk aversive, who view each financial event as grimly significant, the risk affinitive see each risk as just one event in a much larger game.

Sublimely confident in their own ability (sometimes too confident), they dabble in entrepreneurial businesses, speculative real estate ventures, and aggressive stocks, and they tolerate fluctuations in these assets well.

To their more conservative partners, the fiscally aggressive are a constant menace, always keeping financial life on the brink of calamity. The risk affinitive stand to make huge amounts of money. Most millionaires, at some point, gambled big with everything they had. The problem is, so did many paupers. Those who err on the side of fiscal aggression can—and very frequently do—lose it all.

Profile of the Risk Aversive

Those who are risk aversive spend their time hunting for the sure thing. Sacrificing high yields for safety at every juncture, they move slowly and cautiously through their financial lives toward retirement.

These conservatives perceive money as a pool of assets that, once risked and lost, is not easily replenished. They'll tell you how hard they worked for that money. Their risk comfort zone is narrow and well defined. Any movement toward the extreme trips an elaborate network of emotional alarms.

Risk averse investors stash their money in treasury bills, bonds, certificates of deposit, conservative utilities, or blue-chip stocks. They tenaciously resist debt, "creative financing" maneuvers, and even capital investments to start their own businesses.

To more aggressive partners, the fiscally conservative seem stagnant and plodding. Terrible setbacks are rare, but so are big, adrenalized successes.

The risk aversive err on the side of safety. By putting on the brakes when they spot anything that looks unsafe, they fail to take risks that will benefit their financial well-being and retirement security. The too-timid investor actually squanders money in the form of lost potential income and missed opportunities.

When Risk Is Out of Control . . . and When It Isn't

There's a significant difference between prudent risk (say, putting money in a well-performing stock) and wild gambles (such as investing in a ski resort in the arctic circle). Know the difference. A prudent risk has the following characteristics:

- Risk is calculated based on highly probable financial returns, not on ego.
- The investment changes slowly; it's difficult to lose your entire investment quickly.
- Your investments are tailored so you can limit losses. For example, using a "stop-loss order" on stocks gives you a way out of your investment before you lose an unacceptable amount of money.

In a wild gamble:

- Risk is a form of entertainment, not founded on methodical financial reasoning.
- You stand to lose large amounts of money—fast.
- You have little or no control over the outcome.

When contemplating an investment or significant financial move, you and your partner should ask yourselves the following questions:

1. What is our financial objective in taking this risk, relative to our mutual goals?

2. Does the objective of this investment match our present financial needs?
3. What is the potential return on this investment?
4. Are the assumptions used in determining this potential return realistic?
5. How good is the investment's track record?
6. What could go wrong?
7. Is the potential reward worth the risk?
8. Are we overcommitting our resources to this one investment at the expense of a balanced portfolio?
9. Can we both live with this investment?
10. If one of us is uncomfortable with this investment, is there a way to offset the risk with greater security in some other area, such as committing more money to low-risk bonds or savings?

Specific types of investment risks and what to watch out for are discussed in chapter 4.

How Do You Make Decisions?

The "80–20 rule" says that 80 percent of what you get comes from 20 percent of what you do; conversely, 80 percent of your efforts produce little benefit. When it comes to making financial decisions, doing too little (acting in haste with no attention to details) or doing too much (overplanning and overcontemplating) produce diminishing returns.

What happens when the stalling of one spouse enrages the other, or when the impetuousness of one results in unsound decisions? On the continuum of decision making, most people fall between the extreme of reflective and impulsive. Take a moment to determine where you and your partner might be on this continuum, and then let's look at these extremes.

Decision-making Style

Impulsive . . . . Reflective

Profile of the Impulsive

"You snooze, you lose," the impulsive will caution. It's better to act and pay the consequences than to wallow in uncertainty and do nothing.

Impulsives anchor onto the major features of any financial choice, sailing past all of the subclauses and small print. The fewer alternatives offered, the better. Sorting through options is agonizingly dull for impulsive investors.

Magnificent examples of selective memory, impulsive decision makers see and hear what they want. If their first impulse is that a business deal "looks good," they tend to ignore all later evidence to the contrary. Don't bother them with the facts, they've made up their minds.

In their zealous flight from decision to decision, impulsives trip up in their own unreasonable expectations and incomplete assessments, as overlooked specifics of financial choices come back to haunt them.

Profile of the Reflective

Reflective financial decision makers, on the other hand, weigh all the facts before they put down a dollar. They gather information slowly and consider every option against all other possible options.

Unlike the impulsive, reflectives consider everything, study every angle, and always read the fine print. The problem is, left to their own instincts, they get lost in details, often unable to take action. "Should I or shouldn't I?" "What if . . . ?"

Reflectives wait for all the facts to be in. The problem is, all the facts are never in. Their partners experience emotions from excitement to disgust as the reflectives make up their minds and change them again. Opportunities pass by while they postpone, hesitate, delay, debate, and wait for the optimum time to invest.

Making Decisions Effectively

Making decisions effectively, in a timely manner, comes down to the following four rules:

1. **Know only what you need to know.** You'll never have all the information. In fact, by the time you have all the knowledge you think you need to make the right choice, the environment will have changed. Narrow your knowledge to include only essential information, and know that information thoroughly.

2. **Cultivate your intuition and use it.** Gut instinct is crucial for cutting through mental ambivalence. When you have an important finan-

cial decision to make, friends will give you good, bad, and contradictory advice. You will be stalled in a mental polemic if you don't know how to trust your own instincts.

3. Agree on how mutual decisions will be made. Not every decision must be made by first consulting your partner. Some decisions can, and should, be made unilaterally—by mutual agreement. Others must be made together. Work out a strategy between you. To avoid procrastinating, make a time line: Decide on what date you will reach a decision, whether it is about when to retire or where to invest your money.

4. Don't look back. "Why didn't I think before I did that?" may plague the impulsive, and, "I should have moved faster, I've lost the opportunity now," will bother the reflective. You will make millions of financial decisions during your lifetime, some profitable, some educational. Once you make your decision, move on. Monitor your investment, but don't dwell on the investment decision. "Shoulda', woulda', coulda' " doesn't work any better in investing than it does anywhere else.

How Do You Handle Change?

In any one day, week, or month, we are bombarded by change. Pick up any newspaper and you'll be faced with diverse yet interrelated changes; for instance, what happened in Tokyo's stock exchange last night affects the value of your pension plan this morning. Our global marketplace is overwhelmingly complicated. Stocks rise and fall at such giddy speeds, sometimes it's hard to keep up. Paper fortunes are made and lost faster than ever before. Corporate jobs too are more precarious as mergers, takeovers, and cutbacks become the norm. Industries booming one year can be obsolete the next. And government does its part: new tax laws instituted in the last few years have effected more changes than this nation has known in the previous fifty years. Investments have also changed: there are now more mutual funds in the United States than there are stocks trading on the New York Stock Exchange. As you read this, even retirement plans are changing. Some 401(k) plans, which formerly offered five or six investment choices, now offer hundreds, even thousands, of choices.

Accelerating change is a permanent part of our lives. Your retirement will be a profound and significant change. Will you fight the change or will you take it comfortably in stride? In many ways it depends on how easily you cope with change in general. How are you and your partner positioned on this continuum?

Flexibility

Change adaptive. . . . . Change avoiding

If handling financial change and dealing with information overload makes you feel stressed, you are neither inept nor alone. You didn't miss some all-important day in school when everyone else learned the tax code, how to decipher the hieroglyphics of the financial pages, and how to read a 401(k) statement.

Be gentle with yourself. Financial stress should not be taken lightly. Upswings in domestic violence, stress-related illness, and suicide often accompany sudden changes in the economic picture. Here are some strategies you can use to increase your flexibility in thinking and enhance your retirement decision making.

1. **Define the problem.** Begin by listing your major concerns. They may include where to live, when to retire, how to save, or how to invest. Get them all on paper clearly. Many times, obvious solutions are overlooked because the problem isn't well stated.
2. **Brainstorm.** Start brainstorming solutions to your concerns—any and every solution you can think of, no matter how absurd or impractical. Don't evaluate—not yet.
3. **Do a cost-benefit analysis.** What would each solution cost you, compared to how much of the problem it would solve?
4. **Select one solution.** Inevitably, one solution will appear better than the others. Choose it and implement it.
5. **Monitor and modify.** During the following weeks or months, monitor your solutions. How are they working? Make changes as necessary and continue to move toward your goals.

Jim and Nancy, ages fifty-five and forty-nine, found themselves in a quandary. Jim wanted to take early retirement from his employer, who was offering a very good package. If he stayed on and a proposed merger went through, the same package might not be offered him later. But if he took early retirement, could he get another job and could Nancy start the computer-tutoring business she wanted to? They defined the problem by listing all of their concerns. Would there be enough money to live on? What would the initial capital requirements be for Nancy's business? How would they invest the lump sum if they took the early retirement? What job opportunities would Jim pursue?

Next they spent a Friday evening brainstorming every solution and every alternative they could think of to come to a decision. Saturday morning they made a list of the pros and cons of whether to take or not to take the early retirement package. From their discussions it seemed pretty clear that the advantages of taking early retirement outweighed the disadvantages. They agreed that Jim would have six months to look for a new job and that Nancy would stay in her current position, delaying her resignation and the start of her business by six months. During the early weeks and the months that followed, they monitored their finances carefully to determine if the plan was working. Jim had not found a job at six months, and a month later he was still out of work. After deliberating carefully they decided that Jim had enough encouraging leads that they both felt comfortable with Nancy quitting her job to start her own business. The happy ending came in the ninth month with a job offer for Jim, which turned out to be better than his prior position.

The Perils of Procrastination

There will be two groups of baby boomers at retirement time—those who prepared and those who should have.

"There's so much to do to prepare for retirement, no time to do it, and I don't want to do it anyway. So why start?" So goes the interior monologue of the procrastinator. If that is conversation you recognize, pay close attention. There are basically three reasons why we procrastinate: perfectionism, excusability, and rebellion.

Perfectionism. "I'll do it when I have more information," or, "Until I can afford to do it right, I'm not going to do it." These are the promises of the procrastinating perfectionist. Of course, if you wait until conditions are perfect before you start saving or planning for your retirement, nothing will ever get done. The perfectionist is perennially "about to begin," demanding the best and creating the worst.

Excusability. "I don't have the time to do it." "I'm too tired." "You should have done this for me." "We need a secretary to do this." "My computer is down." The procrastinator will drum up a million excuses why he or she can't meet the commitments. Not only do excuses absolve procrastination, but procrastination itself makes it possible to excuse ourselves. We all know people who put off tasks until the eleventh hour. Then when the job is poorly done, they have a ready-made excuse: "Time was so short—what can you expect?"

Rebellion. "To hell with the IRS. If they want my money, they can wait until I'm ready to give it to them." Procrastination is a passive act of aggression. Procrastinating rebels are paying back their partners, parents, banks, God, and any other authority for heaping upon them a financial responsibility they never asked to handle.

Here's what you can do now to stop procrastinating and begin planning more effectively for retirement:

1. Understand what you are trying to say—to your partner, your boss, or the IRS—by not handling what you know needs to be done. Failing to enter the checks you write in the checkbook or computer may be a way of asking for more attention from your partner. Not filing tax returns on time may be expressing anger at the IRS. Perhaps your procrastination shows you would like more understanding from your partner of how busy and stressed you are. If you feel frustrated, angry, or unappreciated at home or at work, it may seem more acceptable to let things slide than to express the feelings and ask for help.

2. Know the consequences of procrastination in emotional and financial terms. Only the very lucky procrastinator avoids serious financial mishaps from disorganized financial records. Every bounced check, tax penalty, overdue bill, and undetected bank mistake has a financial cost to you—in real dollars. Calculate each expense. It may inspire you to modify your very costly habits.

3. Break the job of organizing your finances into manageable chunks. What really awaits you is rarely as insurmountable as the task looming in your mind. Tackle each of the following separately.

- Checkbooks and bank statements. Note when during the month you receive your bank statement and set aside an hour or two a month to reconcile your checkbook at that time. Computerizing your checkbook on *Quicken* or another personal finance software program may make your life easier and record keeping smoother.
- Tax records. Label files and keep them handy for filing charitable contributions, medical expenses, business expenses, and other deductible expenses as you incur them during the year. Documentation of expenses is essential for saving on taxes, and it is also a way you can audit-proof yourself.
- Receipts. File them as they come in using whatever system works

for you. Organize your files at the beginning of the year and you'll save time and effort when doing your taxes.

- Investment information (prospectuses, brokerage statements). Keep these in one place and review brokerage statements monthly—it should take no more than half an hour.
- Cash flow management. List debts in order of balance due and interest you are paying. Pay down debts that carry the highest interest rate and have the smallest balance. For cash management, the time spent inputting your data into *Quicken* or another software program will simplify your record keeping and save time in the long run.
- Bills (to be paid). Make a list of bills to be paid on the first and the fifteenth of each month, and schedule a bill-paying time on each of these days.

4. Redivide tasks between you and your partner. Delegate work to be done based on talents and interests. Disregard habit ("Oh, but we've always done it this way"); gender ("I'm the woman of the house, so this is my job"); or any other arbitrary standard.

> You can imagine how surprised I was when Janet said that she had not only been willing for these eight years to handle the checkbook, but actually wanted to. It came out during one counseling session we had about how much we should be spending on her kids and my kids. She had been an accountant before we were married and I guess I assumed she was tired of it. So we just fell into the habit of me doing it. But we never really talked about who would do what when it came to our finances. (Jonathan S., age forty-six)

5. Know what you can realistically expect from each other. If there are tasks you know neither one of you will ever do, hire a professional. Though hiring a financial planner, accountant, bookkeeper, or secretary can be costly, what it will save in terms of worry, stress, blame, and argument will be well worth the money.

> I think the best money we ever spent was to get a bookkeeper to pay our bills and keep track of our finances. At the end of the day, it's the last thing either of us wants to do. It's saved our sanity and quite frankly it's probably saving us money too—no more finance charges on our credit cards or bounced checks either. (Marjorie M., age forty)

Are We Speaking the Same Language When We Discuss Money?

While individual differences are most important, there are some gender differences that we should explore to round out the picture. Men and women have different attitudes about money, affecting everything from how they spend it to what drives them crazy about it. While today we are shattering the confines of gender roles more than ever before, differences in attitude and style remain.

That caused us some concern when we first began noticing how differently men and women approached the process of retirement planning. If money means something different to men than it does to women, how can couples make joint financial decisions as they plan their retirement?

Recognizing those differences can create a window of understanding between financial partners. Since these factors can play a major role in how you make your retirement decisions, take a moment to think about how you would answer each of the questions that follow.

Goals

How do you measure success or fulfillment in your life?

Women: Whether or not they work outside the home, most women we speak with often respond, "I feel successful if I'm making a contribution and feel recognized and appreciated for it," or, "I am fulfilled if my relationships with family, spouse, and those I work with are going well." Men: "Success means having money in the bank," say many men.

Men tend to gauge the quality of their lives according to financial satisfaction, women according to personal satisfaction. Relationships are important to women both in their homes and in the corporate world. Money, though important to working women, is secondary to feeling recognized for their contributions and enjoying relationships with those with whom they work.

Passages

What stages have you gone through in your financial life?

In traditional marriages of providers and nurturers, we very often see a midlife switch that can have a significant impact on retirement planning. Men, having left for the office every day for decades, suddenly want to be part of home life. They take a new interest in their children, want to learn James Beard's secrets for baking bread, or decide to build that addition to the house themselves.

Women, tired of culinary advice and Martha Stewart perfection, may want to take a job, manage a stock portfolio, read *Forbes* rather than *Fashion,* watch *Wall Street Week,* or surf the Internet for financial updates.

Fears

What are your worst fears about money?

"No matter how much money I make, I have this gnawing anxiety that one day it might disappear," confided Anita, a thirty-three-year-old dentist. This bag lady syndrome, which conjures up images of wandering the streets with clothes in a shopping cart, troubles many women, even as they successfully advance in their careers. An irrational fear of loss and destitution can lead to paralysis when it comes to investing, or cause women to put their funds into super-safe CDs or treasury bills. Inaction or an overly cautious attitude can be a real detriment to building a substantial retirement nest egg.

Men generally tend to have more specific income-related fears: What if I'm injured? What if I get laid off? What if this stock takes a dive? Men's fears focus on specific changes in financial circumstances rather than on sudden general poverty. Their fears often revolve around "losing face" when there's no rent or mortgage money, or letting down their family and friends.

Risk

How well do you tolerate risk?

The typical macho male response to risk is, "No guts, no glory." Countered one woman we talked to about risk taking, "I don't want to get creamed financially. I'd rather live to invest another day."

Though often stereotyped as financially irresponsible spendthrifts, women, we've found, are more conservative and in some ways more astute investors than men. But overall they still lack experience: While their track record in the investment marketplace is growing, they are not quite as acclimated to the ups and downs of investing as are their male counterparts. Many women treat investment money gingerly, glorifying gains but considering losses catastrophic rather than just part of the rough-and-tumble of the financial marketplace.

Men, often more accustomed to the fluctuations of the market, have a greater emotional threshold for risk. But this does not always serve them well. When they err—especially early on in financial life—they usually err on the side of risk folly, plunking down their money without thoroughly checking out the investment.

We've noted an interesting phenomenon that takes place in many couples in their late forties, when retirement planning begins in earnest: risk switch. Many men, previously very comfortable with equities and aggressive investments, become more conservative as they look toward retiring. They become acutely aware that as their work years dwindle, money won't be flowing into their lives as regularly as the twice-a-month paycheck. Meanwhile, their wives, buoyed by increased interest, knowledge, and confidence in investing, become more comfortable with higher-risk investments. With children grown and gone, their instinct for protecting the nest lessens, and women in their forties are now starting new businesses at an ever-increasing pace. Designing a portfolio that meets both partners' changing needs is a challenge. Diversification among stocks, bonds, and cash is the key.

Self-confidence

How do you assess your financial competence?

Men like to appear to know it all, even when they don't. Women often doubt they know it, even when they do. When clients come to us for financial planning, men are less likely to ask questions or to appear unsure. When they are convinced it's all right to let down their guard, they seem relieved. Their lives have depended on looking capable and in command, even when they were shaking in their shoes.

Women have had society's permission to not know the answers. They can ask questions, backtrack, or hesitate without suffering a blow to their self-worth. But often they underestimate or ignore their considerable abilities.

Adviser Relationships

How do you choose and relate to your financial advisers?

A person should choose a financial adviser "based on their track record and performance," says Henry, a retired management consultant. "By whether they answer my questions, how they relate to me, how attentive they are to my concerns, and whether I can trust them," says Sally, his wife.

Men traditionally don't mix business and pleasure in relationships with their advisers. But for women, a sense of having a close relationship is essential. Women take the process personally and look for affiliation and trust in their advisers. If they don't like an adviser, it can end the relationship. Men are more likely to evaluate their advisers on technical merits such as credentials, how well they sell their services, and the bottom-line promises.

Decision Making

How do you make financial decisions?

Women tend to manage their money based on a combination of linear reasoning and intuition, with intuition and "feeling" leading the way. To proceed they must trust their adviser, and the decision must feel right.

Men are a different story. Sometimes they make their decisions by reasoning through the facts, but just as often they stake their money on tips from friends. Many of the money moves that created fortunes came from someone's comments on the golf course or at the club. So have staggering losses.

Attribution

When something goes wrong, whom do you blame? When something goes right, whom do you congratulate?

Men tend to attribute positive consequences to their own ability ("I'm glad I saw that opportunity") and negative consequences to outside circumstances ("That damned stockbroker!"). Women are just the opposite. They tend to attribute positive results to good luck or to their adviser's recommendation ("Can you believe the stock went up so high?"), while negative consequences are their own fault ("I should have been more careful").

As you analyze how you and your partner answered the above questions, you'll gain insight into how to navigate your next fifty years. In the next chapter we look at some of the roadblocks that can get in your way as you plan for retirement.

3

• • • • • • • • •

Retirement Roadblocks

What do you mean, save for retirement? With my financial obligations, it's all I can do to get to next month. (Susan G., age thirty-five)

I've been a loyal employee at AT&T—they darn well better give me a good retirement package. (Fred D., age forty-five)

These 401(k) options are all so confusing—it's easier just to put it all in a fixed rate of return fund. (April J., age thirty-seven)

Sure I'm in a high-powered position—but so is our lifestyle. Even though I have great options for saving, we use all my income now. (Larry F., age forty-four)

Your Preparation Profile

Do any of these statements sound familiar? In the previous chapter you saw how your views and those of your spouse might affect how you spend, save, and plan for retirement as you interact with others on the subject of money. We find that as people begin to prepare for their next fifty years, they tend to follow one of the five basic styles of preparation: Would If I Could, Others Will Do It, Avoider, Freewheeler, and Perspective. Read on to see which of these profiles most closely fits you.

Would If I Could

Profile

You are aware that you are not saving enough, even though retirement is on the horizon. The future figures into your long-range plans, but present expenses are in clearer focus. Supporting children, parents, or your current lifestyle is making it impossible to save. You feel pressure and guilt because you know you should save.

Would If I Coulds are burdened with unpredictable financial obligations and feel they simply don't make enough money. It is interesting to note that this style does not just apply to lower-income individuals. Many of our clients complain they are overwhelmed by the financial demands of the moment, no matter what their savings profile or income bracket.

Janine is a single mother who exemplifies this style: "Yes, I know I should be saving, especially since my firm matches our 401(k) contributions. But darn it, there's no way with supporting two children and myself on my salary. I'm lucky that I pay off my credit cards each month. That's the best I can do now. Hopefully I'll be able to contribute next year. I've got enough on my plate, and feeling guilty about not saving for retirement when I really can't doesn't make me feel any better."

Recommendations

If you are a Would If I Could, the first step is to reduce the overwhelm. Perhaps you can't put aside a large amount of money now, but at least you can begin to save. Begin by saving 2 to 5 percent of your take-home pay in a 401(k) plan or any other plan you have at work, or else contribute to an IRA. With each promotion or raise, boost the percentage you put aside. If a bonus comes your way, enjoy 10 to 20 percent of it now and direct the majority to your retirement savings.

Others Will Do It

Profile

An Others Will Do It counts on his or her employer, Social Security, Medicare, pension, or the spouse's retirement. Buying into the traditional American dream, an Others Will Do It thinks, If I'm a loyal employee and give years of my life's hard work to the company, it should take care of me when I retire.

This sounds almost like an attitude problem when Mark expresses it:

"Well, I've worked hard all my life. I can't say I've always enjoyed what I do. I think it's like being entitled to a decent retirement if you play the game by the rules. And I've sure done that—what with paying into Social Security all these years and being at the beck and call of my company for twenty-two years, I deserve a comfortable retirement."

Recommendations
Thoroughly investigate the retirement income resources you have available. Check your employer's annual benefits statement and see what your benefits will be when you (voluntarily or involuntarily) stop working there. Check your accrued Social Security benefits and any other expected income sources. Chances are these sources alone won't provide adequate retirement income, especially in the event of unforeseen circumstances—divorce, disability, or an unexpected layoff. Realize that in order to take charge of *your own retirement,* you probably need to save in addition to your company's retirement plans.

Avoider

Profile
Like Others Will Do Its, Avoiders perceive someone else as more responsible for their own retirement planning. Avoiders also tend to avoid involvement with money altogether. They dislike dealing with money at all and avoid budgeting, balancing the checkbook, keeping records, and planning for their financial future. At the extreme, their anxiety about money can lead to financial paralysis and a pervasive feeling that they can't understand anything relating to finances.

> I don't know, it's all so confusing, those choices we have to make on the 401(k). There used to be four different options from fixed income to aggressive-growth type things. But now there's lots more. I don't have the time to study all these brochures. I wish they would just pick something for me and let it go at that. (Pat S., age forty-nine)

Avoiders also include the happy-go-lucky, who believe retirement will take care of itself, all in good time—no need to save now, it's too far away, maybe I'll win the lottery or get an inheritance.

Recommendations

If you are an Avoider, you must take one step at a time until you are comfortable being involved. Learn what you need to learn; take classes in personal finances, retirement planning, and investing at your local college. Discount brokerage firms, like Charles Schwab and Company and Fidelity, offer a multitude of seminars and materials. Knowledge will help relieve your anxiety.

For the happy-go-lucky Avoider: *get real!* Add up the numbers and you'll see the kind of life you'll have when you retire if you continue your current rate of savings.

Freewheeler

Profile

For the Freewheeler, it's lifestyle now, as power and success take priority. Freewheelers spend every penny they make on freedom and an expansive lifestyle. They don't like to budget, balance checkbooks, or keep track of credit cards, and are often in debt. They usually value liquidity in investments, although they may need illiquid investments to keep them from spending all of their savings. They may define their self-worth by the possessions they have accumulated. In their lives, Freewheelers may portray an attitude that seems decidedly more lighthearted than Would If I Coulds, Others Will Do Its, or Avoiders.

> OK, so maybe we do spend too much on trips and fun things, but what's money for if you don't enjoy it? I'm sure we'll get serious about saving for retirement when it gets closer, but for now, my job pays well and we're doing fine. (Jackie M., age forty-four)

Recommendations

If you're a Freewheeler, chances are you are in a high-power position in your firm and able to take advantage of pretax retirement savings plans such as 401(k)s, deferred compensation plans, and profit-sharing plans. The more money you are able to put aside before you receive it, the less tempting it will be to spend it. Take a close look at why spending is so intoxicating. Find some expenses you could cut back on without reducing the quality of your life. Set priorities. As you age, you may find that toys like cars, stereos, and electronic gadgets are no longer as important as they once were. Figure out what the debt you have amassed through extravagant spending is really costing you.

Perspective

Profile

Those who have money in perspective have a clear and realistic picture of finances, a sense of control, and a feeling of confidence that they are on track to a secure retirement. As planners, they know what they own and owe currently and they've computed what they are likely to need to cover retirement expenses. Perspectives have the discipline to save regularly for retirement. They worry less than Would If I Coulds, Others Will Do Its, and Avoiders about their future because they feel more comfortable with the amount they are saving now. They educate themselves about investment strategies. But Perspectives aren't perfect. A Public Agenda survey found that only 26 percent of those we have identified as Perspectives choose investments appropriate to their long-term goals—investments that, while they may have higher risk, also have greater potential reward over the long haul. The majority of Perspectives, despite their discipline in utilizing the retirement plans available to them, may ultimately find their savings eroded by inflation.

When Susan and Michael came into our offices, they were very clear on when they wanted to retire and what retirement income they would need from their investments. With well-organized financial records and details of their cash management that Susan had generated using the software program *Quicken,* they were surprised to learn that there was something more they needed.

> Well, I see what you mean about being diversified, but we really don't want to take much risk. We thought it was a good idea to start moving everything into fixed income, but that sure isn't going to give us much growth, is it? (Michael S., age forty-three)

Recommendations

If you are a Perspective, congratulations—you're on track. You can afford to take more risks to achieve more return, so consider increasing the stock portion of your investments. Your diversified portfolio should include both U.S. and international equities, bonds, and cash. Within the equities groupings include large and small capitalization stocks as well as value and growth styles of investing. In chapters 4 and 12, we show you how to design your own portfolio to meet your retirement goals and live comfortably in retirement.

Whether you are married or single, it's important to be clear on your own style in how you prepare for retirement. Knowing whether you are a Would If I Could, Others Will Do It, Avoider, Freewheeler, or Perspective can be a valuable insight and may give you the nudge you need toward becoming a Perspective. If you are married, talking openly and honestly with your spouse about your retirement thoughts, feelings, and plans is crucial to enjoying your years ahead. It's rare when we find both individuals in a couple equally involved in their finances. Usually one or the other has taken a more active role in gathering information, interfacing with advisers, and making the decisions. In some cases the other spouse is just as knowledgeable but may not be as actively involved in the day-to-day finances. In other couples, one partner takes a backseat to the other's financial decisions and knows little or nothing about their money.

Preparing for Retirement With Your Partner

What to do if one partner is "clueless" about family finances? Whether retirement is imminent or in the distant future, it is essential that both you and your spouse are capable of taking over family finances quickly and easily if need be. Here are some steps to follow now:

Schedule a financial summit meeting as soon as you can. Update your net worth statement (what you own versus what you owe) and cash-flow statement (income versus expenses), and go over it in detail with your partner.

Get organized. Keeping and maintaining good records will help the uninvolved spouse. In the event of an emergency, the task at hand won't be too overwhelming.

Don't just think it, ink it. Do yourself and your family a favor. Start by developing an "operator's manual" listing everything you own, where it can be found, and what you would like to have done with it. A good operator's manual will cover everything from Social Security, insurance, and company benefits to what is in the safe deposit box. Update it once a year at the same time. (See the worksheet "Where to Find It: Asset Location Inventory," in the resources section at the back of the book.)

SMART TIP

KEEP SAFE IN YOUR SAFE

These are the items that you should keep in your safe deposit box:

Personal Papers

- Birth certificates
- Death certificates
- Marriage certificates
- Citizenship papers
- Adoption papers
- Veteran's papers
- Social Security verification

Ownership Papers

- Stock and bond certificates
- Deeds
- Automobile titles
- Household inventories
- Home ownership records (blueprints, deeds, surveys, capital improvement records)

Obligation and Contract Papers

- Contracts
- Copies of insurance policies
- IOUs
- Retirement plan and pension documents

Estate-Planning Documents

- Wills
- Trusts
- Letters of instruction
- Guardianship arrangements

Utilize your strengths. One partner may be great at doing taxes and have a knack for making good investment decisions. The other, a computer whiz, can take the mystery out of family finances by using a home computer to balance the checkbook, print checks, and track investments. Both are involved and both are capitalizing on their unique talents. Our clients Sam and Nancy, both professionals with high-power jobs and little time, worked out the perfect solution for managing their finances. They hired a bookkeeper who input their checks, credit card receipts, and deposits into a software program. Nancy reviews it monthly to make sure entries are accurate. Sam handles the investment ideas and uses an on-line service to update the market values. One evening a month, they come home from work an hour early, change into casual clothes, and hold a financial meeting, each updating the other and making any decisions about insurance, tax planning, bill paying, and investing that need to be made. Whether we asked Nancy or Sam, both felt strongly that this once-a-month meeting helps them avoid money fights and keeps them both "in the loop." (See the resources section for recommendations about retirement-planning and financial-planning software.)

Plant some seeds. Whenever your ill-informed spouse shows an interest in some aspect of your family finances, reinforce that interest with an article or book. There are many financial guides on the market, such as Ginita Wall's *The Way to Save* (Henry Holt), which deals with saving and personal financial management, and *The Way to Invest* (Henry Holt), which covers mutual fund investing. Attending seminars and investment club meetings together can also help. We know one couple for whom this worked well. Gerald always seemed too busy to listen when Margaret talked about the investments she was interested in. She had taken an active role in managing the family finances for the eighteen years they had been married, and Gerald felt he didn't need to be involved because she was doing a good job. But Margaret was tired of shouldering the investment burden alone, and she really wanted more interest and involvement from him. Joining a couples investment club with friends honed Gerald's interest and turned him into an active investment partner.

Put advisers in place. Discount brokers and no-load mutual funds may save a well-informed investor money, but if your less-knowledgeable partner ends up managing all of the accounts, he or she may need help that can come only from a professional. If you have an accountant, financial adviser, lawyer, or insurance agent whom you trust, set up a meeting and introduce your spouse to this professional and his or her services. If you die or become disabled, this adviser can help steer your partner toward other professionals who can help with investments and financial planning.

> When Stan realized he had cancer, he made it a point to introduce me to the financial adviser who was handling our

> investments as well as to the accountant and attorney he trusted. Oh sure, I could have gone to meetings with them before, but I was busy with my job and knew he was taking care of it. Now I see it as really important for me to be involved on every level. (Sarah B., age forty-two)

Trust a trust. Different trusts have different purposes: to bypass probate and pass assets without public scrutiny (living trust), to save on estate taxes (charitable trusts and bypass trusts), to benefit future generations, and even to save on income taxes. If you are worried that your spouse may find it difficult to manage the family finances after your death, set up a trust and name an attorney, a financial adviser, a bank, or a trust company as cotrustee. The burden of managing the money can thus be transferred to someone else's shoulders.

> It wasn't that I couldn't manage the money, but after his death there was so much to do. Sometimes I didn't feel quite up to all of it, so having a trust made it easier because I knew there was a professional who could help me handle things. (Doreen T., age fifty-seven)

Check Social Security. You should be checking your Social Security earnings records *at least* every three years; if you're within three years

---

SMART TIP

CHECK UP BEFORE YOU GET CHECKS

Call the Social Security Administration at 800-772-1213 and ask for the form "Request for Social Security Earnings History." When you receive it, you'll need to provide basic information such as your name and Social Security number, and also an estimate of expected annual earnings until retirement. Within a few weeks you should receive an "Estimate of Benefits" statement, which will tell you how much you can expect to receive at your full retirement age. It will also tell you at what age you can file for early retirement benefits, and how much to expect to receive if you do so. A history of your earnings as reported by your employers is what your benefit amount is based on, so compare it to your W-2s or tax returns for any discrepancies.

---

of your target retirement date, you should check *every* year. Social Security does make occasional mistakes, such as not crediting you with the correct amount you earned in a given year. The statements will also help you in your planning, because they'll give you a projected monthly retirement benefit. Within the next few years, these benefits statements will begin to be sent to you automatically by the Social Security Administration. Until they are, it's a good idea for you to request them.

The Outlook for Social Security

> I've heard that the Social Security and Medicare systems may be bankrupt by the time I'm supposed to start receiving benefits. Could this be possible—that I won't get anything after all I've paid into the system over the years? (Andy J., age forty-seven)

According to a 1994 report by Social Security's trustees, the system will remain solvent until the year 2030. (However, experts predict that Medicare part A, which provides hospital benefits, will start running in the red soon after the year 2000, unless adjustments are made.) Demographics dictate that serious changes *do* need to be made, but it is unlikely that benefits will be eliminated in the near future. Social Security is just too much of a political hot potato—a few years back, Congress attempted to cut out the annual cost-of-living increase for just one year, but quickly gave up the idea after a coordinated uproar from voting retirees and the politically powerful American Association of Retired Persons (AARP).

As politically difficult as changing Social Security is, however, it *is* likely we will see some or all of the following adjustments to Social Security in the coming years.

- **Earning limit increase.** Currently, beneficiaries ages sixty-five to sixty-nine lose one dollar for every three dollars they earn above $13,500 a year. Social Security recipients under the age of sixty-five lose one dollar in benefits for every two dollars in earnings above $8,640. It has been proposed that this earnings limitation be increased gradually to as much as $30,000.
- **Increase in the amount of Social Security benefits subject to income taxation.** Under current law, up to 85 percent of your benefits

may be taxable, depending on your total income, including tax-exempt income. In time this will probably be increased so that 100 percent of your benefits are taxed.

• **Needs-based test required in order to receive full benefits.** Right now anyone, regardless of income or net worth, can receive Social Security benefits if fully "insured" in the system (generally ten years of participation). This is likely to change to exclude the wealthy from receiving full benefits. After all, the original purpose of Social Security was to provide a safety net to those who had little else for retirement.

• **Increase in the age at which you are entitled to maximum retirement benefits.** A gradual increase in the age limit from sixty-five to sixty-seven is already in place for those born after 1937; as life expectancies continue to increase, the system will be able to justify further increases in the age limit. When Social Security was first enacted and the normal retirement age was set at sixty-five, most people did not live more than a few years beyond their retirement date. Now the average life expectancy for retirees at age sixty-five is fourteen years for men and eighteen years for women, with half of retirees living longer than that. No wonder the system has gotten into trouble! It's paying benefits for many years longer than anyone envisioned when it was first created.

CURRENT AGE REQUIREMENTS FOR FULL SOCIAL SECURITY BENEFITS

Year of Birth	*Full Retirement Age*
1937 or earlier	65
1938	65 and 2 months
1939	65 and 4 months
1940	65 and 6 months
1941	65 and 8 months
1942	65 and 10 months
1943–54	66
1955	66 and 2 months
1956	66 and 4 months
1957	66 and 6 months
1958	66 and 8 months
1959	66 and 10 months
1960 and later	67

Feeling a Triple Squeeze? Welcome to the Sandwich Generation

> It's hard to save from what we earn. Each month about $700 goes to the kids' college, car, or insurance expenses and $1,100 goes to supporting my mother in a retirement home in Florida. (Annabelle Q., age forty-nine)

Chances are, several hands are reaching into your wallet at this moment. If you feel caught in the middle, supporting generations on both sides of you at the same time as you're trying to save for retirement, know that you are not alone. Here's what to do:

1. **Be realistic about what you can and cannot do.** Develop a list of expenses, prioritize them, and compare with your income. Put your own retirement planning, if not *at* the top, at least near the top of the list.
2. **Hold an intergenerational family meeting.** Gather parents and children to go over all anticipated expenses and all sources of income. If it sounds too ambitious to have everyone present simultaneously, meet with each party individually, but cover the same issues. Get a mediator or professional counselor involved if need be.
3. **Look at ways of cutting expenses and saving tax dollars.** If you support parents whose income is low, declare them as dependents and take a tax deduction. At work, use a flex plan—or Section 125—to pay for elder care with pretax dollars.
4. **Brainstorm creative ways to meet expenses.** Can the children work? Can one of your parents supplement their income? If the children and grandparents get along well, perhaps an investment in real estate to house them both—like a duplex near the college—might make sense.

Our Retirement or the Children's College Education—Which Shall It Be?

It may surprise you that saving for your retirement instead of saving for your child's college expenses may actually pay more of the education bills. That's not what you generally hear, but here's the scoop.

Although recently published studies project that the cost of a four-year college education will spiral toward $250,000 in less than two decades, saving for college may hurt more than it helps in one vital aspect: financial aid. More than 50 percent of students enrolled in post-secondary education receive some form of financial aid.

Calculating the amount of aid families qualify for involves determining their expected family contribution (EFC). The EFC is the sum of the student and parents' available income and assets that must be spent on college before the student is eligible for financial aid. If the cost of college is greater than the EFC, the student is eligible for aid. Eligibility for financial aid is determined by a host of factors, including the parents' income, family assets, and the number of family members currently enrolled in school.

Now for a bit of irony: families whose incomes and assets would technically qualify them for financial aid may be rejected because of how they have allocated their savings. Money set aside specifically for college may count toward the EFC. But savings in retirement plans, life insurance, and home equity are excluded from the calculation of EFC. Consider the Joneses and the Smiths, both with identical incomes and both with a son who will enter college next year at the cost of $13,000.

	Jones Family	*Smith Family*
Husband's income	50,000	40,000
Wife's income	30,000	40,000
Son's income	3,000	3,000
Family savings	32,000	32,000
Retirement savings	40,000	0
College savings in son's name	4,000	44,000
Cost of college	13,000	13,000
Less EFC (expected family contribution)	(8,498)	(22,498)
Financial aid	4,502	0

It's clear that the Joneses are the winners in this situation, because they have stashed $40,000 in their 401(k) plan and still maximized their eligibility for financial aid for Jim Jr.'s college expenses. If necessary they can dip into their retirement funds to meet the remainder of Jim Jr.'s college expenses.

The Smiths, however, do not qualify for any financial aid for Sam Jr. The only difference between the Joneses' and the Smiths' financial situation was the amount saved specifically in Sam Jr.'s name rather than in a retirement plan. The financial aid paperwork that parents complete asks for details on assets owned by parents and child but specifically exempts information on the value of retirement plans, including pensions, annuities, IRAs, and Keogh plans.

Starting with parents' adjusted gross income (AGI), the Department of Education, through either of two agencies, the College Scholarship Service of the College Board or the American College Testing program, will deduct certain allowances:

- federal taxes paid
- a state tax allowance ranging from 2 to 11 percent, depending on the state
- Social Security taxes
- income protection allowance, ranging from $9,240 to $23,670
- employment expense allowance, generally $2,500

Parents are expected to spend a percentage of the net income after allowances on their child's educational costs. That percentage ranges from 22 to 47 percent and is the first element of the EFC.

Keep in mind, though, that money you contributed toward a retirement plan in the year before the child enters college *is* counted as available income, and therefore figures into the EFC. For example, if you've contributed $5,000 to your 401(k) during that time period, it will not be sheltered.

College financial aid is a complex area, and many parents miss out

---

SMART TIP

DON'T CASH OUT

Consider giving appreciated stocks to your children rather than selling the stocks and giving cash. If your child is older than thirteen, this is a tax-smart way to come up with money for education expenses. Remember, if you sell the securities yourself, you'll pay tax on any long-term gains at the 28 percent rate. By giving the stocks to your child and letting him or her sell them, the gain will be taxed at the child's rate, which is presumably lower than yours. But be aware that your child must hold those stocks for two years before selling them, or the gain will be taxed at your tax rate, not theirs.

---

because of a poor understanding of the system. Check with a financial adviser who specializes in advising parents regarding financial aid sources. This is one situation where saving diligently for your retirement may pay more bills than you think.

Your Parents and Your Finances—Balancing Their Needs with Your Obligations

> They're very private about their finances. I don't know if they have enough to live on or what plans they've made if one of them gets sick or dies. It's so hard to talk about money. (Hal A., age forty-five)

> I guess we've put off asking about her finances. I hate the thought of her getting sick or, worse yet, dying. I'm also a bit afraid that she'll think we're after her money if we bring up the subject. She's a very proud person and she could take it wrong. (Stephanie R., age fifty)

The day may soon come when your parents can no longer handle finances on their own. Then you will have to take over. If you don't plan for that day now, you may regret it—and pay for it as well—for the rest of your parents' lives and possibly your own. A debilitating illness can sap family fortunes as money is needed for health care.

> Mom had been in an assisted-living-care facility, but she was declining. When the facility could no longer take care of her needs, we had to move her to a convalescent hospital. Insurance didn't cover her care and there were no government subsidies for either of these places. When I wrote out a check for $3,500 for one month to the convalescent home, it really hurt. And neither my brother nor sister had any money to contribute to Mom's care. (George P., age forty-nine)

To avoid problems like these, here are some steps you'll want to take now:

1. Be sensitive and caring, but do broach the subject of finances. You might be a role model, showing Mom and Dad a financial plan you've recently done for yourself. Say that you just want to make sure they aren't worried about finances, and if they are, you want to help. If they bring up a friend who has had financial difficulties or steep bills, use the opening to ask whether they are confident that their own financial affairs are in order. Ask what you can do to ensure that their wishes will be carried out if they should die or cannot make decisions themselves.

2. Develop with parents a clear picture of their net worth, income, assets and liabilities, bank accounts, insurance, and so on. Make sure they have—and you can find—key documents such as tax returns, pension and retirement plan records, insurance policies, and wills, trusts, and durable powers of attorney for both financial and medical decisions. These powers of attorney may be more important than you realize. They certainly were for Edwin, a fifty-nine-year-old retired engineer who survived a brain aneurysm: "Waking up from a six-month coma and hearing that neither your spouse nor your children could sign checks or pay bills, so your home has been repossessed, is not what most of us want."

3. Get names, addresses, and phone numbers of advisers your parents have worked with: estate-planning attorney, insurance agent, accountant who has prepared past tax returns, and financial planner or investment adviser.

4. Discuss with your parents some of the sticky, tricky issues: What if there is a potential shortage of cash? Are there uninsured risks? Do they have or could they get long-term-care coverage? Are there any tax problems you should know about? Are their investments appropriate given their ages, needs, and economic circumstances? Are their wills or trusts current?

5. If they don't have long-term-care insurance, look into getting a policy. This type of coverage is most appropriate for those with $200,000 to $2 million in assets, not including their home. Depending on the rules in your state, people with less than that may be eligible to have long-term care paid for by Medicaid, while multimillionaires can probably afford to pay for such care on their own.

6. You'll want to ask where your parents would like to stay if they become incapacitated. Home health care may seem appealing, or moving in with family members, or living in a nursing home or community care complex. Start researching possible facilities now through your city or state's department for the aging.

7. If your parent is already in need of help, consider a geriatric-care manager. For adult children who can't take the time off from work to make arrangements or who aren't able to be with their parent to supervise care, a geriatric-care manager will do it for a fee. Private geriatric-care managers, often social workers or nurses, can help you with everything from arranging for home repairs and for meals to be delivered, to hiring someone to care for Mom or Dad at home or finding a nursing home. They also may provide counseling for patients and family members.

Two good resources: *Before the Other Shoe Drops*, by Penny Fall, is a twelve-page worksheet available for three dollars from Fall (Washington College, 300 Washington Ave., Chestertown, MD 21620). Profits go to Washington College's annual fund. *One of These Days, We'll Have to Get Organized*, by Donald Upp ($21.95, JADLU Press, Box 554, Jenision, MI 49429), is a helpful workbook you can use to make sure you and your parents don't overlook any important information.

The Starting Place—Your Retirement Assets

Now that we've considered some of the personal aspects of the retirement challenge, let's consider your retirement assets and how much income you'll really need to live comfortably.

The first step in making sure you can still afford your standard of living after twenty or thirty years of not working is to get a snapshot of your retirement assets. Let's assume you'll have a pension from your employer, Social Security payments, and some funds from various sources such as 401(k)s, IRAs, and your own savings and investments. You also may have significant equity in a home.

For someone retiring now at sixty-five who has been earning at or above the maximum Social Security earnings base ($65,400 in 1997), the top monthly Social Security benefit will be $1,200. For a worker and spouse the same age, the benefit will be $1,800.

Your Social Security check increases along with inflation, at least for now. Benefits ratchet up at the same rate the consumer price index rises. As for company pensions, if you have been earning at or above the maximum Social Security base and are retiring at sixty-five with twenty-five years of service, your annual payout likely will be $25,000 or more. Unfortunately, pension plan benefits almost never increase with inflation.

For some, pension plans don't even exist. The retirement mainstay

Worksheet 3.1

A SNAPSHOT OF YOUR ASSETS THAT WILL PROVIDE RETIREMENT INCOME

SOURCES OF REGULAR ANNUAL INCOME	
Social Security annual benefits	$______
Pensions, including spouse's, if applicable	______
Annuities	______
TOTAL REGULAR ANNUAL INCOME	$______
ASSETS STRICTLY FOR RETIREMENT	
Profit-sharing accounts (total)	$______
Employment savings plans (401(k), 457, ESOP, etc.)	______
Tax sheltered annuities (403(b) plans)	______
Individual retirement accounts (IRAs)	______
Keogh accounts	______
OTHER ASSETS AVAILABLE FOR RETIREMENT	
Bank accounts	______
Money market funds	______
CDs	______
Treasury bills	______
Common stocks	______
Bonds	______
Mutual funds	______
Business interests	______
Real estate investments	______
Vacation home	______
Other	______
TOTAL VALUE OF ALL ASSETS AVAILABLE TO GENERATE RETIREMENT INCOME	$______

of our parents' generation—pension plans that pay a benefit based on years of service combined with the employee's earnings—are becoming scarce. They are being replaced with employee savings plans, such as 401(k) plans, 403(b) plans, and TSAs—plans that rely on employees foregoing part of their current income and stashing it in the plan tax-deferred. In many of these plans the employer matches part of the employees' contributions. Because the plan is funded primarily by the employee, it is far less expensive for the employer. And because many employees decline participation, it is cheaper still.

Complete Worksheet 3.1 on page 57. With a snapshot of your assets, you'll be ready to crunch some numbers with the retirement-planning software listed in the resources section at the end of the book. If that thought doesn't appeal to you, check out the worksheets in chapter 5 or visit a friendly financial planner who will run the numbers for you. The goal is to compare how much income you will need when you retire—taking into account the number of years until you retire, the rate of expected inflation, and the expected annual returns on your investments—with how much income your total assets will generate.

Sizing Up Your Retirement Needs

The way things are going, it is estimated that nearly eight out of ten Americans will have less than half of the annual income they need to retire comfortably. To ensure that you'll have enough for the next fifty years, here are some things you should do now.

1. **Determine the size of your nest egg.** You may be saving money in a variety of investment vehicles and be unaware of your total retirement assets—or what income you can expect from those assets.

2. **Contact your employer regarding the amount vested in your pension plan.** Find out how and when the funds will be disbursed. An employee usually has a choice at retirement of a lump-sum distribution, a rollover into an IRA, or some form of annuity. The best choice will depend on your individual circumstances.

3. **Determine what it costs you to live now.** If you find it hard to follow a budget before retirement, we can guarantee it won't be any easier after. Practice budgeting for retirement by living on the amount that you plan for retirement. If that's a struggle, you may not be ready to retire.

4. **Estimate your after-retirement expenses.** This is simple budget planning. Start with your current expenses but subtract those that are

work related, such as office wardrobe and commuting expenses. Be sure to add expenses you'll have after retirement that you don't have now. For example, health-care benefits formerly paid by your employer may become a personal expense after retirement. If you now drive a company car, you'll have added automobile expenses after you retire.

5. Determine the balance on your mortgage. Will it be paid off when you retire? If not, when? This information is essential for calculating item 4.

6. Contact Social Security to determine your estimated retirement benefits. As we said earlier in the chapter (see page 48), it is wise to contact the Social Security Administration several years in advance of your planned retirement date, and annually for the last three years before retirement, to obtain information about your account. That way if there are any problems, you'll have time to resolve them before you actually retire.

7. Review how current tax laws will affect your retirement income. There are a lot of issues here—how to take assets out of your retirement plan, how those assets will be taxed, and whether you'll be in a lower income tax bracket after you retire. Don't forget state taxes. For example, you may be moving from a state that has an income tax to a state that has none (such as Florida).

8. Plan now to pay off debts before you retire. It might be wise to pay down large debts prior to retirement and get major expenses out of the way—such as buying a new car or remodeling a kitchen.

9. If you're planning to work after retirement, be aware of the income limitations established by Social Security. If you earn more than a certain amount, your benefits will be reduced. If your earnings will exceed that amount, it may pay to delay applying for Social Security, so you can collect a larger benefit later on.

10. Review your insurance policies to determine which policies can be restructured or canceled. After you retire, you won't need disability coverage any longer, but you may need long-term-care coverage. The insurance you need may depend on your retirement age; for example, you won't be eligible for Medicare benefits until age sixty-five. If you retire at sixty-two, you'll need to plan for health coverage during that three-year gap.

11. Update your estate planning. Do you have a will and understand the laws pertaining to inheritance, estate taxes, and probate? How you take distributions from a retirement plan can affect your estate plan, and vice versa. Examine and coordinate all of the various elements of your estate and retirement plans.

12. Inform your spouse, children, relatives, or a close friend where your important records are kept. This is a good time to get organized, if you aren't already.

13. Consider where you want to live after retirement. If you plan to move, have you taken into account possible changes in your cost of living?

14. Coordinate plans with your spouse. Is your spouse planning to retire at the same time you do? A wife may have entered the workforce later than her husband and may be at her peak earning years just as he is ready to retire. Their lifestyles may not be in sync. What about yours?

In the pages that follow, we give you the information you need to get ready in earnest for your retirement, whatever form it may take during your next fifty years.

PART II

GETTING READY

4

• • • • • • • • • •

Retirement Planning Begins with Investment Planning

> When the people in my company were offered a retirement package, the company did some brown bag lunches and had stockbrokers and financial planners come and speak to us. It was interesting, but I don't think I really got good, solid information about the investment options. Both Jeanne and I felt confused and frustrated because we know how important this decision is for the rest of our lives. (Mark E., age forty)

In today's world, more and more of the responsibility for saving and for investing for retirement falls squarely on the shoulders of workers. Study after study shows that baby boomers don't save enough or feel confident about their investment know-how when making decisions about how their money should be invested in their 401(k) plans or other retirement savings.

So whether you are thirty-something, fifty-something, or something in between, keep in mind three key concepts:

• **You're younger than you think.** A long-term investor expects his or her money to stay invested and grow for at least ten years, and your retirement assets may be in place for as long as forty to fifty years. Since your life expectancy is considerably longer than that of your parents, if you are anywhere south of seventy-five you are a long-term investor and should plan your investments so that they can provide both growth and income during the rest of your life, whether you choose to retire, work part time, or work till you drop.

• **Investing successfully is simpler than you think.** During the last several years you've been bombarded with information from mutual funds, stockbrokers, financial advisers, even your local bank. By now you may feel overwhelmed by information, confused by choices, and frustrated by decisions you must make. But if you understand just a few basic concepts, you can cut through the jargon and mystique of Wall Street and develop an effective portfolio of investments.

• **You can afford to take greater risk to get more return.** Four-letter words sometimes makes us feel uncomfortable, and "risk" is no exception. But "safe" should make us squirm even more. If you invest solely in bond funds, CDs, and treasury bills, which are generally considered very safe investments, you are actually putting yourself at more risk than you would be by adding "risky" stocks and international mutual funds. Why? Because if you are a long-term investor, you know that over the long haul, taxes and inflation are the most constant risks of all, and those "safe" fixed-income investments just don't make enough to achieve growth in your portfolio over time.

While it may be nice to know you're younger than you think, investing is simpler than you think, and you can take more risk than you think, why does planning and saving for your next fifty years sometimes seem overwhelming? It doesn't have to be. In the pages that follow, we look at various types of investments and some simple strategies for investing. The process of investing should become easier, whether you choose to go it on your own, use a professional adviser, or choose some combination of the two. By the end of this chapter you'll have a clear picture of what investments you should have if you are targeting retirement in twenty years, or in fifteen, ten, five, or two years.

Mistakes to Avoid

Most people have it backward. They think that they must begin the investment process by picking individual stocks, bonds, and mutual funds. Not true.

To determine how to invest for your next fifty years, start by asking yourself three questions: What are my goals in terms of income and lifestyle when I retire? How much time do I have before retirement? What's the best mix of investments (stocks, bonds, cash) to produce the return I need and yet not take undue risks? How you answer the first two questions determines the answer to the last question.

> For most of my adult life, I've looked around for the "best" investments. How do they fit with my own goals? I guess I didn't really think about it. It's sort of like packing a suitcase for an unknown destination. (Sandra M., age fifty-one)

When it comes to investing money for retirement, many of us haphazardly pack our suitcases with an unclear picture of where we're heading and when we expect to arrive. Imagine opening a suitcase with all casual clothes when you like the symphony and dining out. Or a suitcase with all shoes rather than a variety of clothing items that would serve you better. So often this is true of our portfolios—either they are filled with investments with such low returns that they won't allow us to enjoy the good life or they are not diversified enough to protect us from risks. We don't seem to have a plan as to when we want to retire, what it will cost to live the lifestyle we want, how much we need to save now, or what rate of return we need to earn on those savings. Without a clear focus, we are vulnerable to making mistakes in investing that can cost us dearly over time. Consider whether any of the following are getting in your way as you plan for your next fifty years.

Our timing is off. We know the stock market goes up and down, but unfortunately, we can't accurately predict the peaks and valleys. As you approach retirement, you've experienced many business and market cycles. Many people seem to have a knack for selling a stock just before it goes up and for buying just prior to a downturn. It goes something like this:

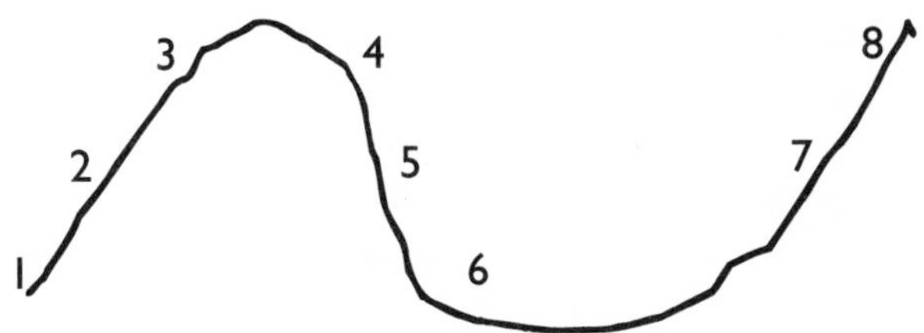

1. "The market is risky. I'm not interested."
2. "This market is getting interesting, I had better watch it more closely."
3. "I'll lose a great opportunity if I don't buy now."
4. "This is just a minor correction. It will be back up soon."
5. "I'll just wait till it gets back to where I bought it, then I'll sell."
6. "This is a loser, I'd better get out."
7. "No way am I getting back in the market."
8. "I'll lose a great opportunity if I don't buy now."

And so it goes. This episodic panic selling on downturns and overoptimistic buying when the market is soaring will ultimately mean lower returns, costly transactions, tax consequences, and last but not least a lessening in the self-confidence we have about our investment skills and acumen. Market timing accounts for only 1.7 percent of the performance in a portfolio, according to the Brinson, Singer, Beebower study in 1991. Yet we spend a lot of time trying to psych out the market turns. A buy-and-hold strategy will produce superior results most of the time for most people.

The thought of losing money scares us. Stocks generate superior returns over the long haul, so it makes sense for anyone with a time horizon of more than three to five years to own stocks. Yet many investors who are decades away from retirement wouldn't dream of putting their money in the stock market. People suffer more pain from losses than they receive pleasure from gains, so they tend to be more risk averse than is good for them.

We drive by looking in the rearview mirror. The 1987 stock market crash which occurred after the market had gone up, up, and then some was precipitated by rising interest rates. Investors' expectations had bid prices up, but earnings of corporations were not moving up at the same rate that share prices were. Many investors were swept up in optimism as stock prices went higher and became more nervous as prices began to fall. What happened in 1987 terrified many novice and not-so-novice investors. While a crash like that occurs infrequently, many people have been paralyzed with worry about a correction happening again.

We miss the big picture and the long term. Most of us don't look at our entire portfolio. Instead we focus on each investment in isolation. We see the risk of individual securities rather than viewing the overall picture over time. As a result we may fret over short-term performance, which can lead to excessive trading and bad decisions. During a recent correction in the stock market, many clients, such as Cassandra, age forty-nine, expressed their fears to us: "Stocks are going down the tubes. We're definitely in a bear market now and I'm thinking of selling out my entire portfolio. What do you think?"

We asked Cassandra when she would need to spend her money, although we knew the answer. Most of her investments were in her IRA, set aside for retirement, and she couldn't touch those assets without penalty for another ten years. Selling now when stocks were in a valley instead of waiting for later peaks made no sense. Cassandra's short-term myopia would have cost her dearly had she sold when she wanted to. But it's human nature to feel panic, and novices often sell at the wrong time. Luckily, Cassandra had level-headed professional advisers to help her through the crisis.

Choosing a Financial Adviser

At this age and stage in your life, you may already have had some experience with financial planners, stockbrokers, and investment managers. Some of the experience may have been good, some bad. As you plan for retirement, whether it's a few years away or many, here are some tips on evaluating, selecting, and monitoring a financial adviser.

Start your search for professional advice in your employer's pension and benefits office. Many employers maintain a list of financial advisers in the area who have an excellent reputation. Also ask friends and associates who are using advisers themselves.

Check with the Institute of Certified Financial Planners (800-282-7526) for a list of names of certified planners in your area. The International Association for Financial Planning will give you names of their members nearby. Write the IAFP at Two Concourse Parkway, Suite 800, Atlanta, GA 30328, or call 800-945-4237.

Find out in advance how your planner is compensated. Commissioned planners charge for their services by collecting commissions for funds, annuities, and insurance policies they sell you, while fee-only planners charge an hourly fee or an overall fee for their services—no commissions. Many planners charge a combination of fees and commissions. You can get a directory of fee-only practitioners from the National Association of Personal Financial Advisers at 1130 Lake Cook Road, Suite 105, Buffalo Grove, IL 60089, or call 800-366-2732.

After you've assembled a list of prospective advisers, call or visit several. Ask them these questions:

- *How long have you been providing financial-planning or investment management services?*

Those who have been in the business for eight to ten years or more have experienced the ups and downs of the market. They may bring a maturity and a sense of what works and doesn't work from their dealings with a number of clients over the years. Don't completely discount advisers who are relatively new, though. They may have fewer clients than more established advisers and be more motivated to provide a higher level of personalized service.

• *What are your credentials and qualifications?*

Many qualified advisers have "CFP" after their names. These letters mean that the adviser is a certified financial planner who has completed the courses required to earn the designation. CFPs must also complete thirty units of course work every two years to keep the designation current.

• *Have you ever had a complaint filed by a client?*

Steer clear of advisers who have had frequent complaints filed against them. You can find information on part 1 of the adviser's ADV, a disclosure form the adviser should furnish you. You can also call your state securities department and the federal Securities and Exchange Commission in Washington at (202) 942-8088 to find out if there are any investigations pending or disciplinary actions taken against the adviser. If the adviser works for a National Association of Securities Dealers (NASD) member firm, you can call the NASD at 800-289-9999 to get this information.

• *How much money do you have under management?*

The money managed by the adviser's firm should be at least $100 million, large enough that you'll benefit from economies of scale, such as institutional-trading rates and access to research and other services. But beware the busy adviser who personally manages that much, particularly if the firm manages over $1 billion. If you are a small client, you may not get the attention you deserve.

• *What is your investment philosophy?*

Advisers should be able to clearly explain why they make the investments they do, and their approach should mesh with your investment philosophy. The adviser's style should be in sync with what you would do if you had the knowledge, the time, and the access to research that he or she does.

• *How diversified are your clients' portfolios?*

Some professionals specialize in stocks or bonds, mutual funds or individual issues. Search out a money manager who puts together portfolios with a blending of stocks and bonds, using mutual funds, individual issues, or a combination of both. A well-diversified portfolio should include stocks in domestic and international large, midsize, and small companies, as well as bonds. To achieve diversification you can select different managers for stocks and for bonds and coordinate it all yourself, or consolidate your investments under one manager who will design, select, and monitor the investments you have.

• *What rates of return have you achieved for your clients?*

The adviser should be able to furnish you a five-year track record with returns within the range of appropriate benchmarks such as the Standard & Poor's 500 index for stocks and the Shearson-Lehman bond index for fixed-income investments. A good manager may outperform the index in up markets, but that isn't as important as how well the adviser protects your portfolio in down markets. Remember, it is steady, consistent growth that you are looking for.

- *How often do you communicate with clients, and in what format?*

Your adviser should furnish you a performance report at the end of each quarter. Many advisers also call their clients regularly, and publish regular newsletters or other written correspondence. Tell the adviser just how involved you want to be in the investment process and how often you would like to be contacted.

- *What is your minimum account size?*

Some managers take accounts as low as $50,000 and use mutual funds for the investments. Although this minimum amount is effective to get the diversification you need, most managers require a minimum account size of $200,000 or more.

- *What is your average account size?*

With this information you'll be able to judge whether you'll be a big fish in a little pond or a tadpole. In the ideal world, service would not vary from client to client based on the size of the account, but the investment world is far from ideal.

- *What is the profile of your typical client?*

If the typical client is not even remotely related to who and what you are, this professional is probably not for you. The closer the typical client fits your profile, the more likely your concerns will be understood and addressed.

- *How are you compensated?*

A professional who charges a commission will make money only if you buy or sell something. Beware of the financial adviser who is anxious to churn your account and who has only his or her own interests in mind. On the other hand, if the commission-based financial adviser is trustworthy, once he or she has invested your assets, there probably will not be major shifts in your assets, and so you will continue to receive the adviser's professional expertise at little cost to you. If the financial adviser charges a fee for service, either at an hourly rate or as a percentage of the amount of money being managed, you are less likely to find that the adviser's interests are in conflict with yours. If the adviser is compensated at a percentage of your invested portfolio, when your account does well, he or she makes more money; when it goes down, he or she makes less. But be aware that you will be paying for the services year after year, even if relatively few changes are needed.

• *Given my situation, what might you recommend?*

Explain your current investments, your ability to save, when you expect to retire, and what you'll need in terms of income. Then let the professional give you some ideas and recommendations. Do they make sense in terms of what you think you need? Is the adviser's rationale for the recommendations clear?

• *Can you provide me with references?*

Ask the adviser for the names of a few of his or her clients whose financial goals resemble yours, and for permission to call them. Do call those clients and ask about their satisfaction with the adviser's services and how well their investments have performed.

Major Classes of Investments

Magazines such as *Money, Kiplinger's, Forbes,* and *Mutual Funds* may leave you more confused than when you started reading, because each one gives different advice on which mutual funds to buy now. If you are thinking of buying an annuity, you're bombarded with brochures, ads, commercials, and advisers, all touting different annuities. At best you are overwhelmed and frustrated by too much information, but information overload may even cause you to procrastinate making investment decisions.

To relieve your frustration, realize that you don't need to learn about all of the investments that are on the market to pick good ones that fit your goals. Investments aren't as tricky as they appear at first blush. There are really only three basic investment classes to consider: stocks, bonds, and cash. You can purchase individual stocks and bonds or choose mutual funds that invest in both. Your cash investments may include savings accounts, money market funds, certificates of deposit, or short-term treasury bills.

Stocks

Growth stocks are shares in companies that have in the past grown faster than the economy and are expected to continue to grow rapidly in the future. Most are large companies, like Microsoft, that pay little in dividends because they plow most of their profits back into the business to maintain growth. Growth stocks are generally medium-risk investments.

Small-company growth stocks, such as those offered by bioengineering companies or new telecommunications technology companies, offer a chance for faster growth, but they're more volatile and therefore riskier.

Income stocks pay out dividends, which are a percentage of earnings, to shareholders in the form of cash or fractional shares. These companies are generally large, well-established companies with reasonably reliable earnings, such as public utilities or banking institutions. Because of the dividend return, income stocks are generally lower-risk investments than growth stocks.

Bonds

Bonds come in two primary varieties. *Corporate bonds* are loans you make to corporations. The interest rate you are promised on that loaned money depends on the financial strength of the issuing company and the length of the loan, as reflected in the bond's maturity date. In general, the longer the maturity date, the higher the stated interest rate. Weaker companies with a greater risk of default will also pay higher interest rates. These bonds are called "high-yield" or "junk" bonds, in contrast with high-quality bonds issued by companies with stronger financials. If safety is important to you, buy only bonds rated AA or better by Moody's and Standard & Poor's, the major rating services.

Tax-advantaged bonds include municipal bonds issued by states and municipalities and U.S. Treasury and other federal agency bonds. We call them "tax advantaged" because the interest you earn is tax-free, as states don't tax interest paid by the federal government and the IRS doesn't tax interest paid by the states. Most states don't tax bonds issued by municipalities within their states, so, for example, if you live in California and buy California "munis" you will not pay state *or* federal taxes on the interest you earn. Consequently, expect the stated interest rate on such bonds to be lower than the rate on corporate bonds. Bonds issued by the U.S. Treasury are the safest fixed-income securities because they are guaranteed by the full faith and credit of the federal government. They also pay somewhat less than top-rated corporate bonds with similar maturities. If you are in a low tax bracket, you won't save as much by investing in government bonds as someone in a higher bracket, and so the tax savings may not make up for the lower interest paid by those bonds. If you are in a low tax bracket or are investing money within a retirement plan that pays no current income tax on earnings, you should invest in higher-paying corporate bonds.

Mutual Funds

> I like mutual funds. They're easy to invest in, and through them I can own more different stocks. I feel like there's a professional team selecting and monitoring those stocks. (Rita L., age forty-eight)

You can gain access to both stocks and bonds through mutual funds. A mutual fund is a pool of money from investors with goals similar to yours. You buy shares in the fund, and the fund manager or investment committee invests your money in stocks or bonds of many different companies or government entities. As the investments go up or down in value, the value of the fund shares fluctuates.

Mutual funds rate a close look if you're managing your own retirement money. Owning shares in a fund gives you instant diversification, a slice of a professionally selected and managed portfolio tailored to your objectives. This is true of mutual funds you own through your 401(k) account as well as those you own individually. Here are the more common types of mutual funds, one or more of which almost certainly matches your investment objectives.

Stock Funds

Aggressive-growth funds seek maximum capital gains by investing in speculative stocks. These funds sometimes use high-risk investing techniques such as options and futures contracts, so they aren't for the faint of heart. Although their returns are sometimes staggeringly high, they can also dip precipitously. Over many years, the gains far outweigh the losses, so they best fit the investment objectives of people years from retirement. For example, Fred and Monica, both in their early thirties, are years from retirement, so aggressive-growth funds fit the bill for them. These funds are also right for Ted, who wants to establish a college fund for his six-year-old son.

Growth funds stress capital gains rather than income, by investing in stocks of companies likely to grow faster than average. Because they look for better-established companies than do aggressive-growth funds, they tend to be less volatile. Margo, age forty-two, moved her 401(k) funds from fixed income into growth—a smart move, as she did not plan to retire until fifty-five at the earliest.

Growth and income funds balance the objectives of long-term growth and current income by investing primarily in established companies that are growing while maintaining a solid record of paying dividends. Growth and income funds tend to be more stable than growth funds because their steady dividends cushion market falls. *Equity-income funds* are similar to growth and income funds, but a little less risky. They pursue current income by investing in the stock of companies that pay reliable dividends.

Balanced funds invest fairly equally in a mix of stocks and bonds in order to meet three objectives: to conserve principal, to pay current income, and to seek long-term growth of both principal and income. These more conservative funds have more conservative expectations for returns as well. Samantha and Richard chose the balanced fund option in each of their 401(k)s both to satisfy their conservative nature and because they planned to retire in about three years and would begin drawing money from their 401(k)s.

International funds invest their money in stocks of companies located outside the United States. These funds generally have the word *international* as part of their name or bear the name of the country or region in which they invest, for example Harbor International, Oakmark International, or Fidelity Latin America. *Global funds* are similar to inter-

---

SMART TIP

NINE IMPORTANT REASONS FOR INVESTING GLOBALLY

- Seven of the ten largest automobile manufacturers
- Eight of the ten largest electrical and electronics companies
- Seven of the ten largest insurance companies
- Eight of the ten largest chemical companies
- Eight of the ten largest machinery and engineering companies
- Eight of the ten largest financial services companies
- Eight of the ten largest electrical and gas utilities companies
- Eight of the ten largest appliances and appliance manufacturing companies
- Ten of the ten largest banking companies

... are located *outside of the United States!*

---

national funds but may also hold stocks issued by U.S.-based companies. We strongly recommend to our clients—and to you—that you invest 20 to 50 percent of your stock or mutual fund portfolio in international funds. International funds and global funds can be risky on their own, but when you mix them with other assets, such as U.S. large and small companies and bonds, you'll actually *lower* the overall risk in your portfolio. You'll see why in the section on diversification (page 75).

Sector funds concentrate their investments in a particular part of the economy, such as transportation, energy, or biotechnology. These funds can be extremely volatile, and success in this arena generally takes specialized knowledge of an industry. The Fidelity Fund family has more sector funds than any other fund family. Called Select Funds, they focus on such diverse investments as automotive, gold, financial services, energy, environmental, food, health care, technology, telecommunications, and utilities, among others.

Bond Funds and Other Fixed-Income Funds

Bond funds, which come in a variety of objectives, are far duller than stocks, because they are less volatile and offer lower long-term returns. Although bond funds provide ballast for your portfolio, they shouldn't be your sole investment. Bond funds and stock funds fit the tortoise and the hare scenario: it will take a very long time for the tortoise to reach its goals using bonds alone!

High-grade corporate bond funds are conservative investments that seek current income by investing primarily in investment-grade corporate bonds. Investment-grade bonds are rated AAA to BBB by Standard & Poor's or Aaa or Baa by Moody's. *High-yield corporate bond funds* invest most of their portfolios in lower-rated bonds, nicknamed "junk bonds," that pay a higher rate of interest. These are higher-risk investments, although fund managers attempt to minimize risk through diversification.

U.S. government income funds invest in bonds and notes issued by the U.S. Treasury or other governmental agencies. Because they are backed by the U.S. government or its agencies, these funds are the most conservative of the bond funds. They have some tax advantages as well, as income from U.S. bonds generally not is taxed by your state.

Municipal bond funds invest in tax-exempt bonds issued by state and local governments or their agencies, such as bridge or highway authorities. Municipal bond income isn't taxed by the U.S. government or by the state of issuance. If your state has high taxes, look for municipal bond funds investing solely in bonds from your state, so that the income will be free of both federal and state income taxes.

GNMA, or "Ginnie Mae," funds invest in pools of mortgage-backed securities issued by the Government National Mortgage Association. Although they may offer higher income than other bond funds, they often experience wide price swings as interest rates rise or fall.

Money market funds are perhaps most familiar to investors and savers. These funds buy short-term IOUs from corporations and the government and pay interest. The rate of interest fluctuates from week to week, but the principal does not. Because these funds return one dollar for each dollar invested, they are not true investments but are instead "parking places" for your money, just as are savings accounts and certificates of deposit.

Diversification

> Everything I read talks about diversification, so I've put my money in a lot of different funds, both in my 401(k) and my mutual fund investments. But I'm never sure I've made the right choices, or diversified enough, so I keep adding. Now I've got so many different investments it's hard to keep track. (Raymond F., age thirty-eight)

Diversification allows you to manage downside risk while you enjoy the upside of investing, by allocating your investment funds among different types of assets, such as stocks, bonds, real estate, and cash. Within the stock investments, you should go a step further and spread your dollars among large, midsize, and small company stocks and international stocks. Your portfolio should include stocks that reflect the growth style and the value style of investing.

Margo and Timothy were afraid of the stock market, so most of their investments were in bond funds—California municipal bond funds, some corporate bond funds, and two different GNMA funds. They also had a sizable amount in money market funds because they just didn't know what to invest in next. We analyzed their returns and found that in the first half of 1996, they experienced discouraging returns as interest rates rose and bond prices dropped. With a long time-horizon, Margo and Tim should have invested most of their money in stocks. But recognizing their conservative nature, we recommended a shift of only part of their investments to stocks. By changing to a more balanced mix of 50 percent bonds and 50 percent stocks, their returns would be substantially higher over time.

Diversification is not so much about increasing return as it is about reducing risk. Diversification reduces (but does not eliminate!) the risk of loss by blending your investments among assets that do well at different times. A well-diversified portfolio should provide moderate returns, and should minimize the downside risks so that you can sleep at night.

As you make investment decisions about your retirement funds, be mindful of how much your portfolio may grow each year and what risks you must take to achieve that growth. The annualized return for the investments you make reflects the growth, and the risk is measured by annualized standard deviation, which represents the variance or volatility in the annual return. For example, if your annualized return over twenty years is 10 percent and the standard deviation is 5 percent, two-thirds of the time you can expect a return that will be no more than 5 percent higher or lower than the 10 percent annualized return. In other words, the range of returns will fluctuate between 5 percent and 15 percent for two-thirds of the years. During the rest of the years you may have returns that are either higher than 15 percent or lower than 5 percent.

The trick, then, is to get the highest return possible with the least variance (standard deviation). Most institutional money managers maintain portfolios that are about 40 percent in long-term bonds and 60 percent in large-cap stocks, because research shows that that combination will have the highest returns over time. For that combination of investments, historical data show the annualized return would have been 13 percent and the standard deviation would have been 10 percent for the years 1976 to 1996. That means the annual returns on the portfolio would range between 3 percent and 23 percent in most years. The average return of 13 percent is pretty good, but you'll want to reduce the volatility if you can. You'll be ecstatic in the years you earn 23 percent or more, but in the years you earn 3 percent or less, you'll wish you'd left your money in the bank.

Here's what you can do to reduce the risk. By adding some shorter-maturity bonds, such as one-year and five-year bonds, and dividing the stock holdings equally between U.S. and foreign stocks, the historical returns increase to 13.4 percent and the standard deviation, the measure of risk or volatility, is reduced to 9.7 percent. Now your returns will generally be 3.7 percent to 23.1 percent, a less radical swing from year

PORTFOLIO 1

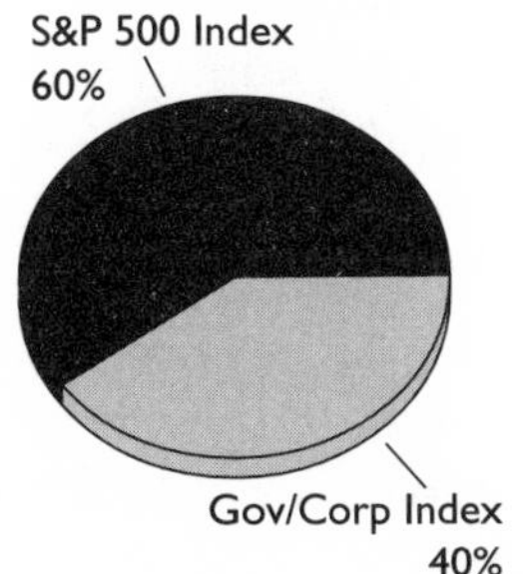

1976–96	Annualized return	Annualized Standard Deviation
Portfolio 1	12.99%	10.09%

PORTFOLIO 2

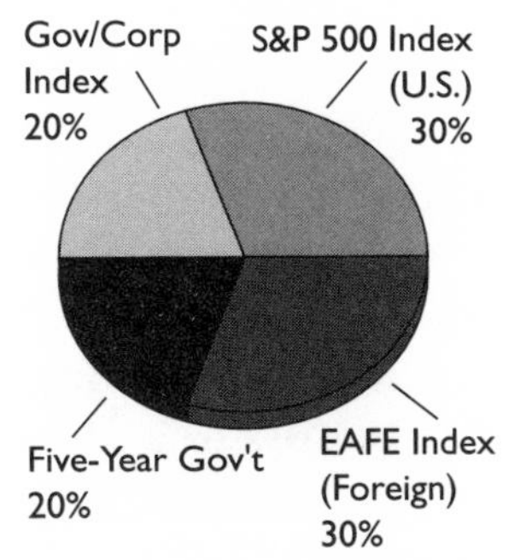

1976–96	Annualized return	Annualized Standard Deviation
Portfolio 1	12.99%	10.09%
Portfolio 2	13.38%	9.67%

PORTFOLIO 3

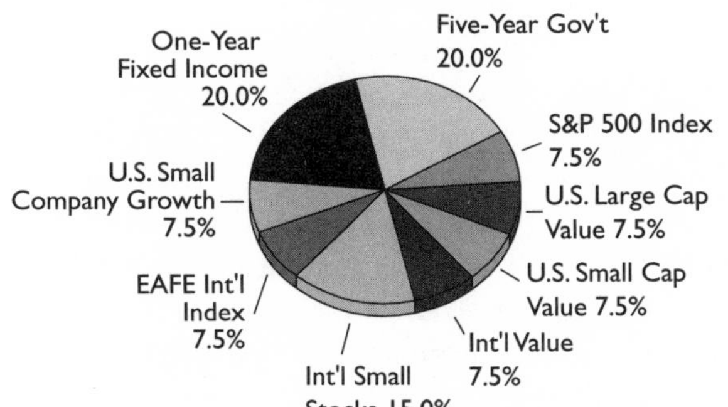

1976–96	Annualized return	Annualized Standard Deviation
Portfolio 1	12.99%	10.09%
Portfolio 2	13.38%	9.67%
Portfolio 3	14.98%	8.84%

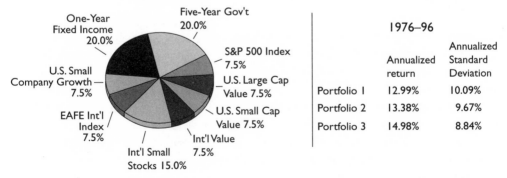

Data are from the University of Chicago, Ibbotson Associates, and Ibbotson and Sinquifield Associates.

to year. You may want to diversify even more by adding small stocks to both the domestic and international segments of your portfolio.

You can further enhance returns by adding value stocks, which are selling below their book value. Just as the bargain hunter peruses department store racks seeking top quality at a discount, the value investor looks for an out-of-favor company that is trading for less than the total value of its net assets, or one whose earnings represent a greater-than-average return on its current price.

The charts on page 77 show the benefits of effective diversification. By adding a variety of different investments to the standard mix of 60 percent stocks and 40 percent bonds, you improved your historic returns from 13.4 percent to 15 percent a year, while reducing the risk from 9.7 percent to 8.8 percent. The improved portfolio 3 offers historic returns most years of 6 percent to 24 percent compared to those of 3 percent to 23 percent for portfolio 1.

Managing Risk

No one likes to take unnecessary risks with their money, but every investment is associated with some risks. Certain investments, such as derivatives, commodities, and speculative stocks, are too risky for your retirement funds. But putting all of your money in savings accounts, certificates of deposit, and bonds is also a risky way to invest for your retirement needs. Because there is no such thing as a risk-free investment, the key to long-term growth is properly balancing risk.

Here are some of the risks you face as you invest.

Inflation risk. If you play it safe by putting all of your money in treasury bonds and certificates of deposit, you'll have less buying power in the future. Your principal may be safe, but the after-tax income it generates won't keep pace with rising prices. For example, the consumer price index (CPI), a measure of inflation, averages about 3 percent per year. That means each year 3 percent of your money has eroded in terms of purchasing power. So if you are getting 6 percent in a CD and the rate of inflation is 3 percent, your real return for that year is only 3 percent.

Interest-rate risk. When interest rates rise, the higher rates make the interest rates of existing bonds less attractive, so their market values decline. Rising interest rates also hurt stocks by making their dividend yields less appealing. Higher interest rates also reduce the profits of those who invest with money borrowed on margin accounts.

Economic risk. When the economy slows, shares of small companies may decline because they need a booming economy to sustain their growth. Cyclical companies, such as automakers and chemical producers, can't easily cut costs during a recession, so the value of their shares may nosedive. Economic downturns can also undercut junk bonds issued by financially weak firms that might default.

Market risk. Political developments, natural disasters, and Wall Street fads can batter investment markets. Tax law changes, trade agreements, program trading, even the quirks of investor psychology, all contribute to market risk, which accounts for much of the stock market's day-to-day volatility.

Specific risk. Poor management or bad luck can dampen earnings or even bankrupt a specific company, as can adverse government regulations. Earnings disappointments may ground high-flying growth stocks. Individuals assume high specific risk when they buy stock in a firm with a heavy debt burden or when they concentrate their holdings in a single industry. That is why sector funds are riskier than more diversified funds.

Your ability to tolerate risk will change as your temples gray and your career moves through different stages. To determine how much of each type of risk you have in your investments, look at the makeup of your retirement plans as well as your individually owned portfolio to answer the questions in Worksheet 4.1 on pages 80 and 81.

If your portfolio is perfectly balanced for risk, you will end up with a score of zero for each category. If not, it may be time to make some changes. Here is a list you can use to determine how to control each type of risk:

Type of Risk	*How to Control Risk*
Inflation risk	Invest for greater potential return such as stocks
Interest-rate risk—rising rates	Invest in short- or intermediate-term bonds
Interest-rate risk—falling rates	Invest in long-term bonds
Economic risk	Include several types of assets
Market risk	Invest for the long term
Specific risk—credit	Diversify bond issuers
Specific risk—poor performance	Diversify among different industries
Specific risk—bond defaults	Invest in high-grade or insured bond funds

Worksheet 4.1

HOW RISKY IS YOUR PORTFOLIO?

Questions	*Inflation Risk*	*Interest-Rate Risk*	*Economic Risk*	*Market Risk*	*Specific Risk*
Are you invested in fewer than four of these five categories: stocks, real estate, gold, bonds, and cash? If yes, score one point for each risk.					
Are more than 30 percent of your assets invested in any one of the five categories? If yes, score one point for each risk.					
Do you generally keep at least 15 percent of your portfolio in cash equivalents such as treasury bills or money market funds? If no, score two points for interest-rate risk.					
Do you have at least 30 percent of your portfolio in investments such as growth stocks and real estate, geared for long-term capital gains that can outpace inflation? If no, score two points for inflation risk.					
Is more than 30 percent of your portfolio in long-term government bonds, CDs, or annuities? If yes, then score three points each for inflation and interest-rate risk.					
Do you try to time the market and catch the highs and lows of different investments? If yes, score two points for market risk.					
Are you invested in small-growth stocks or junk bonds, which may fall sharply in a recession, for more than 25 percent of your portfolio? If yes, score three points for economic risk.					

Questions	*Inflation Risk*	*Interest-Rate Risk*	*Economic Risk*	*Market Risk*	*Specific Risk*
Do you use dollar-cost averaging or a similar plan that involves adding money to your investment portfolio at regular intervals? If no, score two points for market risk.					
Do you have more than 20 percent of your portfolio in a single industry? If yes, score three points each for economic risk, market risk, and specific risk.					
Does a rental property account for more than 30 percent of your portfolio? If yes, score one point for economic risk and three points for specific risk.					
Do stocks and bonds issued by one company (including the one that you work for) or shares in a single mutual fund comprise more than 15 percent of your assets? If yes, score three points each for economic risk, market risk, and specific risk.					
Do foreign stocks and shares of domestic companies with significant overseas sales account for less than 10 percent of your portfolio? If yes, score one point for economic risk.					

Adapted from *Investing for a Secure Retirement,* Junius Ellis and editors of *Money* (New York: Money Books, 1995).

Annuities—What Your Broker May Not Tell You

Annuities are similar in some ways to mutual funds, but they have the added feature of tax-deferred growth. Annuities offer you a way to build up a retirement fund without paying current taxes (a deferred annuity), and then they guarantee an assured income stream until your death (an immediate annuity). They are usually sold by insurance companies, although some mutual fund families now offer annuities too. You invest a lump sum or make regular payments over a number of years. The company will invest the money for you at a fixed rate of return (a fixed annuity), or invest in the subfunds of your choice (a variable annuity). Your money grows tax-deferred until you withdraw it, either in a lump sum or in a series of payments over a specified period of time. This tax-sheltered buildup of your money is the annuity's chief attraction. Although the money you invest isn't deductible on your tax return, it offers the same tax-deferred income advantages as an individual retirement account, and there's no limit to how much money you can put in.

Another benefit of a variable annuity is the guaranteed death benefit, which is sometimes coupled with a guaranteed income benefit. These guarantees provide that your total investment will never be worth less than the amount you invested plus a specified rate of return. That guarantee sounds great, but there's one hitch: It becomes effective upon your death, so you have to die to get it. It protects your heirs, not you.

Annuities have become very popular retirement savings vehicles, but they're not right for everyone. Be careful before you take the plunge. Here's what your broker may not be telling you:

• *If you own an annuity, when you die, your heirs can get hit with a big tax bill.* There is no step-up in basis for annuities as there is for mutual funds, stocks, or other assets. For example, if you invest $50,000 in an annuity and it is valued at $100,000 at your death, your heirs will owe income taxes on the $50,000 appreciation. If the same investment were in mutual funds, stocks, and other assets, there would be no income taxes on the $50,000 gain, because under current law there is a step-up in basis for such assets when you die. That means that when your heirs sell the stocks or mutual funds, they will be able to treat the $100,000 value at your death as their original cost for income tax purposes, and so they will owe income taxes only on the difference between the sales price and the $100,000 stepped-up basis.

• *The "guaranteed death benefit" won't completely protect your investment.* If your annuity loses money and you die before earning it back, your heirs get only the original principal you put in. Your heirs may never see any earnings or appreciation on your account, unless the guarantee extends to a guarantee of a specified income return as well as the original investment. In addition, the annuity must be in place at the time of your death. If you purchase an annuity and then liquidate your investment during your lifetime, there is no guarantee that you will get all of your money back.

• *Tax deferral has a downside.* When you withdraw from the annuity, the income portion is taxed as ordinary income, even if it is capital gains from the appreciation of the investment rather than from dividends. If you are in the maximum tax bracket, you'll be paying 39.6 percent plus state taxes on your withdrawals rather than 28 percent, the long-term capital gains rate.

• *The fees are higher in annuities than in comparable mutual funds.* Although you pay no commission when you buy, commissions of 4 to 6 percent paid to the broker come from two sources: the annuity's mortality and expense-risk fees, which typically run 1.25 percent annually, and the surrender charges, which typically begin at 7 percent in the first year and decline by one percentage point annually until they reach zero.

• *You'll pay a 10 percent penalty if you withdraw your money before age fifty-nine and a half.* This penalty is similar to the penalty for early withdrawals from IRAs.

The tax-deferral benefits of a variable annuity may make sense if it has strong returns, low expenses, and you pay no surrender charges. You should plan to hold it for at least twenty years and withdraw the money when your income tax rate is 28 percent or lower.

If you already own annuities and are not satisfied with the performance or you believe the insurance company may not be as financially solvent as you would like, you can roll the money over into another annuity tax-free under Internal Revenue Code section 1035. If you do a 1035 exchange, you'll pay no penalties and no income taxes, but there may be surrender charges if you are still within the surrender charge period on your current annuity.

Strategies for Growing Your Investments

Now that you know the basics on investment vehicles, financial advisers, diversification, and risk, here are some strategies that will serve you well as you plan for the next fifty years. You can apply these strategies to investments in your 401(k) plan and other retirement plans as well as investments you hold individually.

Start Early

Let's look at two hypothetical investors. Assume Janet and Jim each earn an 8 percent annual return on their investments over thirty-five years, from age twenty-five to age sixty. Janet invests $2,000 a year beginning at age twenty-five, but after ten years she stops adding to her investments, and so her total investment is $20,000. Jim doesn't invest a dime until he's thirty-five, but then he begins investing $2,000 a year and continues to do so for twenty-five years, for a total investment of $50,000. When she turns sixty, Janet's investments will have grown to $214,295, while Jim will have only $157,909, despite his having invested an additional $30,000. This hypothetical example demonstrates the power of starting to invest as early as you can.

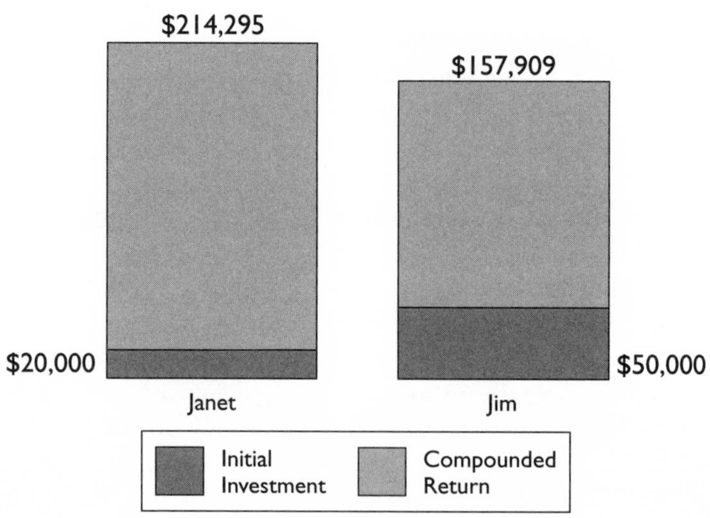

Go for Growth

Avoid bond funds for your long-term investments. The biggest mistake most people make in planning for retirement—besides not starting—is being too conservative and keeping most of their money in bonds, certificates of deposit, money market funds, and savings accounts. These fixed-income investments never deliver what you really want—a high total return over time. To maximize your return, invest for growth through stock equity funds rather than investing for income through bonds and bank deposits. For example, if George invested his $100,000 portfolio in bonds in 1975, by 1995 his holdings would have grown about 10 percent a year, to $846,000. If Harriet invested her $100,000 portfolio 85 percent in stocks, 10 percent in bonds, and 5 percent in cash, her investments would have grown about 20 percent a year, to $4,500,000. The longer your money has to grow, the more aggressive your investment stance should be toward growth.

Invest in the Northwest Quadrant

Your investment returns will range from low to high, and so will your investment risks. Just where is the northwest quadrant of investing? It's that quadrant in which we find investments with consistently above-average returns and consistently below-average volatility. To invest in the northwest quadrant, determine which of the risks we've discussed make it work for you and consider the relationship of risk to return for each of your investments.

PORTFOLIO—ROCKO AND SUZANNE

Return	Risk: *Low*	Risk: *High*
High	Income and Growth Fund S&P 500 Index Fund Blue Chip Stocks	Foreign Stocks Emerging Markets Fund Small Company Stocks
Low	Treasuries Money Market, CDs	New Business Venture Gold Penny Stocks

Worksheet 4.2

YOUR PORTFOLIO

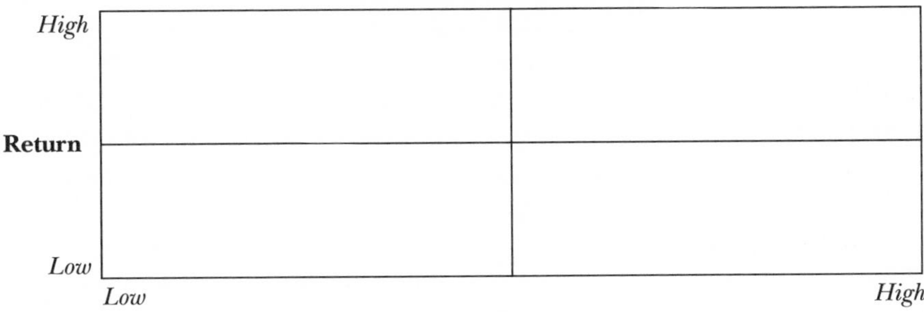

For example, we've analyzed the investments of a couple who expects to retire in three to five years. The quadrants on the chart on page 85 represent the level of potential risk they are taking as well as the potential return they can expect from each of their investments.

To see how close you are to the northwest quadrant, use the blank worksheet and plot your current investments. Include real estate, certificates of deposit, international stock funds, over-the-counter stocks, blue chip stocks, mutual funds, municipal bonds, and all retirement assets. This will give you an idea of whether you need to take more risk to get more returns.

Use Dollar-Cost Averaging

Dollar-cost averaging is a natural strategy for investing in 401(k) plans and other employee savings plans. This strategy involves investing a set amount of money into a mutual fund each month. Using this strategy, you'll actually benefit during market declines, because your monthly investment will buy more shares when the market is down than when the market is up. Studies show that you can achieve a better rate of return by using dollar-cost averaging than by trying to time the market and sell at the peaks and buy at the low points. Through steady monthly investments, you'll avoid the natural tendency to buy when the market is up and sell when it takes a dive. However, since this strategy involves regular investment, you should have the financial ability to continue purchases for a number of years, to take full advantage of market cycles.

Follow the Cocktail Napkin Strategy

Don't invest in anything you don't understand. Picture a cocktail napkin. If you can't draw a simple picture of what the company does or how the investment works on a piece of paper the size of that napkin, the investment isn't right for you. If you can't explain the investment to your child or spouse, don't buy it.

Let me share a personal story that coauthor Ginita Wall and I think demonstrates the cocktail napkin strategy. In 1986, needing a last-minute gift for a friend, I visited a new department store in Walnut Creek, California. The store furnishings were attractive, the products well displayed, and classical music was floating through the air. After a trying day at the office, the sight and sound of a pianist in a black tux created a wonderfully relaxed atmosphere for shopping. Delighted by the helpful treatment of the sales staff, I left feeling that this department store was not only innovative in approach but superior in service.

The next morning, after some careful research, I invested $18,000 in three hundred shares of Nordstrom Department Stores. Since then the stock has split several times, and my investment is now worth more than $50,000, a 178 percent increase. The moral of the story: If you are observant when you shop or eat out or just live your daily life, you too will be able to spot good stocks in growing industries.

Go for the Dogs

One successful investment strategy is to go for the so-called dogs of the Dow, the Dow-Jones industrial average stocks that pay high dividends but are out of favor with the market and trading at lower prices than one might expect. This strategy involves buying shares of the ten highest yielding stocks of the thirty stocks in the Dow-Jones industrial average. (You will find a list of those stocks in the *Wall Street Journal* as well as some other financial publications.) Hold these stocks for one year, then replace any that no longer make the list with new ones that do. Performance of this investment strategy over the past sixty years has bested almost every other investment strategy, with the dogs of the Dow exceeding 90 percent of all general equity funds.

Consider Costs and Expense Ratios

What you pay to make an investment has a direct impact on how much you will make on that investment. Costs include loads (brokerage commissions) and internal costs within mutual funds for management and for marketing. Let's look at the different kinds of costs you might pay.

Front-load funds

Most mutual funds purchased through a stockbroker, and some funds purchased directly from the mutual fund company, carry a front load, which means that a sales commission, called a load, is included in the sales price. Those loads generally range from 4 percent to 8.5 percent. For example, if you invest $1,000 in a mutual fund with a front load of 5 percent, $50 of your investment will go for the sales commission, so your net investment in the fund will be only $950.

For front-load funds, the load is included in the price of the fund. Funds are priced each day by computing the net asset value per share, known as the NAV, and then adding the load to the NAV. That becomes the "offer price," which you must pay to buy the fund. When you sell the fund, however, all you will receive is the NAV. For no-load funds, the NAV and the offer price are the same, because there is no markup for load.

No-load funds
Most of the mutual funds that sell their products directly to the public are no-load funds, which means that none of your money goes toward paying a sales commission—100 percent of the money you invest is put to work for you. No-load funds now account for more than half of the total assets in mutual funds, including money market funds.

Low-load funds
Some fund families, such as Fidelity, have added loads of 3 percent or so to some of their funds, although the loads are frequently waived for retirement accounts. Some low-load funds periodically have "specials" during which no load is charged, or they let investors in a new fund invest free of load, with loads being charged to subsequent investors.

Slow-load funds
Slow-load funds charge small annual fees. These 12b-1 fees, named after the 1980 Securities and Exchange Commission rule that permits them, cover distribution costs, a fancy term for the cost of advertising and selling the fund to you. At least half of all funds levy some sort of 12b-1 fee. The fee cannot be higher than .75 percent of assets per year plus an additional .25 percent service fee, for a total of 1 percent. Funds charging 12b-1 fees can't call themselves no load unless the fee is .25 percent or less.

The fee may not seem like much, but it is charged each year on the fund value, so it goes up as the value of your fund grows. However, an investor cannot pay more than an aggregate of 8.5 percent in 12b-1 fees for each fund. Some funds cap the 12b-1 fee at an aggregate of 3 or 4 percent.

Go-load funds
Some funds charge a commission not when you buy shares, but when you sell your shares. To encourage people to hold on to their investments longer, you might pay 5 percent if you sell in the first year, 4 percent the second year, and so on. If you sell after the fifth full year, there is no deferred load or redemption fee.

Free-loading
If you invest in a family of funds that charges a load, you may be allowed to switch from one fund to another without additional charge. This is called free-loading, and generally applies if you buy a fund within ninety days of selling another fund within the same family.

Other fees

Be alert to other fees charged by no-load funds. Some funds charge a redemption fee when the shares are sold or a transaction fee when the shares are purchased, to cover the transaction costs of investing or liquidating shares. Because these fees are paid to the fund itself (that is, to the existing shareholders), the fees are equitable and should not be viewed in the same light as loads, which are paid to a sales force and not to the fund.

Expenses

All mutual funds charge operating expenses and management fees, which are deducted from the total return you receive each year. These expenses include the investment advisory fee or management fee, which ranges from .3 to 1 percent of fund assets; administrative costs of .2 to .5 percent; and other operating expenses of .1 to .4 percent. Added together, those fees range from .6 to 1.9 percent.

The fee table near the front of a fund's prospectus lists the annual expense ratios for recent years. This is the fund's operating expenses divided by the fund's net assets. Obviously, the lower the expense ratio the better, as expenses reduce the annual performance of the fund. Just because the fund's total return quoted in publications has those expenses already subtracted, don't think they don't matter. In a down year, when profits range from slim to none, a low annual expense ratio can mean the difference between making a small profit or losing money.

The funds offered by the Vanguard Group have, by far, the lowest costs because the funds own the management company, so management administrative services are provided at cost, reducing those charges considerably.

Countdown to Retirement

The amount of time that you have until you'll draw on your retirement savings has a great deal to do with how you should invest the funds. Use the following allocations for your overall investments, including 401(k) plans and other retirement savings.

If you have twenty years until retirement, keep 80 to 100 percent of your investments in fast-growing stocks. You want to accumulate as much as possible for your nonworking years.

Twenty Years to Retirement

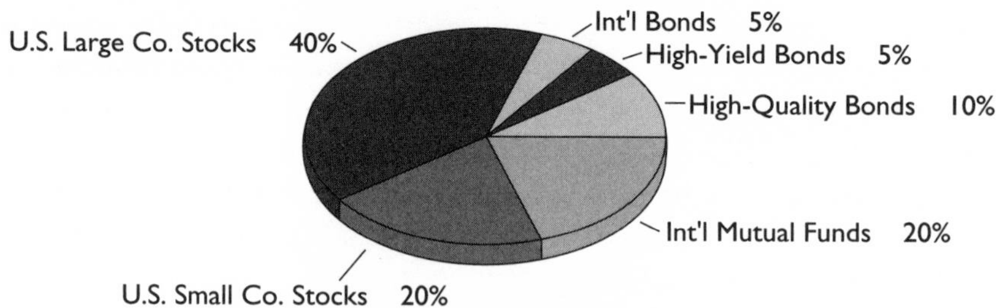

With ten years to retirement, you'll want to increase safety by ratcheting down your equities to 70 to 75 percent.

Ten Years to Retirement

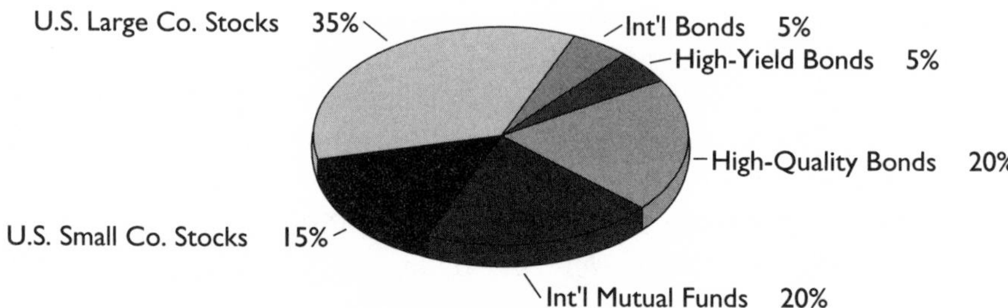

With two years to retirement, you may have some income needs and want to be more defensive as well. Here are the changes to make:

Two Years to Retirement

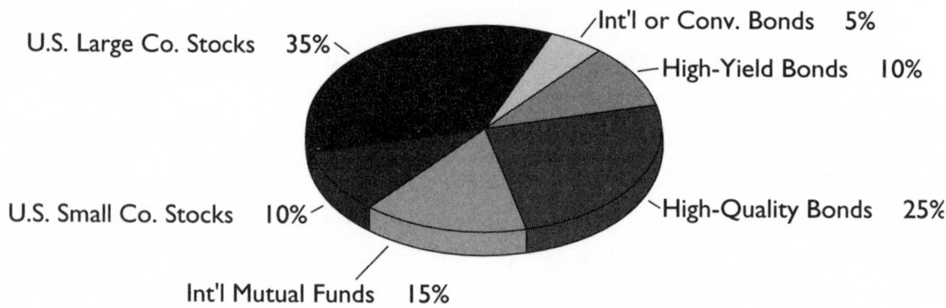

Your own allocation will depend on how long you anticipate being retired, how much income you will need to draw from your investments, and how large your portfolio is. If you are two years away from retirement and are counting on income from your investments to start immediately, you may need to increase the bond portion from 40 percent to 50 percent.

Turn to chapter 12 to learn how to invest after retirement. In the resources section at the back of the book you'll find a glossary of investment terms you should know.

Now that you know how to invest your funds, it is time to find out how to tailor your retirement plan to fit your goals.

5

• • • • • • • • •

Tailoring Your Retirement Plan to Fit Your Goals

Joe and Mary Ellen are sure they'll enjoy retirement. Joe, an engineer who celebrated his fiftieth birthday last year, anticipates days on the links and nights on the town. Mary Ellen, forty-six, is equally optimistic. Though she's enjoyed their family years, she's looking forward to a time when the kids will be grown and she and Joe will be free to travel and to entertain. "In a lot of ways, I feel as though our lives have been on hold—all we do is go to work, come home, fix dinner, and watch TV with the kids," she says. "Weekends we catch up on household chores, and then rest up a little so we can do it again the next week."

When do they plan to retire? "No later than sixty-two," says Joe, "and hopefully sooner." But they haven't saved much toward retirement. Joe has changed jobs several times, and each time he's forfeited most of his pension. His current employer offers a 401(k) plan, but Joe hasn't put in as much as he could, and he's borrowed nearly half of the money out for the children's education costs. Right now he has $46,000 in the plan, but $22,000 has been taken out as a loan, leaving only $24,000. Mary Ellen works as a secretary for a company that has no retirement plan at all. Joe and Mary Ellen put money into IRAs until their tax benefit was eliminated in the mid-1980s. Today they have nearly $60,000 in IRAs. Joe also qualifies for a small pension from a previous employer, but it is only a couple of hundred dollars a month.

Like many Americans, Joe and Mary Ellen believe that the current Social Security system is doomed. And yet, like 61 percent of Americans surveyed recently, they believe they are entitled to a comfortable retirement as one of their rights as citizens. Where will that retirement come from? "I don't know," says Joe. "I've just always felt we'd be OK. But now I'm starting to wonder." And that is what brought Joe and Mary Ellen into our offices.

Fact of life: 30 percent of baby boomers feel at a loss when it comes to planning for their retirement.

Inheritance isn't the answer for Joe and Mary Ellen, and it isn't the answer for most people planning retirement. The net worth of the parents of the average baby boomer is just under $300,000. If that pie is divided among four children, it will provide just $75,000 of inheritance to each.

Like Joe and Mary Ellen, most Americans simply have not thought through their next fifty years. Despite what they believe, retirement in the traditional sense may not be in the cards for them. They will probably continue working years beyond the early retirement they dream of.

When we first met with Joe and Mary Ellen, we reviewed their assets to see what they had saved for their retirement. Though they were doing well financially, much of their net worth didn't count as retirement savings. For example, their home is worth considerably more than the mortgage, but they plan to continue living in the home after retirement, so we didn't count the equity as a retirement asset. Fortunately, they have only thirteen more years of payments to make on the home, and so it will be paid off when Joe is sixty-three. That means that mortgage payments won't be a drain on their finances in retirement. They also have a small vacation cabin that was given to them by Joe's grandfather, but they don't intend to sell it, so that too won't provide any money on which to retire.

Here's what Joe and Mary Ellen have saved so far for retirement: 401(k) plan, net of loan, $24,000; IRAs, $60,000; mutual fund, $12,000; and pension from a prior employer, $200 a month at age sixty-two.

Next we worked with Joe and Mary Ellen to figure out what they would need in retirement. Many financial planners use a rule of thumb that retirement expenses will be 75 percent of what they are currently, but that rule of thumb isn't always accurate. We figured out which expenses would no longer be relevant in retirement (the children's school expenses, a home mortgage that will be paid off by the time Joe is sixty-three, commuter train costs, and business lunches). We then added the new expenses they would have in retirement (country club dues, additional travel, theater tickets). We calculated their total monthly retirement expenses to be $3,000, in today's dollars. Adding 20 percent for income taxes (less if they lived in a state with no income taxes), their total needs in retirement will be $3,696 a month in today's dollars.

Our next task was to figure out the income they would have in retirement. They wanted to assume that Social Security would produce nothing. "If we end up getting benefits," said Joe, "that will ice the cake, and we'll be more comfortable. But I don't want to feel pinched if we get nothing."

They have a $200-a-month pension coming when Joe is sixty-two, Mary Ellen earns about $1,200 a year selling handmade ornaments at craft shows, and Joe figures he can earn another $700 a month doing consulting for his current employer and others. The rest of the income they need will have to come from retirement plan income and savings.

Finally, we put it together to find out what Joe and Mary Ellen would need, in future dollars. See Worksheet 5.1 on page 96.

The tables on page 95 provide amounts needed in the Retirement Planning Worksheet calculations.

"Wow," said Joe and Mary Ellen simultaneously when we reached the conclusion that they would have to save over $3,600 a month to retire in ten years. It was clearly unrealistic. "There's no way we can do that," Joe protested. "We'd have to sacrifice everything."

And that's true—in order to retire that soon, with as little saved as they have so far, Joe and Mary Ellen would have to pare their expenses to practically nothing. That was impossible to do, so something had to give.

"Since you can't save that much, we'll have to make some changes to make your retirement plan work," we said. Here are some of the possible changes we suggested:

1. We could assume that Joe and Mary Ellen would qualify for Social Security based on today's laws. In Joe and Mary Ellen's case, that might not be a bad assumption. We predict that future changes to Social Security for those nearing retirement age will be to make benefits fully taxable for most people and to reduce benefits for the wealthy. Joe and Mary Ellen are within striking distance of retirement, and they are far from wealthy, so they may indeed qualify for full Social Security benefits.

2. We could assume that Joe will retire at age sixty-seven rather than at sixty-two. An extra five years to save for retirement would lessen the strain on their current budget enormously.

Table 1

YOUR SOCIAL SECURITY BENEFITS (MONTHLY SOCIAL SECURITY BENEFITS YOU WILL RECEIVE IN TODAY'S DOLLARS)

Your	*Your Current Income*				
Age	*$20,000*	*$30,000*	*$40,000*	*$50,000*	*$60,000+*
30	$819	$1,099	$1,242	$1,373	$1,520
35	819	1,099	1,242	1,373	1,517
40	819	1,099	1,242	1,373	1,505
45	819	1,099	1,242	1,373	1,489
50	819	1,099	1,241	1,359	1,452
55	819	1,099	1,226	1,322	1,391
60	819	1,094	1,193	1,282	1,330
65	814	1,080	1,173	1,231	1,259

Spouses will receive half of the above amounts at age 65 to 67, or benefits based on their own earnings records, whichever is greater.

Table 2

INVESTMENT GROWTH FACTOR (AMOUNT ONE DOLLAR INVESTED NOW WILL GROW TO)

Years to	*Rate of Return*			
Retire	6%	8%	10%	12%
5	1.3	1.5	1.6	1.8
10	1.8	2.2	2.6	3.1
15	2.4	3.2	4.2	5.5
20	3.2	4.7	6.7	9.7
25	4.3	6.9	10.8	17.0
30	5.7	10.1	17.5	30.0
35	7.7	14.8	28.1	52.8

Table 3

MONTHLY SAVINGS FACTOR (MONTHLY AMOUNT NEEDED TO SAVE ONE DOLLAR)

Years to	*Rate of Return*			
Retire	6%	8%	10%	12%
5	0.0143	0.0136	0.0129	0.0122
10	0.0061	0.0055	0.0049	0.0043
15	0.0034	0.0029	0.0024	0.0020
20	0.0022	0.0017	0.0013	0.0010
25	0.0014	0.0011	0.0008	0.0005
30	0.0010	0.0007	0.0004	0.0003
35	0.0007	0.0004	0.0003	0.0002

Worksheet 5.1

RETIREMENT-PLANNING WORKSHEET—
JOE AND MARY ELLEN MILLER

How much you will need (in today's dollars)		$3,000
Add 20 percent for income taxes		600
Total needed each month (in today's dollars)		3,600
Earnings and retirement benefits:		
Earnings—Joe	700	
Earnings—Mary Ellen	100	
Social Security from Table 1 (assume $0)	0	
Pension plans (defined benefit)	200	
Total earnings and retirement benefits		1,000
Other income needed (in today's dollars)		2,600
Divide income needed by 24 (inflation = 3 percent)	108	
Times years until retirement	× 10	
Additional income needed due to inflation		1,080
Future monthly income needed		3,680
Multiply by 240		× 240
Investment needed at retirement to produce future income*		883,200
Amount saved so far:		
401(k) plan	24,000	
IRAs	60,000	
Mutual fund	12,000	
Total saved so far, in today's dollars	96,000	
Times investment growth factor from Table 2 (ten years, 8 percent)	× 2.2	
Amount saved so far, in future dollars		211,200
Investment still needed, in future dollars		672,000
Monthly savings factor from Table 3 (ten years, 8 percent)		× 0.0055
MONTHLY SAVINGS NEEDED		**$3,697**

*Assumes that investments will earn 4 percent more than inflation and will be exhausted in forty years.

3. We could assume that their investments would earn at a higher interest rate, say 10 percent rather than 8 percent.

4. We could assume that their retirement income needs would be less, either through penny-pinching in retirement or through greater earnings from employment.

Joe and Mary Ellen did not think it was realistic to reduce their retirement needs, and Joe said that he'd rather work an extra five years before he retires than work harder during retirement. Mary Ellen said she just wasn't comfortable assuming that their investments would earn more than 8 percent. "If they do, that's great," she said, "Joe can retire that much sooner. But I don't want the stress of worrying that we aren't meeting our goals." Because they agreed with our logic regarding Social Security, we decided to include an estimated $1,000 a month in Social Security benefits for Joe and $500 a month for Mary Ellen as a factor in their retirement.

Here's what their retirement worksheet looked like once we modified it for their changed assumptions. See Worksheet 5.2 on page 98.

"Wow," said Joe and Mary Ellen again, and this time we joined in. The amount they needed to save each month had plummeted from $3,700 a month to only $350. It is *amazing* how much difference it makes to change some of the assumptions, especially those regarding the retirement income needed from investments and the length of time needed to save.

"I know we can save more than $250 a month," said Joe. "If Social Security will really be there for us, let's see how much I would have to save to be able to retire at sixty-two, as I wanted to do in the first place. I can always continue working longer if they make drastic changes in the Social Security system between now and then." We recalculated the retirement-planning worksheet and found that $900 a month would do the trick. See Worksheet 5.3 on page 99.

"I think that $900 a month is doable," said Joe, and Mary Ellen agreed. We cautioned Joe and Mary Ellen that they wouldn't qualify for full Social Security benefits until age sixty-six, and so they would have to make up the difference in Social Security with earnings until then. "That's OK," said Mary Ellen. "I'd be willing to keep working for a few more years, and my salary will be more than enough to cover it."

What do you need to save for retirement? Use Worksheet 5.4 on page 100 to compute the money you must put aside each month to meet your retirement goals, just as Joe and Mary Ellen figured theirs. If the

Worksheet 5.2

RETIREMENT PLANNING WORKSHEET, MODIFIED— JOE AND MARY ELLEN MILLER

How much you will need (in today's dollars)		$3,000
Add 20 percent for income taxes		600
Total needed each month (in today's dollars)		3,600
Earnings and retirement benefits:		
Earnings—Joe	700	
Earnings—Mary Ellen	100	
Social Security from Table 1 (assume $1,500)	1,500	
Pension plans (defined benefit)	200	
Total earnings and retirement benefits		2,500
Other income needed (in today's dollars)		1,100
Divide income needed by 24 (inflation = 3 percent)	46	
Times years until retirement	× 15	
Additional income needed due to inflation		690
Future monthly income needed		1,790
Multiply by 240		× 240
Investment needed at retirement to produce future income*		429,600
Amount saved so far:		
401(k) plan	24,000	
IRAs	60,000	
Mutual fund	12,000	
Total saved so far, in today's dollars	96,000	
Times investment growth factor from Table 2 (fifteen years, 8 percent)	× 3.2	
Amount saved so far, in future dollars		307,200
Investment still needed, in future dollars		122,400
Monthly savings factor from Table 3 (fifteen years, 8 percent)		× 0.0029
MONTHLY SAVINGS NEEDED		**$355**

*Assumes that investments will earn 4 percent more than inflation and will be exhausted in forty years.

Worksheet 5.3

RETIREMENT PLANNING WORKSHEET, MODIFIED AGAIN—JOE AND MARY ELLEN MILLER

How much you will need (in today's dollars)		$3,000
Add 20 percent for income taxes		600
Total needed each month (in today's dollars)		3,600
Earnings and retirement benefits:		
Earnings—Joe	700	
Earnings—Mary Ellen	100	
Social Security from Table 1 (assume $1,500)	1,500	
Pension plans (defined benefit)	200	
Total earnings and retirement benefits		2,500
Other income needed (in today's dollars)		1,100
Divide income needed by 24 (inflation = 3 percent)	46	
Times years until retirement	× 10	
Additional income needed due to inflation		460
Future monthly income needed		1,560
Multiply by 240		× 240
Investment needed at retirement to produce future income*		374,400
Amount saved so far:		
401(k) plan	24,000	
IRAs	60,000	
Mutual fund	12,000	
Total saved so far, in today's dollars	96,000	
Times investment growth factor from Table 2 (ten years, 8 percent)	× 2.2	
Amount saved so far, in future dollars		211,200
Investment still needed, in future dollars		163,200
Monthly savings factor from Table 3 (ten years, 8 percent)		× 0.0055
MONTHLY SAVINGS NEEDED		**$898**

*Assumes that investments will earn 4 percent more than inflation and will be exhausted in forty years.

Worksheet 5.4

RETIREMENT-PLANNING WORKSHEET

How much you will need (in today's dollars)		$______
Add 20 percent for income taxes		______
Total needed each month (in today's dollars)		______
Earnings and retirement benefits:		
Earnings	______	
Social Security from Table 1	______	
Pension plans (defined benefit)	______	
Total earnings and retirement benefits		______
Other income needed (in today's dollars)		______
Divide income needed by 24 (inflation = 3 percent)	______	
Times years until retirement	× ______	
Additional income needed due to inflation		______
Future monthly income needed		______
Multiply by 240		× ______
Investment needed at retirement to produce future income*		______
Amount saved so far:		
401(k) plans	______	
IRAs	______	
Mutual funds	______	
Total saved so far, in today's dollars	______	
Times investment growth factor from Table 2	× ______	
Amount saved so far, in future dollars		______
Investment still needed, in future dollars		______
Monthly savings factor from Table 3		× ______
MONTHLY SAVINGS NEEDED		$______

*Assumes that investments will earn 4 percent more than inflation and will be exhausted in forty years.

results don't fit your ability to save, think through the options that you have for modification: working part time in retirement, delaying retirement, investing more aggressively to pursue a higher return on your investments, including Social Security in your computations, reducing your spending in retirement, and so forth. Then incorporate these modifications into your retirement-planning worksheet and calculate your savings needs again. The worksheet can be a tool to guide you toward realistic thinking about your retirement needs, your ability to meet them based on your current financial course, and your willingness to make current sacrifices to reach your retirement goals.

Fact of life: 66 percent of Americans approaching the age of retirement say they should have started saving sooner.

Like Joe and Mary Ellen, you may not be putting aside enough to retire as soon or as completely as you had planned. The solution is to integrate your retirement goals into your life, taking a little time now to enjoy some pleasurable pursuits, and planning to work well into retirement to supplement your future retirement income with employment. To make ends meet in the future, start now to save. Put aside as much as you can into retirement plans. But what retirement plans? The purpose of the rest of this chapter is to try to take the confusion out of retirement plans and tell you how you can use them for maximum benefit.

Retirement Plans: An Overview

> Just three years ago I started to get serious about putting money into my 401(k) plan. It was a struggle at first, but now it's addictive to see how my money has built up. I'm pumped! (Randy L., age forty-one)

Contributing to a retirement plan that is tax deductible makes a lot of sense. When you contribute to such a plan, everything that you put in is deducted from your income for tax purposes, and everything you earn in the plan is tax-deferred as well. Of course, you will have to pay taxes on the money when you retire and draw income from the plan. For example, if you are in a 33 percent combined federal and state tax bracket, it's as though your uncle said to you, "I'll tell you what, for every two dollars you put away, I'll loan you one dollar interest-free. You can invest that dollar along with your own, and years from now you can pay me the dollar back. Everything the money earns will be yours." That's quite a deal your uncle offered. The good news is that Uncle Sam is willing to make that same pact with you. If you were to put two dollars into your savings account, you would have to earn three dollars to do it—income taxes would eat up the missing dollar. But with a tax-deductible retirement plan you can put away the entire three dollars—two dollars of your own and one of Uncle Sam's. When you draw the money from the retirement plan years from now, you will have to pay the taxes, but meanwhile, all of the money has been earning, tax-deferred.

How much will you get when you retire? It depends. There are two basic types of plans, the defined benefit pension plan and the defined contribution plan. A defined benefit plan defines the retirement benefit you will receive. If your plan is defined contribution, the amount you will be able to draw on retirement will depend on the contributions you and your employer make to the account, its earnings between now and retirement, and the manner in which it is invested after retirement.

Times have changed, and so have retirement plans. In your parents' day, employers provided for their employees' retirement primarily through defined benefit plans that paid a pension based on age, salary, and life expectancy. Employees who had spent their whole career with one company could expect to have all of their needs met in retirement, even if they'd never saved a dime. Today only the very fortunate have a defined benefit pension plan that will pay a monthly benefit sufficient to live on. According to the Employee Benefit Research Institute (EBRI), only 56 percent of today's workers are covered by such plans, down from 70 percent as recently as 1988. The trend is toward defined contribution plans that shift part of the cost to you.

Defined Benefit Plans—The Granddad of Them All

Your employer—especially if it's a large, older company—may have a defined benefit plan, often called a "pension plan." Long-term employees are promised a lifetime monthly retirement benefit based on years of service and salary level. As a plan participant, you don't contribute any of your own funds and you don't have any say in the investments the plan makes. Your employer guarantees the benefit, and that guarantee is backed by a government agency, the Pension Benefit Guaranty Corporation. The PBGC (nicknamed "Penny Benny") will pay part or all of your benefit should your company go bankrupt or become otherwise unable to meet its pension obligations. The maximum amount PBGC will pay ranges from $11,097 to $31,705 a year, depending on your age when you begin to receive payments.

One problem with pension plans is that they have been chronically underfunded; and the money in the plan is not sufficient to cover the demands that will eventually be made on it for employees' retirement. If your employer's pension plan goes bust, as did more than 150 plans in 1996, the guarantees offered by the PBGC ensure that you will receive most or all of the benefits you have been promised. But if your plan is merely underfunded, not bankrupt, the PBGC will not step in. However, if your pension plan is less than 90 percent funded, 1994 legislation requires your company to send you a notice each year that shows the portion of the plan that is underfunded and the portion of the plan that is insured by PBGC's benefit guarantee.

SMART TIP

DON'T LET LIGHTNING STRIKE TWICE

Even if your employer goes out of business, your money is protected, since it is held in trust for you and is not subject to the claims of your employer's creditors. If your employer does go bankrupt and shuts down its plan, however, you are likely to receive your pension in a lump sum from the PBGC rather than over your lifetime.

Alternatively, an annuity can be purchased for you from an insurance company to replace the monthly benefits you would have gotten from the employer's plan. In the unlikely event this happens to you, make sure that the insurance company issuing the annuity is financially solvent. Remember, lightning *can* strike twice, and you don't want to be hit first with the failure of your employer's plan and then with the failure of your annuity provider.

Just because money has been put into the plan in your name does not mean that the money is yours (vested) even if you leave the company. If you leave the company before your rights are fully vested, only the vested portion of the money will belong to you. Your employer should give you an annual benefit statement that tells you how much is vested, the current benefit you would receive if you retired today, and, possibly, the projected benefit you will receive at retirement.

With a defined benefit plan you know exactly what you are going to get. It offers a guaranteed benefit on retirement that is established by a formula taking into account your earnings, years of service with the company, and your age at retirement. If the plan is integrated with Social Security, any Social Security payment you receive may reduce the benefit you receive from the plan.

All pension plans are required to offer joint and survivor annuities, which means that after you die, your partner receives 50 percent or more of what you were getting while you were alive. If you and your spouse waive the survivor portion, you will receive a greater amount while you are alive; but then when you die, the payments will cease. To make an effective waiver of the survivor benefits, your spouse has to sign a written release within ninety days of the annuity start date.

Defined benefit plans have become costly. That's because they pay a monthly retirement benefit *for life*—and people are living a lot longer, costing the companies much more than in the past. A few plans still allow for cost of living increases to compensate for the effects of inflation, but to save money, many employers have eliminated these increases. Other companies have done away with expensive defined benefit plans entirely, replacing them with economical 401(k) plans. Because the 401(k) plan is a salary-reduction plan, the employee, not the employer, makes most of the contributions.

> Dad retired from General Motors with a pension and health benefits fifteen years ago. He keeps telling me I shouldn't worry about retirement, that Susie and I will be fine. But *we* don't have a pension plan. I don't think Dad realizes how much we have to juggle today's financial responsibilities with tomorrow's needs. (Hamilton S., age forty-eight)

This shift in responsibility for employees' retirement from the employer to the employee has potentially disastrous consequences. Only three-quarters of workers eligible to contribute to 401(k) plans actually do so, and few of those contribute the maximum they are allowed. In short, the employer has shifted the burden for retirement planning to the employee, and many employees have not yet picked up the mantle. To make things worse, at the same time that employees are having to fund more of their own retirement savings, statistics show that people are retiring earlier and living longer. That means that the money in the accounts, although less than ever before, will have to last even longer.

Government and Military Retirement

If you work for the government, be it at the federal, state, or local level, you are probably covered under a defined benefit plan sponsored by that governmental entity—for example, the state teachers' retirement fund or the civil service program. If you participate in the Federal Employees Retirement System (FERS) you can contribute up to 7 percent of your salary, which will be matched by your employer. Other government plans are also contributory, but the contributions you make are generally not tax-deductible. To make up for that disadvantage, the plans often have more favorable terms than most employer defined benefit plans. For example, the benefits paid by many governmental plans are automatically adjusted for inflation, and many plans allow you to retire after thirty years of service, regardless of your age, and receive about 50 percent of your basic pay. About half of all government plans include cost of living increases, compared to fewer than 5 percent of private plans.

If you are in the military you can receive benefits for life after twenty years of service, and you'll get a cost of living adjustment each year as well. If you joined the service after 1986 you will receive 40 percent of your base pay if you retire at twenty years, or 75 percent if you retire at thirty years. If you joined before 1986, after twenty years of service you'll receive 50 percent of your base pay and up to 75 percent if you stay longer.

Defined Contribution Plans—Shifting the Burden with a Multitude of Options

In addition to or in lieu of a defined benefit plan, you may be eligible for some type of defined contribution plan. These include profit sharing, money purchase pension plans, stock bonus plans, employee stock ownership plans (ESOPs), tax-sheltered annuity (TSA) plans, savings and thrift plans, and the most popular type of plan, the 401(k).

Profit-sharing plans provide contributions by the employer that can equal up to 15 percent of your salary, at your employer's discretion. In a good year you may see a large deposit to your account. But if the company has a bad year, there may be no contribution at all. Profit-sharing plans are common in all sizes and types of businesses.

Money purchase pension plans provide contributions by the employer that can equal up to 25 percent of your salary. Unlike profit-sharing plans, the percentage is a fixed amount; once determined, it cannot be changed without amending the plan. More common in smaller businesses, money purchase plans are often paired with profit-sharing plans for maximum flexibility. For example, the company may offer a 5 percent fixed money purchase plan and add a profit-sharing plan whose contributions could range from 0 percent to 15 percent each year. This way the employee is guaranteed at least a 5 percent contribution but may be credited with as much as 20 percent of his or her salary as a retirement plan contribution in any one year.

Stock bonus plans and *ESOPs* are variations of profit-sharing plans. ESOPs are generally noncontributory, and they are entirely funded by your employer's contributions. Such plans can also be structured to be part of a 401(k) plan, allowing you to contribute your own money on a tax-deferred basis.

Generally, an ESOP owns the employer's stock, and it is a way that you can invest in your employer's stock. At your retirement, the stock may be distributed to you or you may receive your benefits in cash. An ESOP is a nice addition to a retirement plan package, but it does not make a good stand-alone retirement plan because it is too closely tied to the fortunes of the company, generating an all-your-eggs-in-one-basket problem.

> When we divorced, my ex-wife cashed out of my ESOP plan. She got quite a bit, as I recall. But times have been hard and my employer is struggling, so the stock price is way down. If things don't improve before I retire, I'll get hardly anything. (Erik H., age fifty)

Savings and thrift plans, 403(b) (TSA), and *401(k) plans* are all salary-reduction plans to which you may contribute tax-deferred income. If your employer matches a portion of your contribution to your 401(k) or other salary-reduction plan, you'll find that your contribution costs you comparatively little. For example, if you contribute $100 to the plan and your employer matches half of that, you will have $150 in your plan. The net reduction in your paycheck is the $100 of wages less the $30 or so of income taxes that would have been withheld, for a net reduction of only $70. That means you have garnered a $150 investment at a cost of only $70. Of course, income taxes will be due when you receive distributions from the plan, but that will be years from now, and your money will have grown, tax-deferred, in the meantime.

401(k) Plans—Your Retirement Piggy Bank

Fact of life: More than eighteen million people participate in 401(k) plans.

The 401(k) plan is quite the rage. These plans are now offered by most major employers and are becoming common in many smaller companies with more than nine employees. The 401(k) plan allows employees to reduce their compensation by a certain percentage, up to 15 percent of their salary. Total contributions to the plan by the employee cannot exceed $9,500 a year. Some plans also provide an employer-matching contribution. For example, the employee may be eligible to contribute up to 4 percent of his or her salary to the plan and the employer will match 1 percent. If this type of plan is available to you, you should contribute the maximum you can afford. The 401(k) is one of the best vehicles for retirement savings, since all contributions you make are tax deductible.

SMART TIP

BE ALERT TO 401(K) THEFT

Some companies use their employees' retirement contributions illegally for cash float rather than depositing them directly into 401(k) accounts. A sign of trouble is that your contributions don't match the totals that appear on your pay stubs.

Here's what to do: Ask your plan administrator for an explanation—it may be a mistake. If it can't be explained or corrected, ask the regional office of the U.S. Department of Labor to investigate. New legislation has shortened the time your employer can legally delay turning your contributions over to the plan administrator.

Fact of life: Participants in 401(k) plans typically cite a spouse or other family member as the single most important source for financial advice.

If your employer offers a 401(k) plan, check it out thoroughly. Read the summary plan description, which explains the terms of the plan, including the percentage of your salary you can contribute to the plan and the employer-matching contributions. You will also find a discussion of the investment choices available and how often you can redirect your investments. At a minimum you can invest in a stock fund, a bond fund, a money market fund, or a balanced fund that includes both stocks and bonds. The plan may also allow you to invest in your company's stock.

If you have great faith in the company's prospects for future growth, and the company does well, the company stock may be the best investment you can make. Remember, however, that if the company's fortunes change, your investment will decline. You'll lose part or all of your retirement, and you may even find yourself out of a job. This happened to employees of Carter Hawley Hale/Broadway Stores a few years ago. Some employees who were retiring or who lost their jobs at the time the company was going through bankruptcy lost up to 75 percent of their 401(k) account value because they had everything invested in CHH stock. Had they put their money into other investment options offered under the 401(k) plan, such as growth stocks, bonds, international stocks, and the like, they would have lost none of their retirement funds.

SMART TIP

ASSEMBLING YOUR NEST EGG

If you have some type of stock ownership or stock bonus plan available to you, or if your 401(k) plan offers the choice of investing in company stock, be careful of investing *too much* in it. You already have a lot of your "eggs" in that basket simply by being employed at the company, so direct the company plan to put more of your money into other investments. As much as you may believe that the outlook for your company's stock is positive, it pays to diversify.

When you change jobs, if you have at least $3,500 in your 401(k) plan, you are not required to remove your money from the old plan, though there is rarely any advantage to leaving your money with the old employer if your new employer has a plan available. You may want to roll the money from your old employer's plan into your new employer's plan once you are eligible to participate, or into a rollover IRA account and then into your new employer's 401(k). If you roll your funds into an IRA and leave them there, be aware that if you take a lump-sum distribution later, you'll lose two advantages. You won't be eligible for special lump-sum averaging, which allows you to figure the taxes on a lump-sum distribution from the plan as though you had received the money over a five-year period. Remember, too, you can't borrow against an IRA as you can against some 401(k) plans. For that reason, if your new employer has no IRA rollover provisions, you may wish to leave your money in your old employer's retirement plan.

SMART TIP

KEEP 401(K) MONEY SEPARATE

If you receive benefits from a 401(k) and roll them into an IRA, make sure that it is an IRA that you set up exclusively for that purpose. That will allow you to roll those benefits from the IRA into a new employer's 401(k) plan, should you decide that that would be in your best interests. If you commingled the 401(k) proceeds with other IRA funds, you will not be eligible to roll the 401(k) proceeds into a new employer's plan.

If you don't roll your 401(k) proceeds into another retirement plan or an IRA, you may regret it. Not only will you owe income taxes plus a 10 percent penalty tax if you are under age fifty-nine and a half, but also your retirement savings will be wiped out. All the progress you've made toward saving for retirement will evaporate, and you'll begin at ground zero with your new employer. Because people change jobs frequently today, this means retirement-planning disaster for many Americans.

Although your 401(k) plan money is set aside for your retirement, about 70 percent of companies allow you to borrow from your 401(k) plan for certain expenditures, such as the purchase of a home, medical expenses, a car, or even a vacation or paying off debts. Federal regulations let you borrow one-half of the balance up to $50,000; if your account is less than $20,000, you can borrow the full amount of the account, up to $10,000. You have to repay the loan at the going interest rate within five years, unless the loan is to purchase a new home, in which case you have longer to repay. Some employers let you borrow money for any purpose, while others restrict the loans to purposes such as medical bills, college, or housing.

Borrowing from a 401(k) Can Be Easy . . . and Dangerous

Fact of life: 20 percent of 401(k) plan participants say they have one or more employee loans outstanding.

Borrowing money from your 401(k) plan is pretty easy—your signature on a simple document will garner you the check. The interest rate is generally prime plus one or two percentage points, which is considerably lower than the amount charged by most credit cards. Even better, you pay the interest to yourself, so that your retirement plan continues growing.

Although borrowing from your 401(k) plan is easy, it may not be your best move. The interest you pay on your 401(k) loan is generally nondeductible, so you may find that tax-deductible interest on a home equity loan will cost you less. Also, consider the lost opportunity for investing in stocks. For example, if you pay yourself 9 percent interest on the money borrowed from the plan, and yet investing in stocks would earn you a 12 percent annual return, you are reducing your investment growth by 3 percent.

It even can be downright dangerous to borrow against your retirement plan. When you leave your current employer you will have to settle up all loans. For example, if you owe the plan $10,000, you can pay off the loan by leaving $10,000 of your 401(k) behind to settle up the debt, but that money will be treated as though you had withdrawn it. That means it will be subject to income taxes *plus* a 10 percent penalty if you are under age fifty-nine and a half. To avoid this painful result, you will have to ante up the money you owe to your 401(k) plan from some other source. That may be difficult to do, particularly if you are now unemployed.

Of course if the 401(k) is the only source for the money you need, by all means borrow from the plan. It is considerably cheaper to do so than to withdraw the money from the plan and then pay income taxes on the distribution plus a penalty for early withdrawal.

> I needed some money to put a new roof on the house, and I was going to borrow from my 401(k) plan. But my accountant showed me how much I'd save by getting a home equity loan instead so I could deduct the interest on my taxes. (Marcy A., age thirty-nine)

403(b) Plans—A 401(k) for Nonprofits

The 403(b) plan, also known as a TSA, is similar to the 401(k) plan except it is available to employees of nonprofit organizations, hospitals, educational institutions, and churches. As with a 401(k) plan, you designate that a certain amount be taken out of your pay every month to be contributed to the plan.

The normal limit is 20 percent of salary, up to $9,500 a year. However, the rules are fairly complex, and there are special catch-up provisions that allow larger contributions in later years if you've not participated or have undercontributed in early years. These plans are not quite as appealing as 401(k) plans: most employer sponsors of 403(b) plans do not match employee contributions, and funds contributed to your 403(b) plan can be invested only in insurance annuities or mutual funds.

Other Retirement Plans

Thrift Plans

Federal employees are eligible for a thrift savings plan (TSP), which operates much like a 401(k) plan. Though a thrift plan is in general much like a 401(k) plan, the terms of the plan may make it dissimilar in many ways. For example, the plan may provide that your contributions are not tax deductible, so you are contributing after-tax pay. Your employer may match your contributions in a percentage or a flat dollar amount, and the amount that the employer matches may depend on the number of years you have worked at the job.

Nonqualified Deferred Compensation Plans

These are special plans available only to upper management and key employees. Employers are allowed to discriminate in favor of certain employees because these plans do not receive the same special tax breaks that qualified plans do. If properly set up, they may allow you to defer the taxation of current salary, or they may even provide an added benefit payable at retirement, on top of your regular salary. Nonqualified deferred compensation plans may not be rolled into IRAs.

Simplified Employer Pension (SEP), or SEP-IRA

Smaller employers may find that the SEP-IRA is the simplest way to provide benefits to employees. A SEP-IRA allows business owners to contribute up to $30,000 to their SEP-IRAs. Any employer, including a corporation, a partnership, or a self-employed individual may establish a SEP-IRA. The only hitch is that all employees must be covered under the plan if they are at least twenty-one and have performed service during the last three years. For this reason, SEPs are more popular among self-employed individuals who have few or no employees. The employer may contribute up to 15 percent of the employee's wages to the plan, and an owner-employee may contribute up to 13.04 percent of his or her earned income, up to $30,000. A SEP-IRA is easy to establish, and the plan sponsor will provide the necessary forms. Best of all, there are no annual reports to file with the government. SEPs can be set up and funded after the tax year ends, as late as your tax-filing date, including extensions.

> I sell real estate part time, and I was shocked at how much I owed in taxes last year because of the extra income. Thank goodness I was able to sock some of my real estate profits into a SEP at the last minute to knock my taxes down. (Jerry C., age forty-four)

SMART TIP

A SEP BEATS AN IRA . . . SOMETIMES

Set up a SEP if you have self-employment or consulting income. Even if you or your spouse is an active participant in an employer plan, you may still take a deduction for a SEP based on outside income, whereas an IRA contribution might not be deductible. But if your net self-employment income is less than about $15,350 and you are not covered by an employer plan, you'd be better off with a tax-deductible $2,000 IRA.

An employer with just a few employees may want to start a more sophisticated version of a SEP called a savings incentive match plan for employees (SIMPLE). A SIMPLE is a low-cost alternative to a 401(k) plan and allows employees to make tax-deductible contributions up to $6,000 to their IRAs each year, which employers must match.

Keogh Plans

A Keogh plan is somewhat more complex than a SEP-IRA but less of a burden than a pension or profit-sharing plan. The Keogh plan allows smaller employers to install defined benefit or defined contribution plans that are less cumbersome than the plans installed by larger employers. Defined benefit Keogh plans allow greater contributions than do defined contribution plans and are a good way to build up a retirement plan quickly, although they are considerably more complex than defined contribution Keoghs, as they require the services of an actuary.

Unlike a SEP-IRA, which requires no annual filings, if you establish a

Keogh plan, you must file a Form 5500 with the IRS on a regular basis. In exchange for that extra trouble, Keoghs do have advantages over SEP-IRAs. When you withdraw the money, you can use five-year averaging to decrease the income tax burden (the taxes are due all at once, but they are computed as though you had taken the income over a five-year period.) In addition, you can borrow from a Keogh plan, and you can continue to contribute to a Keogh plan even after age seventy and a half.

A Keogh plan can be set up at a bank or through your broker or insurance agent. Be careful: the Keogh plan must be in place by December 31 for you to get a tax deduction for the current year. You have until April 15 of the following year (or later, with extensions) to contribute to the plan.

Even if you are covered under your employer's retirement plan, you can contribute money to a Keogh or a SEP-IRA if you earn any money on the side. Generally, Keogh plans and SEP-IRAs are set up by people who are in business for themselves or who have supplemental income from consulting or freelancing. They are not available to people who are strictly employees with no self-employment income.

Individual Retirement Accounts (IRAs)

You can contribute up to $2,000 a year to an IRA. If you make less than that, you can contribute 100 percent of your earned income or alimony income. If you have a nonemployed spouse, you may contribute an additional $2,000 on behalf of your nonemployed spouse, if your earned income is at least $4,000. Once you reach age seventy and a half, your contributions to an IRA must cease.

You can contribute only earned income or alimony income to an IRA, not income from interest, dividends, capital gains, and so forth. Your IRA can be invested in almost any type of investment, from CDs to mutual funds, from insurance products to individual stocks and bonds. You can't borrow from your IRA or use it as collateral for any loan.

> I've never made much, so I haven't been able to save, but I've put $2,000 a year into my IRA since they came into being. I'm sure glad I did—last year I passed the $200,000 mark. Imagine that! (Helen F., age fifty)

Created by Congress in 1974, IRAs were initially available only to those who had no employer-sponsored retirement plan. In 1982 the laws were liberalized so that *anyone* with earned income could make a tax-deductible $2,000 IRA contribution. Until 1987, all IRAs were deductible and could be funded up to $2,000 a year. Since then, IRAs have come in two varieties, deductible and nondeductible. Whether you can make a tax-deductible contribution today depends on your income *and* whether you are a participant in a company retirement plan. Fully deductible IRAs are available only to people earning less than $25,000 a year or not covered by an employer plan.

DEDUCTIBILITY OF IRAS

- *Regardless of income,* if neither spouse is an active participant in a qualified plan, you may fully deduct an IRA contribution.
- If you or your spouse is an active participant in an employer plan, you can fully deduct your IRA contribution if you are:

  1. filing as **single,** your adjusted gross income **is under $25,000,** or
  2. **married filing jointly** and your adjusted gross income **is under $40,000.**

- If you or your spouse is an active participant in an employer plan, you may take *no deduction* if you are:

  1. filing as **single** and your adjusted gross income **is over $35,000,** or
  2. **married filing jointly** and your adjusted gross income **is over $50,000.**

If you or your spouse is an active participant and you fall in between these income levels, a *partial deduction* is allowed. The table on page 115 illustrates how the partial deduction is calculated.

IRAs may also be used as a receptacle for rollover funds from another retirement plan. For example, if you terminate your employment with an employer and receive money from the employer's 401(k) plan, it can be rolled over to an IRA without penalty or current taxes.

We are often asked if it makes sense to make an IRA contribution that's nondeductible. In certain cases, yes. IRA contributions that are not tax deductible will nonetheless earn tax-deferred income until with-

PARTIAL DEDUCTION CALCULATION

	EXAMPLES		
	Single	*Married, with Nonemployed Spouse*	*Married, Both Spouses Employed*
Limiting Amount	$35,000	$50,000	$50,000
–Adjusted Gross Income	–33,000	–47,000	–47,000
Difference	$2,000	$3,000	$3,000
÷ $10,000	÷ $10,000	÷ $10,000	÷ $10,000
= Deductible Percentage	20%	30%	30%
× Maximum Contribution	× $2,000	× $4,000	× $4,000
= Deduction	$400	$1,200	$1,200

NOTE: There is a $200 minimum contribution allowed, even if calculation results in less.

drawn. Nondeductible IRAs are good investments, particularly for younger taxpayers, because the money will grow for many years free of tax. But if your employer offers a 401(k) or other tax-deferred savings plan, it makes much more sense to contribute tax-deductible dollars to such a plan than it would to continue to fund a nondeductible IRA.

SMART TIP

INVEST IN YOUR 401(K) INSTEAD OF YOUR IRA

In general, your 401(k) plan makes a better investment than your IRA. Here's why:

- You can contribute over four times more to your 401(k) plan than to an IRA.
- Your employer may make matching contributions for some or all of your investment.
- Contributions to the 401(k) plan are by painless payroll deduction.
- Most 401(k) plans allow you to borrow from the plan for medical expenses and other hardships, and sometimes for nonemergencies as well.
- 401(k) plans offer professional management that may be absent from your IRA.
- Withdrawals from your 401(k) plan may be eligible for five-year averaging.

Taking Early Withdrawals from Your IRA

Although generally you can't take money out of your IRA until you reach fifty-nine and a half without paying a 10 percent penalty, there are some exceptions to that rule, most of them not pleasant: you can take money from your IRA early if you die (or rather, your beneficiaries can take the money) or if you become disabled and unable to work.

One final exception will benefit you if you intend to retire early. If you take regular payments from the IRA that are calculated using your life expectancy, and you continue taking those payments until you are fifty-nine and a half, and for at least five years, those payments will not be subject to the 10 percent penalty. For example, if you have $30,000 in your IRA, you are fifty years old, and your life expectancy is thirty years, under the straight life expectancy calculation, taking $1,000 a year each year until you are fifty-nine and a half will comply with the exception, and your withdrawals will not be subject to the 10 percent penalty. You can also calculate the payment using any reasonable interest rate, which could be based on loans granted by banks, the prime rate, or the IRS rate for annuity calculations. In addition, you can use either the IRS's mortality figures or those published by the insurance industry. The size of the annual payment will depend on which of these variables you use. That gives you an opportunity, within a broad range, to set the payment to meet your circumstances. For example, if you need a small amount to supplement a payment that you are receiving from some other source, you may wish to use factors that result in a lower payment. However, if the payout from the IRA will be a pri-

---

SMART TIP

THE EARLY BIRD IS PENALIZED LESS

If you must withdraw a lump sum of money from an IRA before age fifty-nine and a half, do so early in the year so that the penalty won't apply to the interest or dividends earned on the account during the year. If your withdrawal is for buying your first house, time the purchase so that you close early in the year during which you take the withdrawal, so the mortgage interest and real estate tax deductions can help offset the taxes you will have to pay on the IRA withdrawal. As a general rule, withdrawing funds early from an IRA account should be a last resort if you need money.

THE CONFUSING WORLD OF RETIREMENT PLANS MADE SIMPLE

	Defined Benefit	Money Purchase	Profit Sharing	401(k)	ESOP/ Stock Bonus	SEP	403(b)	IRA	SIMPLE
Benefits which employees most?	Older	Younger	Younger	Younger	Younger	Younger	Younger	Younger	Younger
Maximum Contribution	Actuarially determined—100% of salary to a maximum of $125,000 in 1997	25% of salary	15% of salary	15% of salary up to $9,500	15% of salary	15% of salary	20% of salary not to exceed $9,500	100% of wages up to $2,000	15% of salary up to $6,000
Are contributions tax deductible?	Yes	Yes	Yes	Yes	Yes	Yes	Yes	Maybe	Yes
Can employees contribute?	No	No	No	Yes	Maybe	No	Yes	Yes	Yes

SMART TIP

PAY YOUR PLAN FIRST

If you make your retirement plan contribution at the beginning of the year instead of waiting until the end of the year, you will shelter an additional year's interest and dividends from current tax.

Assuming your IRA earns 10 percent a year, here is a table that shows the difference in IRA accounts of $2,000 contributed on January 1 each year versus contributions on April 15, fifteen and one-half months later:

End of Year	January 1 Contributions	April 15 Contributions
5	$13,400	$9,800
10	35,100	28,500
15	69,900	58,900
20	126,000	107,600
25	216,400	186,000
30	361,900	312,500
35	596,300	516,100
40	973,700	844,000

mary source of income for you, you may wish to substitute variables that will provide a higher payment. In making your decision, consider the income taxes that will have to be paid on any payment that you receive. Also remember that once you have begun taking the payments, you will not be able to vary them or the factors you have chosen until you turn age fifty-nine and a half (or five years has expired, if that is a longer period). For that reason, be sure that you calculate a payment that is high enough to take into account emergencies as well as inflation.

The table on page 117 will help you compare the features and benefits of each type of retirement plan.

What If You've Saved Too Much?

In the news recently you no doubt have heard that Americans aren't saving enough for retirement. Based on that information, you might think that the government would do everything it could to encourage Americans to save for retirement. Not so. As a matter of fact, under tax legislation passed in 1986, you are penalized if you accumulate *too much* in your retirement plan. The 15 percent penalty, nicknamed "the success tax," applies to the portion of your annual distribution from retirement plans that exceeds $155,000, and is indexed by inflation each year. Fortunately, in 1996 legislation suspended this penalty for money withdrawn in 1997, 1998, and 1999.

Leaving your money in the plan until you die won't eliminate the tax: A related 15 percent penalty tax is levied on your estate if your retirement plan accumulations exceed $750,000. You can't take it with you, and they tax it if you leave it behind!

Generally you will be forced to take distributions from your plan by the time you reach age seventy and a half, unless you continue working beyond that age, and there is a 50 percent penalty for failure to do so. That means that those with large retirement plans are caught in a no-win situation: a 50 percent penalty for failure to take the proper distributions but a 15 percent penalty if they do so and the distributions exceed the threshold. Although the threshold amount will increase each year, you may be headed for trouble and not realize it. If you are fifty or younger, have accumulated $160,000 or more in your IRAs and 401(k), and anticipate earning a 12 percent return between now and retirement, you will likely face penalties if you delay taking money out of these plans until the required age of seventy and a half. As you grow nearer to retirement, it will be important to assess your own circumstances so that you have a plan for how and when to take distributions from your retirement plans to minimize both taxes and any potential penalties.

Eight Questions You Should Ask about Your Retirement Plan

> I read so much about retirement planning lately. I think I'm OK, since I've got several retirement plans through my work. I just wish I knew more about them. (Charley V., age forty-five)

The more you know about your retirement plan, the better off you are. From the documents that your employer has furnished you, you should know the answers to the following questions. If you are in doubt, ask your employee benefits department to help you read the forms and figure out the answers.

1. What is my plan worth?

If it is a defined benefit plan, you need to know roughly the amount of money that you'll receive every month when you retire, or the lump sum you can receive. If it is a defined contribution plan, you should receive a statement at least annually showing the amount that is in the plan.

2. When do I begin participating in the plan, and when am I vested?

Some plans have a waiting period before you are allowed to participate, and there is often a period of time after you have begun participating before you are fully vested. It is important to know the plans you are eligible to participate in, and how long you must be in the plan before you can take early retirement or change jobs.

3. What are my rights if I leave my job?

Some plans allow you to take a lump sum when you leave, which you can roll into another plan or an IRA. Other plans keep your money for you until you reach retirement age. This information is important when you leave your job, so that you can take the proper steps to insure that you don't miss out on any benefits in the future.

4. When can I retire?

Some plans have early retirement benefits that allow you to retire at any age, from fifty to sixty-five. In most plans, retirement benefits grow proportionately the longer you stay on the job, but some other plans don't grow as much, encouraging early retirement. Find out your options under your employer's plan.

5. What happens if I work past retirement age?

It is important to know if your plan will continue to grow or if you will be losing benefits once you pass age sixty-five. If you plan to continue working, that will have a bearing on whether you continue to work for that company or take your benefits and work elsewhere.

6. What if I become disabled or die before retirement?

To plan for adequate family protection in the event of your death or disability, it is important to know what happens in the event of catastrophe. You will also need to know what life insurance benefits have accrued in your name.

7. Where are the plan assets invested?

You need a solid understanding of the past performance of the retirement assets in order to estimate your future retirement benefits. If you are able to direct the investments and you have years until retirement, be sure to invest your funds for maximum growth.

8. How solvent is the pension plan?

If your plan is a 401(k) plan or other defined contribution plan, the annual statement should show your and your employer's contributions, and how they have grown. Look at cumulative statements to make sure that your employer is putting all of your contributions and all of its matching contributions into the plan, rather than spending them on something else. If the plan is a defined benefit plan, your employer can furnish you with Form 5500, filed with the IRS, which will tell you how much is in the plan and how well it is funded for the future retirement needs of the employees.

In this chapter we looked at the many types of retirement plans available to us today. The case of Joe and Mary Ellen helped us see how we can tailor our planning by adjusting the number of years we'll work or the return we get on investments, or by reducing expenses. This information applies to all of us. If you are a woman, though, read on. There are some additional things we think you will find helpful in the next chapter.

6

• • • • • • • • • •

Why Women Need Retirement Planning More than Men Do

> I've worked hard all my life but I just can't seem to save enough for my own retirement. (Ramona S., age forty-nine)

In the olden days, women didn't have to worry about retirement. Many women didn't live that long; they died young, from childbirth, overwork, or disease. In general, women depended on their fathers or husbands to support them all their lives. The rest, often barely self-supporting, could plan on working forever, not stopping until they dropped in their tracks.

It's different for women today, who by and large must depend on their own resources for retirement. The average age of a new widow is fifty-six, and a married woman can expect to outlive her husband by at least seven years. But widowhood isn't every married woman's fate: Many marriages will end in divorce long before that. No wonder more and more women are marrying later or choosing not to marry at all. According to the Census Bureau, in 1993, 26 percent of the women between twenty-five and thirty-four had never married, up from only 9 percent in 1970. By the year 2003, it is predicted that only one-third of women over sixty-five will be married, and women will outlive their husbands by fifteen years. Even today, only 40 percent of women are married when they retire. Put it all together and it means that most women will be on their own financially for at least one-third of their adult lives, and probably for most of their later years. As women are living longer and longer, those years alone will stretch far into the future.

> Divorce isn't easy to think about. We were looking forward to a comfortable retirement, now everything is topsy-turvy and I'm scared to death about not having enough to live on in my old age. (Sue Ann C., age forty-seven)

Women's Retirement Issues

Women face some special issues relating to retirement that may be different from those experienced by most men. Feeling trapped in lower-paying jobs, some women feel they are never able to save enough. This leads to frustration, anger, and resentment, resulting in poor job performance and inability to cope with the everyday drama of life at home. Being the sole provider for the family or being the primary caretaker for an aging parent creates enormous stress as women feel pulled in different directions. Women in this position often don't feel in control of their own destinies.

> I guess I'm counting a lot on his retirement. He's always had jobs with better retirement plan options, and since he earns more, he can put more aside. I just don't have that advantage. (Penelope R., age forty-eight)

Married women who are partners in two-income families often see their retirement plans growing at a slower and lower rate than their spouses'. This can be demoralizing to a woman who works as hard, or harder, than her husband. In addition, to a woman who depends on her husband's income and retirement savings for financial solvency, the possibility of divorce and widowhood can make retirement seem like a horrible specter for which a woman feels both unprepared and inadequate, in terms of money and knowledge.

For women who earn more than their spouses, even that can be a source of trouble. If it becomes a threat to his ego and to their relationship, his subtle ways of acting out "job jealousy" can sabotage her success.

> I earn more than he does, and as partner in my firm I have stock options as well as a great retirement plan. I think Tom may be a bit jealous, and it's coming out in very subtle ways. (Georgiana L., age forty-one)

Survey after survey shows that most women do not feel prepared financially to face the future. They have not clearly identified long-term financial goals, and they are concerned about outliving the money they've put away for retirement. They do not feel properly prepared for making investment decisions, such as selecting among investment options in an employer-sponsored retirement account; they aren't secure enough about their financial future to take the risks necessary to make their money grow. In short, they feel they are not planning adequately for their retirement.

Women's Retirement Planning

For women, retirement planning has both good news and bad news. The good news is that women tend to live longer. The bad news is twofold: Longer lives mean more expense, and women often have less money to begin with. The combination of being on their own and living longer means that women need far more retirement income than do most men. Unfortunately, women's pensions don't measure up to women's needs, says a study by the Older Women's League. This study shows that women are falling further and further behind when it comes to private pension income, receiving only 54 percent as much private pension income as do men.

More women than ever before now participate in an employer's pension plan. That is the first step toward earning a pension, but it isn't the entire answer. The pension you receive depends on whether you stay on the job. Today more and more women are leaving the work force, because of layoffs, poor job prospects, or to spend more time with their families. On average, women are out of the work force for at least ten years, while men, on average, take just one year out of the work force. Many women now participating in pension plans will not be on the job long enough to ever cash a pension check. That means they won't be building the retirement nest eggs that men are building. Social Security will also be affected by years away from the job: Benefit payments increase as the employee's work history builds, and so women will receive less Social Security as a result of that time off.

> When I took time off to have our two children, I lost my place in line. Sure, I had a job when I went back to my accounting firm, but I wasn't on the fast track anymore. (Terri Q., age thirty-eight)

Women often think that they can rely on their husbands' pensions, but they are wrong. If a couple is living on the man's pension, and the wife dies, the man will continue to get his full pension. But if the husband dies first, as is ordinarily the case, his wife will get only 50 percent or so of the benefit the couple was receiving before. These survivor pensions generally don't come close to providing enough income. No wonder 41 percent of older women are living close to the poverty line. "A lot of times, widowhood is what spurs women into poverty," says Debbie Chalfie, a staff member of the AARP's Women's Initiative. Most of the widows who are poor now were not poor before their husbands died.

If a woman is considerably younger than her husband, she will be financially devastated by the "widow's gap" in the Social Security law. If she and her husband are receiving Social Security, when her husband dies, her Social Security benefits will stop, and won't resume until she is sixty. So even though she and her husband had been retired for a number of years, she may suddenly find herself looking for employment with outdated job skills.

"Twenty-three percent of women who work outside of the home now receive some type of pension, while twice as many men receive pensions. The main reason for this disparity is the multiplicity of roles that women carry. Most women, even those with college and/or graduate degrees, do not remain continually in the work force from twenty-two to sixty-five. Most of these women marry, most married women have children, and most women are ultimately responsible for the care of their aging parents.

If a woman can have a financial floor and some control over her business life and can exercise some power, the years after 50 are good years." (Carole Sinclair, *When Women Retire: The Problems They Face and How to Solve Them*)

Consider Dorothy Jones. She has worked for twenty-eight years as executive director of a local charity. She had put some money aside for retirement but now worries she won't have enough to see her through old age. Busy with work, family, and home, she didn't take time to learn how to increase her retirement money. She saved, yes, but she stashed her money in CDs and treasury bills rather than investing it for growth. Dorothy is typical of millions of older American women: She earned less than her male counterparts, and she has no pension other than Social Security. Although she was able to save, she kept her money in the bank because she was frightened of risk. She didn't understand investing and thought she was too busy to learn. She faces old age without a pension and with limited Social Security income.

Filling the Retirement Income Gap

As Bob Dylan said, "The times they are a-changin'." Baby boomer women have the potential to meet the retirement challenge head-on. The statistics show that women, especially small business owners, have many resources to ensure that their next fifty years are comfortable. That is because women are more economically independent than ever before. According to the U.S. Bureau of Statistics, women earn more than $1 trillion annually, and 47 percent of all Americans with more than $500,000 in assets are women. Female-owned businesses employ more people than all the Fortune 500 companies put together, and women are starting small businesses at twice the rate of men. As a matter of fact, it is estimated that by the year 2000, more than half of all small businesses will be owned by women.

Women in business have some definite advantages in planning for retirement. Small business owners have many options for retirement plans, such as Keoghs, SEP-IRAs, and SIMPLEs, that can be used to their advantage. But whether or not you are an entrepreneur with your own business, there are some smart steps you can take now to make sure you don't end up like Dorothy.

Make retirement plans a priority when you consider a job. Consider sacrificing some current salary in return for a good retirement plan—either the traditional type in which the employer pays monthly retirement benefits or a contributory plan, such as a 401(k), that lets you save money for retirement on a pretax basis. Seek out employers who will match part or all of your savings in a contributory plan.

Work as long as you can at the highest salary you can. If you do, you'll have more money to sock away for retirement and you will earn higher Social Security benefits. If you pay into Social Security for at least ten years (or if you qualify for Social Security under your husband's work record), you won't have to pay monthly premiums for Medicare hospital insurance when you retire.

Understand the effect on Social Security benefits of divorce and remarriage. Divorced retirees are entitled to Social Security payments equal to 50 percent of their ex-husband's benefits. For many women, that is more than they would get based on their own earnings. You must have been married at least ten years to claim benefits based on your ex-husband's earnings, and you lose that right if you remarry. If you remarry, you'll be entitled to collect payments equal to 50 percent of your new husband's benefits (with no waiting period). A widow is entitled to her late husband's benefits so long as she doesn't remarry before the age of sixty (or before fifty if she is disabled).

Understand your husband's pension plan. If you have a choice in how benefits are paid, have your husband elect a formula that in the event of his death assures monthly payments to you until your death. The monthly income will be lower during his lifetime under that plan, but the trade-off is well worth it. If the plan's only option is a lump-sum payment, be sure that he reinvests the money wisely rather than spending it imprudently.

Put money away for retirement on a regular basis. Even if it's only ten to twenty dollars a week, small amounts can add up, especially if you start young. The longer the money will be in place, the more growth-oriented your investments should be. For money that you won't need for many years, putting money aside regularly into a growth mutual fund can build a significant nest egg for your future. Savings accounts, CDs, and treasury bills, though good places to stash emergency funds and money you'll need soon, won't get you where you want to go in the long run.

Get credit in your own name. It is important to maintain credit in your own name after you are married. If you don't maintain your own credit, your credit cards may be canceled if you are widowed or divorced. If you are married and do not have credit cards, apply for one in your own name now. The easiest place to start is to apply for a department store credit card. Many stores allow you to open an account when you are making a purchase. Once you have a department store credit card in your own name, you should be able to qualify for a gasoline credit card. With a department store charge account and a gas card, a bank card such as MasterCard or Visa is within reach. If you are told that you need a cosigner, get a cosigner other than your husband, such as a parent, sibling, or friend, so that the credit will in no way be associated with your husband.

Learn about your finances. Don't just sign tax returns, be sure you understand them. Get assistance from your tax preparer if you need explanations. Identify your financial assets and debts, and begin to save for your future by paying down debt and budgeting. If you are married, be sure that you and your husband each understand what you own and what you owe, so you can begin to plan for the future when one of you dies. If the assets you have now are not enough to cover your immediate cash needs, the funds you will need to educate your children, your living expenses until retirement, and your retirement needs, be sure to cover any shortfalls with life insurance. Whether you are married or single, disability insurance that will replace a portion of your income is a must if you are employed: At almost any age, you are far more likely to become disabled than to die.

> I wish there were a way to coordinate or consolidate our retirement plans—I'm not sure whether what I'm doing in my 401(k) works well with what he's doing in his. (Joyce Z., age thirty-five)

Expect respect. Studies have shown that even in today's world, women are treated differently by stockbrokers, and possibly other financial advisers as well. If you feel patronized or do not get your questions answered, it's up to you to expect and get the respect you deserve. To do so, shop around until you find an adviser who will take you seriously and is able to explain his or her ideas in terms you can understand. Bone up on financial matters: Joining an investment club where you can learn to analyze investments (and have a good time besides) is a wonderful idea.

Develop a contingency plan. Know what you would do in the event of death, divorce, or disability. You will find a more comprehensive discussion of these unplanned crises in chapter 9.

SMART TIP

WOMEN'S PENSION RIGHTS MADE SIMPLE

Women may find two booklets very useful: *Your Pension Rights at Divorce,* published by Pension Rights Center, 918 Sixteenth Street N.W., Washington, DC 20006; and *A Woman's Guide to Pension Rights,* published by the American Association of Retired Persons, 601 E Street N.W., Washington, DC 20049. For facts and research, contact the National Center for Women and Retirement Research, Long Island University, Southampton Campus, Southampton, NY 11968, or call them at (516) 283-4809.

7

Off to a Late Start

The sooner you start planning for retirement, the better. But let's face it, most people in their twenties and thirties have other things on their minds than retirement. The only good thing about planning later rather than sooner for retirement is that you've got lots of company. Two-thirds of those approaching retirement are in that same place because of procrastination or just plain lack of money.

Don't despair. Even if you've procrastinated in planning for your retirement, you may not be as far behind as you think. Your employer may offer a traditional defined benefit retirement plan, which will provide you a monthly benefit when you retire. In addition, you may have saved some money in salary deferral plans, such as 401(k)s, 403(b)s, or TSAs. (See chapter 5 for a discussion of these plans.) You may also have saved money in IRAs. If you've been working for several years, then you may have earned Social Security benefits. And don't forget about your home mortgage—over the years, monthly payments on a mortgage will have created some equity. By retirement time you may have paid off the mortgage completely, or at least have enough equity so that you can move somewhere less expensive or refinance your existing mortgage to reduce your payments. If you have no mortgage, you may qualify for a reverse mortgage, which pays you each month, rather than the other way around. (See chapter 12 for more on reverse mortgages.) Add to all of this an estimate of the amount you expect to inherit from your parents or others, and you will find that you are at least partly on your way to a comfortable retirement.

SMART TIP

DON'T SACRIFICE LONG-TERM GOALS FOR SHORT-TERM SATISFACTION

Take a realistic view of *all* of your goals. Unfulfilled needs make you feel nervous, unprepared, and vulnerable. Emergency funds, retirement income, vacation desires, a new home, a child's education—many of these goals must be addressed to gain true financial security.

Because it is easier to work toward short-term goals than long-term ones, such as eventual retirement, people frequently focus only on their short-term goals. Create objectives for *all* of your goals, and work toward satisfying those goals simultaneously. Otherwise, years from now you will rue the short-term goals that might have been modified or sacrificed altogether, had you realized at the time the importance of your long-term goals.

Now it is time to catch up. Fortunately, it's never too late to jump-start your retirement planning. If you are off to a late start, you will have to save until it hurts and manage your growing investment portfolio wisely, but you can do it. Here are eight things you should do now.

Pay Off Credit Cards as Soon as You Can

The high interest you pay on credit cards greatly reduces the amount you have available to save for retirement. To extinguish credit card debt, first quit using the cards, or at least charge only what you can pay for *in full* within thirty days, when the bill comes. When the bill comes each month, pay all of the current charges plus the monthly finance charge. In addition, pay 5 percent, 10 percent, or even more, if you can afford it, on the old balance due. Within a year or two you'll be off the credit card treadmill and out of debt. The financial relief you feel as your credit card balances disappear will be well worth the sacrifice.

> My fourteen credit cards were out of control, but with the help of a credit counselor I figured out how much I could afford to pay off each month. I started with the cards with the smallest balances and the highest interest rates. As each old balance disappeared, I gained more and more confidence. I finally believed I could do it—*and I did!* (Renee V., age thirty-seven)

SMART TIP

You have too much debt if:

- your monthly consumer credit payments, such as car payments and credit card payments, exceed 25 percent of your monthly take-home income;
- you borrow from one credit card to pay another;
- your credit cards are always borrowed to their limits;
- you shop places that will take credit cards to avoid having to pay with cash;
- a solicitation in the mail for a new credit card is cause for celebration;
- you don't open the bills when they come each month, and you have missed several payments;
- you don't know how much you owe and can't name all of your creditors;
- your debt is increasing each month instead of decreasing.

Scale Down Rather than Up

All your life you have been working toward achieving a better lifestyle. Now that you are scrambling to create a retirement nest egg, scale down your lifestyle and get used to living on less. Don't buy a more expensive car, buy a more economical, used car. When you get a raise, don't increase your spending—sock it away for retirement. Use your income tax refund to pay down credit cards and get rid of expensive monthly interest rather than splurging on a new wardrobe.

SMART TIP

AVOID THE URGE TO SPLURGE

If impulse buying is a problem for you, try this exercise. For three weeks, every time you have the urge to buy something, ask yourself, "Do I really need this?" If the answer is no, don't buy it, and add it to a list of money saved. At the end of the three-week period, add up the money you've saved and write a check to your savings account as your reward for being frugal. Saving is a habit, and this exercise develops habits that will help you attain financial security for life.

If your spending is out of control, find out why (see chapter 2) and make the changes necessary to start saving. Small savings can make a big difference, and big savings can mean more income in retirement. For example, if you spent just $1,000 less each time you bought a new car during your lifetime, and you invested that money instead, you would have $120,000 more when you retire. Spending $15,000 less for a new home will save about $120 a month in mortgage payments over the next thirty years. Invest those savings and they will grow to $220,000.

If college expenses for your youngest children are eating up your current budget, remember that those expenses won't go on forever. Once they end, redirect those dollars from tuition bills into your retirement savings. Do the same thing with any other expense that will stop, such as your car payment, your home mortgage, or a student loan.

Fact of life: 6 percent of Americans cite supporting their twenty-something children as a reason for not saving for retirement.

Put as Much as You Can into Retirement Plans

It's important to put money into retirement plans, for several reasons. The money will grow faster, since you don't pay tax on it currently and it continues to earn tax-deferred. In addition, and perhaps even more important, the money is taken directly from your paycheck, so you never see it. Tucked away in a retirement plan, you simply don't have the opportunity to spend it because there are penalties and taxes on premature withdrawals to dissuade you from drawing it out. Invest as much as you can in 401(k) plans, 403(b) plans, TSAs, and any other savings plan available to you at work. If your employer does not offer such a plan, encourage him or her to start one, or look for a job that offers better retirement benefits. If you do not have retirement plans at work, put $2,000 a year, or as much as you can afford, into an IRA. If you are self-employed, set up a SEP-IRA or a Keogh plan.

Fact of life: 52 percent of Americans who save for retirement say they put their money into a 401(k) plan, compared with 44 percent who say they put it into regular savings accounts.

If you are investing in a retirement plan, you don't need to worry about paying a tax each year on the interest, dividends, or capital gains. You won't pay taxes until you ultimately withdraw the money. Because retirement plans are already tax-deferred, it doesn't make sense to put tax-free investments such as municipal bonds, or tax-deferred investments such as annuities, into a retirement plan.

But if you have invested as much as you can in retirement plans and would like to make additional investments for your retirement, consider tax-deferred annuities. Although contributions to a tax-deferred variable annuity are not tax deductible, the money will grow tax-deferred, so you won't have to pay a tax each year on its earnings. Growth stocks may also fill the bill. Most growth stocks provide tax deferral because they pay small or no dividends and there are no capital gains taxes due until you sell them at a profit.

Boost Your Income

One way to make up for lost time is to find a better job, especially one with enhanced benefits. You may also want to take on a second job, stashing all of that money away for retirement. The sacrifices you make now will have a direct effect on the quality of your life later on. Work hard now, so that in the future, when you have less energy, you won't have to.

SMART TIP

HOW BENEFICIAL ARE YOUR BENEFITS?

Retirement benefits are important, but so are other fringe benefits. If you are weighing the merits of two or more job offers, add up the total value of your current fringe benefits and compare them to the benefits package offered by each of your prospective employers.

Some of the benefits to consider are health insurance and dental plans, vacations and sick leave, life insurance plans, educational programs, variable employee benefit programs (VEBAs) for child care, medical expenses, and so forth, that you fund through salary reduction, and such other benefits as free parking, a company car, dining and athletic facilities, legal and financial planning, club memberships, and the like.

There are other ways to increase your income. If you have unwanted household items, have a garage sale and invest the proceeds. If you have an extra car you don't need or recreational equipment you can part with, sell them. For example, if you sell an extra vehicle that is worth $10,000 and invest the money for twenty years, you will boost your retirement fund by more than $50,000. If your home is large, take in a roommate or a boarder, perhaps a college student who needs a room to rent or a foreign exchange student. And finally, whenever you get a financial windfall, be it a monetary gift, a bonus, an income tax refund, lottery winnings, or even gambling winnings, earmark the money for retirement and invest it for long-term growth.

Postpone Your Retirement

Find ways to make your employment more enjoyable, and realize that you are going to continue working even during retirement. Plan to stay in your present job beyond normal retirement age, or investigate jobs you can move to when your present employment ends. Perhaps you can continue that evening or weekend part-time job even after retirement.

Another benefit of postponing your retirement is that you may be able to build more retirement assets by contributing to retirement plans and adding working years to the pension benefits formula. Working later will increase your Social Security benefits as well, about 8 percent for every year you delay your retirement beyond normal retirement age.

SMART TIP

RETIRING TO A NEW LIFE

If your goal is secure retirement income, define what that means for you. Analyze your current lifestyle costs, then imagine your life in retirement. Transportation and clothing costs may be less, but travel and hobby expenses may increase. Will you continue to live in the same house, or move to smaller quarters? Will your home be fully paid for, so that your expenses won't include a mortgage payment? Will you be able to work part time to lessen your retirement income needs? Envision your life in retirement, then estimate your expenses in today's dollars. That will give you a realistic picture of your retirement goals.

Go for Growth

To make your money grow faster, you will have to take some risks. That doesn't mean taking a trip to Las Vegas or Atlantic City and putting all your money on the line. But it does mean getting your money out of the bank and investing in growth stocks and growth-oriented mutual funds. You may think that investing in the stock market or in equity mutual funds is too risky, but if you have ten years or more to retirement, you can afford the greater volatility risk of the stock market. As a matter of fact, you would be foolish to invest anywhere else. That's because for the long-term investor, inflation is the biggest risk, and over time will rob your money of its buying power. For example, if you are fifty years old and expect to live another thirty-five years, you will find that inflation will steal 60 percent of your money's buying power over your remaining years. So if you invest your money "safely" in the bank, your principal will remain intact, but your buying power won't. In twenty years everything will cost twice as much, so your money will go only half as far.

Mutual funds are the perfect way to diversify so that you can reduce the risk in your retirement portfolio and yet keep your investments simple. If you invest in a 401(k) plan or another type of employee savings plan, the underlying investments are probably mutual-fund-like pools of investment assets. If you invest in an IRA, SEP, or Keogh plan, mutual funds are an excellent investment vehicle. Not only will your investment be diversified, but you won't have to keep track of the underlying investments and decide when to sell one security and buy another. The fund manager will take care of that. You'll have a knowledgeable team of experts on your side to make daily decisions about what to buy or sell.

Growth funds can help you beat inflation by investing in stocks of large, often well-known companies that have a history of steady growth. Maximum growth funds invest in stocks of companies that are smaller and less well known—companies whose profits are often not currently high but whose earnings are growing rapidly. Growth stocks and funds can give you the jitters because they tend to fluctuate more than other investments. The volatility can feel like a roller-coaster ride if viewed too closely. But try to approach your retirement investments from the vantage point of an eagle, not an ant. The eagle can see the road ribbon smoothly into the future. An ant can see only the imperfections in the surface, and each peak and valley looks insurmountable. So it is with stock market fluctuations. Each week your mutual funds will vacillate up and down, giving antlike investors the anxious jitters. But over several years, an eagle's perspective will show a ribbon of steady growth from the same investments.

Add to Your Investments Each Month

If you save and invest for long-term growth each and every month, after a few years the growth of your little nest egg will astound you. Sophie Tucker, the famous singer, said the secret to longevity is to keep breathing; similarly, the secret to financial success is to keep investing.

As you build your portfolio year after year, the market will rise and fall, as do the tides, but your portfolio will grow and grow.

> I hate to admit it, but adding to my mutual funds each month was the only way I managed to save anything. In the old days I used to panic and withdraw all my money every time the market dipped. But now that the money goes automatically from my bank account to the mutual funds each month, I give a cheer when the market is down—I'll get more shares for my money that month. (Tom F., age forty-three)

Adding to your nest egg each month can also help keep your portfolio in balance. Let's say you decided to invest your retirement funds 50 percent in growth funds, 25 percent in international funds, and 25 percent in bond funds. After a year or so you will find that some of the funds have performed better than others, and your portfolio will have changed in its proportions. To maintain your original portfolio balance, direct that future investments go to shore up the lagging funds. For example, if the growth fund has flourished while the international stocks and bond funds have languished, direct future investments to the international stocks and bond funds. This goes against your natural tendency, which is to invest more in growth funds that have had hot recent performance. But remember that each type of fund will have its day in the sun, and the time to buy more is when the price plummets, not when it soars.

Rely on Professional Advice

You may need professional help to get you moving and on track. Just as some dieters do better in a diet program or with a diet coach or group than on their own, many investors do better when they have a professional guiding them. Some investors simply don't have the time to devote to monitoring their investments. Others lack the discipline to follow through. Still others tend to get carried away on a tide of emotions, picking hot funds when the market is rising without regard for proper allocation and selling in a panic when prices drop. If any of these apply to you, you will probably benefit from the services of a qualified, ethical stockbroker, financial planner, or money manager.

The longer you keep your money invested, the more likely you are to reap the potential rewards of positive performance. Get on the right track and keep adding to your portfolio, monitoring and rebalancing as needed, and you'll profit in any economy. Give your investments the gift of time, and you will be rewarded with a retirement fund that will give you a lifetime of financial security.

If you find you are off to a late start, the advice you follow will be valuable even if you find that retirement happens before you anticipated. The next chapter explores the options you have if you choose early retirement—or if your company chooses it for you.

PART III

CONSIDER THE UNEXPECTED, UNPLANNED, AND NONTRADITIONAL

8

It's Never Too Late to Retire Early

> Mark called from work to say he'd be home early with something special. It seemed like a dream come true when he showed me the early retirement package that they were offering him. He's been with Smith-Reilly for twenty years and I guess they are being acquired by another firm. We'll have to think about the advantages and disadvantages I'm sure, but I already know what my vote will be! (Jennifer O., age forty-eight)

The American dream—early retirement. At some point you've probably fantasized about it. Long, leisurely days at the beach, or perhaps hiking the Himalayas, fly-fishing on the river, or just catching up on your reading. Best of all, you could tell your employer to shove the job and all the attendant stress. It sounds divine in concept, doesn't it? In reality, there are two types of early retirement: the early retirement you choose on your own because you want a change, and the early retirement your employer offers you, loaded with incentives to prompt your early retirement fantasies.

The first part of this chapter explores the concept of early retirement generally, and particularly what to do when your early retirement is employer motivated due to corporate downsizing. Next, we'll explore options if you are considering early retirement because you are suffering from Vacation Deficit Disorder or simply want to kiss the rat race goodbye. No matter which situation is yours, you must know what alternatives are available between full-time work and full-time retirement.

Retiring to the Future

Janine had the kind of smile that disarms immediately and an enthusiasm for life to match. She met Victoria Collins at a restaurant halfway between her home near Los Angeles and Victoria's office in Irvine to talk about the early retirement package she was considering. Her soft brown eyes gleamed as she told how excited she was about retiring. At forty-seven, with twenty-six years at Pacific Bell, it was exactly what she wanted. Now she said she needed help determining how much income she could withdraw each year without penalties and how she should invest her nest egg so that it would continue to grow. She had been to several seminars sponsored by Pacific Bell, where she had received an impressive blue-covered binder with the silver letters, *Your Retirement.* She had also visited with account executives from both Merrill Lynch and PaineWebber. Still, she was confused.

> With all the seminars I've been to and stuff I've read, I still don't know how to invest this lump sum or how much I should take as income each month. Meanwhile, it's sitting in a money market at the credit union. And the more I learn, the more confused I feel. It's not only the investments I make now, but what do I do for the rest of my life? Right now I'm so glad to walk away from my job, and Josh really supports me taking early retirement so I can do some volunteer work that's important to both of us. But who knows, sometime I may want to go back to work. Then I won't need income from this rollover. It's hard to plan for the future when I don't know what I'll end up doing, but I see that that's what I have to do. It's really the rest of my life I have to plan for, isn't it? (Janine R., age forty-seven)

As we talked, Janine realized that there were things she hadn't even thought about that needed prompt action. She and Josh, forty-three, had been married for ten years. Neither of them had a will. When she died, Janine wanted any money remaining in her IRA to go to her two sons from a prior marriage. She was uncertain how to accomplish this without jeopardizing the income that Josh would need to continue running the household.

Janine was smart to seek help in dealing with these issues, but by her own admission wished she had begun her planning years earlier, rather than waiting until retirement was imminent. Had she begun earlier, she would have had time to think constructively about her future. But Janine's delay is common. It's hard for any of us to plan for a date that seems to be at some unknown time.

As you read this, Janine's situation is being repeated many times over throughout the country. It used to be that an employer and employee, if all went well, had a long and mutually satisfying marriage. But used-to-bes are no longer the rule, and many employees nowadays are offered early outs. For most people, deciding whether to take an early retirement package is difficult and confusing, and multiple options from which to choose add to the confusion.

Retirement—Past and Present

Retirement as we know it may seem as if it's been around forever. But before World War II, retirement wasn't very common. Social Security didn't exist, and few employers provided pensions. During World War II, unions began negotiating for retirement benefits; under wartime wage freezes they had little else to bargain for. The addition of retirement benefits to wage packages, combined with the advent of Social Security benefits at age sixty-five, made retirement at sixty-five very popular.

But it didn't stop there. Once people acclimated to retirement at sixty-five, they began to think about retiring even earlier. The craze for early retirement began in earnest in 1961, when Social Security payments became possible for men as young as age sixty-two. (Women had been eligible to receive Social Security payments at age sixty-two as early as 1955, but so few women were in the workplace that their early retirement was not statistically significant.) For most people Social Security isn't enough to provide a comfortable retirement, nor do they make their retirement decisions based on Social Security eligibility. The changes in the Social Security program motivated many employers to change their pension systems as well to allow for early retirement at full or reduced benefits.

Fact of life: One in five Americans say they want to retire early.

Early retirement is increasingly difficult as households become more and more expensive to operate in relation to people's compensation. In addition, a study sponsored by Merrill Lynch found that boomers have saved only one-third of what they should save to be on track to retire at age sixty-five, never mind *early*. Why then is the average retirement age only sixty-one and falling? Unfortunately, not for the same reasons as in the past. It used to be a status symbol to be young and retired: It meant you'd made it big, and you'd done so early. Nowadays early retirement is often a euphemism for being laid off and not being able to find another job. Some people have no choice about early retirement due to layoffs or poor health.

Is Early Retirement for You?

Fifty percent of Americans say they want to retire before age sixty-five. But early retirement has many disadvantages. If you are married, will it cause conflicts if one of you wants to quit while the other keeps on working? Would early retirement hamper your ability to return to the mainstream workplace later on? Many people who retire early end up combining part-time or seasonal work with leisure time.

There are financial disadvantages to early retirement as well. Take Social Security. Today's maximum Social Security benefits are about $14,000 per year. Baby boomers won't get *any* benefits until age sixty-two, and even then they'll get only 70 to 75 percent (depending on the year they were born) of what they would if they waited until sixty-six or sixty-seven to retire. And now that people are living longer, that can mean that you will reduce your benefits by hundreds of thousands of dollars over your lifetime. If you work part time, your Social Security benefits may be reduced, so you'll probably want to delay receiving Social Security benefits until you quit work entirely or turn seventy, when your earnings no longer reduce the benefits you receive.

Medical coverage could be a problem too. Under current law, you won't be eligible for Medicare until you reach age sixty-five, but if you retire early, you'll probably lose your employer's medical plan. That means you will have to qualify for medical insurance and pay for it yourself. And medical insurance premiums increase dramatically once you reach age fifty.

You may also need to replace employer-provided life insurance to protect those who are dependent on you, such as your children and your spouse. And if your employer provides college tuition benefits for your children, the loss of that perk through early retirement may be costly.

Inflation is another problem. Even at only 3 percent, inflation can double your expenses over a twenty-five-year retirement. If your retirement is forty years or longer, your expenses may quadruple because of inflation. Though comfortably retired on a fixed income at fifty, you will feel the pinch in your sixties, drastically reduce your lifestyle in your seventies, and face the poorhouse in your eighties and nineties.

For people who had their children late or started second or third families years after the first, the goal of early retirement is complicated by the issue of college tuition for children. And as we are all living longer, our parents are living longer as well. That means people contemplating early retirement may have the added set of financial responsibilities of caring for aging parents.

Consider the Impact of Early Retirement

Whatever your reason for considering early retirement, there are a number of factors to consider before determining whether it is right for you.

> It's hard to get a handle on what early retirement will really mean to us financially. We enjoy our lifestyle now and sure don't want that to change. As helpful as all the stuff we've received from the company is, it still doesn't answer what the bottom line will look like for us. (Gerald S., age fifty-two)

To calculate how much you'll need in retirement, figure how much you are spending today. One way to do that is to take your gross income and subtract Social Security and Medicare taxes, contributions to retirement plans, and annual savings. Then subtract any expenses you have now that you won't have in retirement, such as college tuition and other child-related expenses, or mortgage payments, if your house will be paid off. Now add the extra expenses that you'll have in retirement, such as health insurance, medical costs, hobby expenses, and travel. Of course, if you are married and your spouse is working, you may be covered under your spouse's health insurance plan, so early retirement won't be a problem as long as your spouse continues to be employed and you remain married.

If you are considering saying yes to an early retirement package, think carefully about what you will lose and what you will gain.

- **Lost cash value.** To get a clear picture of what your job is worth in terms of cash value, add your lost income (generally your gross salary), your company's contribution to your retirement plan, and what it will cost you to replace needed benefits, such as health coverage and life insurance.

• **Lost benefits.** If your expense account covers many of your meals, or your job includes lunch, social events, or other freebies, figure out how much of those perks you will still need, and add that to your total.

• **Savings on certain expenses.** Think about the expenses you won't have anymore and subtract them: taxes, work-related clothing, dry cleaning and transportation costs, child care, and any household services you can do for yourself. Needing one less car for the household can save you lots.

You may be able to save expenses simply by having more time. You can volunteer rather than make cash contributions to charitable organizations, shop for bargains, make your own clothes and gifts, plant a garden instead of hiring a gardener, do your own house repairs, and yes, clip coupons.

• **Other gains.** Subtract expenses that will be reduced when you are not working: restaurant meals for the family because you were working late, vacations or luxury items you give yourself as a reward for working hard, extra money you spent on the kids out of guilt for not spending time with them, and any expenses to reduce stress at work: therapy, massages, trips to a spa.

• **New expenses.** Next, add expenses that may come because you'll have more free time. More time with the kids might mean more expenses if you are in charge. If you don't have children, you may be spending more money on leisure activities—classes, movies, travel, and so on—that you didn't have time for while you were working.

• **Intangibles.** In addition to the financial impact, consider intangibles, such as the effect of a career interruption on your promotion prospects and your retirement planning. The intangible costs are harder to calculate. Unfortunately, in some jobs and industries, stepping out for a few years means stepping down on the career ladder should you ever want to return.

Your future retirement prospects may change too, if you take some years off work. Company-paid defined benefit plans are based on years of work and salary, and so are Social Security benefits. Clearly, fewer years of work mean lower benefits when you retire. It's difficult to calculate how much you would lose, without knowing how long you would be gone and how your career would be affected over the long haul.

While you cannot know exactly how these intangibles will affect you, you'd be foolish to ignore them completely. It's important to estimate an impact, giving some thought to a wide range of possibilities.

Your Income in Early Retirement

To begin deciding whether early retirement will provide the income you need, first size up your pension plan at work. Does it allow you to retire early with full or reduced benefits? For example, many plans let you retire at age fifty-five with full benefits if you have spent thirty years on the job. Although most people in our changing society have not spent thirty years on the job by the time they are fifty-five, many plans will allow you to take reduced benefits at fifty-five. Surprisingly, taking reduced benefits may pay off in the long run. Even though the benefits are reduced, over a normal lifetime you will probably receive more than if you waited to collect benefits until you are sixty-five. You may want to start drawing your pension early if you can draw at least 40 percent of your full pension benefits. For example, if you can collect $6,000 (50 percent pension) at age fifty-five or wait until you are sixty-five and collect $12,000 a year, you would be better off waiting to collect your full pension only if you live to be eighty-five or older. But since the average fifty-five-year-old lives to be about eighty, you'll probably be better off collecting at fifty-five.

Be careful, though: Many companies base your monthly benefit on the salary you earned at the date of retirement. That means early retirement will take its toll in the form of reduced checks, even if you qualify for full retirement at fifty-five, because you'll be sacrificing the salary increases of later years that would have boosted your retirement income.

Early retirement poses a problem if you are too young to draw money from your retirement plans. For example, IRAs require you to be fifty-nine and a half before you can withdraw funds without a 10 percent excise penalty. The same rule applies to your 401(k) plan, although it will allow you to take distributions at fifty-five if you fully retire from that employer. So if you retire at age fifty, you will have to wait until you are fifty-five to sixty to begin drawing benefits from these plans. (There is a way that you can begin taking payments early from your IRA, if you take substantially equal payments until you reach retirement age. See chapter 5 for more details.)

The Golden Handshake and the Golden Bridge

Some companies are offering a "golden handshake," the nickname for benefits offered by an employer to motivate employees to retire early. The early retirement package may also include a Social Security replacement, to be paid until you are old enough to start collecting Social Security benefits. That is called a "golden bridge." The sweeteners offered in the early retirement options usually are not enough to make up for a lack of assets stashed away for retirement. For that reason, those packages generally work only for those who are close to retiring anyway.

If you are offered early retirement, refigure your retirement needs and see if they can be met by the plan. And don't forget about your need for medical insurance—is it included in the early retirement option?

If your employer's early retirement package offers you a choice between increased pension benefits or severance pay, one rule of thumb for deciding which is best is to multiply the increased pension benefits by one hundred and then compare the result to the severance pay to see which is higher. For example, if you are offered an increase of $500 a month pension benefits or $60,000 severance pay, which is one year's salary, the choice is clear. Multiplying the increased pension benefits of $500 by one hundred results in $50,000 of benefits. The $60,000 severance pay is a better bargain.

Jumping Back in After Retiring Early

Janine, whom we met earlier, was forty-seven when she received an early retirement package from Pacific Bell. Her goals were to take time off, do some volunteer work, and then go back to "a job." If you retire very early, say in your forties, as Janine did, you too may want to return to work someday, because of boredom, because you stumble across an irresistible opportunity, or because you run low on money. A second career after retirement may be more satisfying than the first. You usually don't have the responsibilities of children, the dependency on your income from your new job, or the need to get ahead. Your new job may be more fun than your former career, or at least less stressful. Perhaps you'll be able to turn a hobby into a vocation, take a reduced salary to work for a cause you support, or take a part-time job. If you do, you won't be alone—a survey by Fidelity Investments shows that 80 percent of people expect to work during retirement.

Fact of life: 2 percent of Americans would like to continue working after retirement, regardless of their financial status.

Your Job Is There, But You'd Rather Be Elsewhere

Perhaps your early retirement fantasies are not motivated by employer downsizing or the offer of an attractive retirement package. You've worked long and hard to be successful, and now you want to kiss the rat race good-bye. Job stress from a variety of sources may be taking its toll, causing you to long for a change—any change. But before you opt for early retirement, ask yourself if you really want to retire or if you simply want to add more enjoyment to what you're doing. You may just be suffering from Vacation Deficit Disorder and need a sabbatical or a travel break.

Let's explore some alternatives for leaving the rat race as well as for changing the race so you enjoy running it. You may benefit from the freedom and flexibility that you could get from flextime, job sharing, or telecommuting. Maybe an extended vacation or sabbatical will do the trick. Or maybe you can turn a hobby into money, go back to school for new skills, embark on a new career, or start your own business.

Here's a simple exercise you can do: If you had a million dollars and didn't have to work, what would you do? Think about it for a few moments and jot down some notes for yourself. Savor the thought of those fun activities, and compare notes with your spouse or partner. OK, reality check—you don't have that million dollars. But how can you incorporate what you wrote down into your daily life? Doing this simple exercise from time to time may help you make changes that will increase your satisfaction as you live out what could be your next fifty years.

To determine just what course of action would be most satisfying, ask yourself:

- Are you tired of doing your current work, or are you tired of all work?
- Do you long to work at home and think telecommuting may be the answer?
- Do you want a more flexible schedule, more personal time, and more freedom than you now have?
- Would you like to share a job with someone?
- If you had three to six months off to study, travel, or do as you wish, would you feel recharged and eager to return to your job?
- Are you drawn to the concept of giving back, of doing work not for profit but to help others?

- Are you just plain tired or burned out?
- Do you have a secret dream of something you've always wanted to do or be?
- Do you think you're too old to make a major career change?

You might want to stay in your current position if you can make some changes to overcome feelings of burnout, stress, or dissatisfaction. Maybe you are not feeling as productive as you would like and need some inspiration. Or maybe you feel life is going by in a blur and you're out of touch with your spouse or family. A long-term change such as downshifting or telecommuting may be in order, or maybe a vacation or a sabbatical will give you the breathing space you need.

Consider Downshifting Your Career

A recent study by the Merck Family Foundation found that an eye-popping 28 percent of respondents said that during the past five years they had made *voluntary* changes that resulted in their earning *less* money. (The study did not include those who had simply retired.) The most common changes were reducing work hours, changing to lower-paying but less-stressful jobs, and quitting work to stay at home. The reasons (and there could be more than one): 68 percent of those who downshifted did so to pursue a more "balanced" life; 66 percent wanted more time; 63 percent were seeking a less-stressful life; 53 percent wanted to spend more time with their children. An astonishing 87 percent said they were happy with their change, and only 35 percent reported missing the extra income.

There are many ways to downshift. Terry, at fifty-two, is a top-level executive with thirty years at Palmolive. He made a conscious and carefully considered decision five years ago that still gives him satisfaction today.

> I woke up one morning and realized—I don't have a life. I had just finished a major project that had taken about two years, and with all the presentations, deadlines, and travel, there was no time for a social life or friends. I decided to be content with what I have and get off the moving sidewalk and let it go by, rather than reaching higher on the ladder. It's been very satisfying. Basically I've had the opportunity to use my talents and skills on projects I want. I not only have more flexibility, but to my mind more job security as well. The higher you get on the ladder, the fewer positions

> there are and the tougher the competition is. By taking a proactive role and creating my own projects, I've stayed ahead of the curve. (Terry L., age fifty-two)

Terry's decision to change his job rather than continuing to climb the corporate ladder was a smart one for him. He was able to use his talent and vision to create results-oriented projects that make him a valuable employee and that give him both job satisfaction and a more realistic work schedule. A similar route is often taken by people who change jobs or reduce their working hours in order to devote more time to their growing families.

Sid's reasons for downshifting were more common, and more negative.

> I'm fed up and I don't want to work for "the corporation" anymore. I gave them eighteen years of my life, did my job well, but lost it. Now I'd rather work less, earn less, and spend less. (Sid H., age forty-nine)

Terry and Sid are among many in the grass-roots movement that trend watchers are calling "voluntary simplicity." Dropping out of the race or at least slowing the pace, giving up pressure-cooker jobs or second incomes in exchange for more free time, more flexibility, more focus on family—that's what it's about for those who espouse voluntary simplicity. The book best known for putting a voice and a plan to this new trend is *Your Money or Your Life,* by Joe Dominguez and Vicki Robin (Penguin Books). The underlying concept is that for every item you decide to acquire, you spend a slice of your "life energy." The program is a different yet straightforward approach to achieving financial independence and quality of life at the same time.

To try this approach in your own life, start by computing how much you've earned so far (the Social Security Administration will send you a statement of earnings) and how much you have to show for it (as shown on your net worth statement or balance sheet). Then convert your pay to a real hourly wage, after taxes and work expenses such as commuting, eating out, wardrobe. You can then track your spending carefully and convert each item that you desire or acquire into the number of hours worked to earn that much money. This can be a real eye opener, and you will want to evaluate whether your spending was worth the work time needed to pay for it. Applying this logic to all spending, you can set priorities of what is really important, reduce budget drain, and divert more income to savings. If you maximize your income and savings and minimize your spending, you'll ultimately reach the "crossover point," that point at which you've achieved financial independence. Your money is now working hard for you and you can choose whether or not to continue working.

While *Your Money or Your Life* was instrumental for so many as a map to voluntary simplicity, there are other excellent resources you will want to check out as well. *Simple Living: The Journal of Voluntary Simplicity* is a quarterly newsletter that profiles downshifters who have made it work and provides a listing of support groups, or "study circles," around the country. You can subscribe for fourteen dollars a year by writing to them at 2319 North 45th Street, Box 149, Seattle, WA 98103. You'll find other resources listed at the back of the book.

You may wish to follow this new trend wholeheartedly or just experiment to see how it feels. You *can* step off and let the moving sidewalk pass you by. The great thing is that you can test out any and all of the alternatives in this chapter—downshifting, telecommuting, taking a sabbatical or refresher break, switching jobs, starting your own business, or volunteering—to see what works for you. You may want to combine two or more ideas or use these to spark your own.

Telecommuting

It is a persuasive ad. A beautiful woman, looking pensive, competent, and satisfied with her life, is half silhouetted in a hotel room with her fingers on a laptop. The words across the bottom of the ad read, "Sheraton's Club level. Everything you have at the office. Except the politics."

With technology expanding so rapidly, we can have the efficiency of an office in hotel rooms, in home offices, and even in our cars. An employer may know we are at some other location, but clients, colleagues, and vendors rarely do.

In early 1996 a blizzard paralyzed the Northeast, but remarkably, work went on—but not in offices. Dan Saloman, a management consultant, stayed at home and worked, taking time off to help his kids build a snowman. Almost all of the staff of thirty-two at the company where he worked stayed at home as well. "We're not finding it a problem, we're finding it a pleasure," he reported.

The storm, which dumped twenty to thirty inches of snow from Virginia to Boston, gave a big lift to the concept of telecommuting, helping to overcome some employer concerns that workers at home don't get much done. The blizzard was the first widescale disruption of work in a few years. During that time, PCs, modems, fax machines, and second phone lines had become commonplace in homes around the nation. With technology we can travel the Internet and tap into research from newspapers and databases around the world. We can link our PCs directly to office networks or participate in conference calls with our colleagues and clients. When the blizzard hit, many professionals found they had all of the necessary equipment to work from home. They decided to stay put, plug in, and still have a productive day.

Both the blizzard of 1996 and the recent Olympics in Atlanta helped push telecommuting deeper into office culture. Concerned about massive traffic jams, frustrated workers, and lost productivity due to the influx of Olympics visitors, an Atlanta telecommuting consultant was engaged to organize twenty workshops over six months prior to the games to help companies plan work-at-home programs. The Olympic Games telecommuting experiment has altered many Atlantans' work habits for good.

You may have thought a lot about the benefits of working from home. You and a lot of other folks, it seems. Find/SVP, a survey firm, figures that the number of telecommuters nationwide has doubled since 1990. This year as many as 4.5 million new people will join the forty-three million Americans who work at home, according to LINK Resources, a New York research firm. The big pluses to home work: no traffic, more family time, more flexibility, and commuting time saved each day to put toward more productive uses.

Businesses are always looking for ways to cut costs and increase productivity. One advantage for companies is that workers who telecommute some of the time are generally happier. Another advantage is that telecommuting can reduce office space needs and overhead. When the cost-saving advantages combine with the added benefits of reducing traffic and pollution and increasing worker satisfaction, telecommuting becomes a win-win situation.

But telecommuting has some disadvantages too. You may not be as proficient a techie as you need to be to telecommute, and connections via modem may be slower than using the office network. Incoming calls may be a problem to answer unless you have secretarial help. Without strict time boundaries, the workday can spill over into family time. But the most significant problem may be lack of personal contact and interaction with colleagues. Many of those we spoke with cited this lack of "face time" as the biggest drawback of their telecommuting lifestyle.

Employers may find disadvantages as well. Telecommuting requires a lot of trust, and managers often worry that staffers aren't working if they can't *see* them working.

If telecommuting appeals to you, try a test run a day or two each week. Does it meet your needs and your employer's needs? Decide how you can structure your telecommuting so you can do your business more efficiently. Despite some disadvantages, telecommuting may mean more flexibility, more time with family, and more freedom from the frustrating aspects of work. It may be just the alternative to the rat race you need.

Recharging with a Sabbatical

We rush home from a ten-hour workday, shop, cook, spend time with the family, walk the dog, and get ready for the next day. Heaven forbid we should take a break. It seems a bit un-American to take time off to study Italian, master the Internet, take a painting class, or go on an archaeological dig. That's not work, and America loves workaholics. We need to get over it.

Working harder doesn't mean working smarter. And you may be at the point where never-ending work is leading to burnout. Or heart disease. Or divorce. Or any number of other unhappy experiences.

> It's amazing how different I feel about work and how relaxed I am. I hadn't taken that much time off since I was a junior in high school. (Claire S., thirty-nine)

Taking time off can help you work smarter. Claire, a benefits manager at a large law firm in San Francisco, has returned from her first minisabbatical—six weeks of paid time off that her firm gives all employees after every five years of service. Six weeks is hardly long enough to be considered a real sabbatical, and Claire, eager for more, has begun planning for a six-month sabbatical two years from now.

For employees who are able to get past the anxiety of stepping off the treadmill, there are great advantages to a sabbatical—restoring scorched brain cells, jump-starting creativity, recouping perspective, and gaining a renewed sense of self.

Companies can benefit from a more committed, healthier worker who is willing to work harder, produce more, and accept the challenges of doing a good job. Employee sabbaticals can be a key benefit that gives companies a strong competitive edge for attracting and keeping skilled employees in this era of brain drain, when the best talent may be the first to leave at any sign of corporate losses or layoffs.

Are you ready to ask for that sabbatical? Before you do, consider the downside. Coworkers who have to cover for you may feel resentful. It may take time to train the person who will fill in for you while you are gone. Then there are the harsher consequences. Will the bosses view you as a slacker for taking time off? Will your career be hurt? Will your job really be there when you return? Can you afford to take an unpaid or partially paid sabbatical?

While only a minority of companies offer paid leaves, a much broader number offer unpaid time off for a variety of reasons. By law now, most companies must allow up to twelve weeks per year of unpaid time off for family and medical leave. Some companies have used voluntary unpaid leaves to temporarily reduce costs during economic downturns or restructuring.

Check out your company's policy on sabbaticals. If it doesn't have

COMPANIES THAT ENCOURAGE TIME OFF

- **McDonald's.** Workers get an eight-week paid sabbatical for every ten years of full-time continuous service and can return to the same job they left.
- **American Express.** Employees with ten or more years of service may take up to one year of unpaid leave. Or they may apply for a limited number of paid leaves to work for three to six months on a community project.
- **Apple Computer.** Since 1987, Apple has offered employees six weeks of paid time off after every five years of work. They can do as they wish with the time, as long as it doesn't conflict with Apple's interests. They forfeit the time off if they don't use it the year it's due.
- **Wells Fargo Bank.** Employees who have been with the bank more than ten years may apply for paid personal-growth leaves of up to three months. Those with more than three years are also eligible for paid social-service leaves of up to six months.

SOURCE: Catherine Romano, "Time Out," in *Management Review,* January 1995.

one, suggest that management consider the benefits they would reap from both paid and unpaid leaves. Here are some data you can use in asking your company to implement a sabbatical option: Nearly 20 percent of American companies offer some kind of sabbatical, and more than 70 percent offer personal leaves of absence, which are often used for the same purpose. According to a recent survey by the International Foundation of Employee Benefit Plans, fully one-third of American companies will begin offering sabbaticals within the next four years. Extended leaves are especially popular with law firms, consulting agencies, and hi-tech companies, where burnout is a problem. Most often, workers can use the time off in any way they choose, though some firms require formal applications and approval. McDonald's, FedEx, American Express, Apple Computer, and Wells Fargo Bank have plans in place that could serve as prototypes.

One of the best resources on sabbaticals is *Six Months Off,* by Hope Dlugozima, James Scott, and David Sharp (Henry Holt). This very practical guidebook gives tips on overcoming such objections as, "I don't have the money," "I can't find the time," and, "My family and coworkers will never go along with it." To negotiate your sabbatical successfully, the authors stress that the starting place is seeking answers to questions such as: What is the company's policy on sabbaticals or extended leaves? If the company allows sabbaticals, how long must I work to be eligible? Have other employees had sabbaticals, what were the terms, who granted permission, who on the management team was for it, who was against it? Who substituted for the employee on sabbatical and who trained the replacement? Did productivity suffer? How and why? How economically healthy is the company? Are any layoffs expected or any constraints that would decrease my chances of getting time off? Are leaves paid, unpaid, or partially paid?

Vacation Deficit Disorder

Perhaps it isn't a full-blown sabbatical that you need. Maybe you are just suffering from Vacation Deficit Disorder. Think about it. Are vacations your most fulfilling times? Do you long for them? Can you combine work and longer, more satisfying vacations as an alternative to fully retiring? Will the race seem less stressful if you detour every now and again to someplace special?

Perhaps resorts, cruises, and bus tours don't give you the relief you need. More and more retirees are opting for active trips and soft-adventure tours offering hiking, bicycling, or white-water rafting.

Others are combining travel and continuing education in an academic setting. Consider the following options:

Study tours. With programs in every state and forty-five foreign countries, Elderhostel rates high for its low-cost, short-term adventures hosted by colleges and universities. The typical program lasts a week, includes three college-level courses, and costs around $300 per person. You could learn in the Galapagos, study Appalachian culture in literature and folklore, or explore the history of art and wine in the Burgundy region of France. Individuals age sixty and older are eligible and accompanying spouses and companions must be at least fifty years old. For a catalog, call (617) 426-7788 or write to 75 Federal Street, Boston, MA 02110.

Senior Ventures (800-257-0577) is popular in six western states and offers similar programs for mature travelers. The cost is about the same, but the minimum age is only fifty.

Many colleges and universities also offer study tours.

International Homestays. Imagine immersing yourself in another culture for a few weeks by living with host families. Seniors Abroad International Homestay offers trips to Japan, Australia, New Zealand, and Scandinavia for U.S. travelers over fifty and arranges for seniors from those countries to visit American families. Participants (usually about twenty per trip) fly to the destination, spend a few days at a hotel for orientation, then embark on several six-day visits to host families across the country.

Homestays can be more enjoyable and more economical than traveling on your own because you don't pay for food or lodging. For information, contact Seniors Abroad, 12533 Pacato Circle North, San Diego, CA 92128.

The Over the Hill Gang International. If you love adventure and are forty-nine or older, this is for you. This "gang" is a travel club that plans ski vacations for members and negotiates special deals on airfares and reduced rates at ski resorts. Summer activities include hiking, rafting, in-line skating, and ballooning. Annual dues are thirty-seven dollars for individuals and sixty dollars for couples. For information, write to 3310 Cedar Heights Drive, Colorado Springs, CO 80904, or call (719) 685-4656.

Outdoor Vacations for Women Over 40. The name makes it clear just who enjoys the two dozen or so nature and outdoor adventures each year. Ten to sixteen participants, many in their late fifties and sixties, take trips ranging from one-day and weekend jaunts in the New

England area to one- or two-week vacations all over the world. Popular trips are cross-country skiing in Big Sky, Montana; a walking tour in the Yorkshires in England; and rafting the Salmon and Snake rivers in Idaho. For a schedule of upcoming events, write to P.O. Box 200, Groton, MA 01450 or call (508) 448-3331.

SMART TIP

INTERNATIONAL MEDICAL COVERAGE

If you travel abroad, consider purchasing a travel insurance policy. This medical coverage typically pays foreign hospital and physician fees up to $10,000. It also covers the cost of emergency medical transportation to an appropriate facility or back to the United States, as well as on-the-spot assistance in finding a doctor, filling prescriptions, and contacting your physician back home.

You can buy travel insurance directly from such companies as Access America (800-284-8300), American Express (800-234-0375), Travel Assure (800-228-9792), and Travel Guard (800-826-1300), or you can purchase it from a travel agent.

Switching Jobs

Many people become underemployed well in advance of permanent retirement. Maybe your company has downsized and you've been laid off. Or maybe you took an early retirement package rather than continuing to work. But then days of golf and unfettered freedom were just not enough, financially or psychologically. Many people who leave their jobs are eager to try something different, build new skills, meet new people, and supplement their income. Here are some options to consider:

• Check to see if your company has any flexible-retirement options. For example, Travelers Insurance and Corning rehire retirees part time. Corning also allows some retiring management and professional employees to phase out over one to three years by working 40 percent rather than full time.

• Consider Operation ABLE (Ability Based Long Experience). This is an umbrella agency for senior employment programs, with offices in eight cities. Helping those over fifty, ABLE has phone hotlines for job search assistance and computerized job-matching systems. Write Operation ABLE, 180 North Wabash Avenue, Suite 802, Chicago, IL 60601, or call (312) 782-3335.

• Check out Senior Career Planning and Placement Service, which places retired executives in full- or part-time positions across the country. Salaries can reach $60,000 for these high-level positions, such as vice president of finance or chief fund-raising officer. Call (212) 529-6660 for details, or send a current resume to 257 Park Avenue South, New York, NY 10010.

• Attend a "Think of Your Future" workshop sponsored by AARP. These workshops help retirees check out employment options. Contact AARP at 1909 K Street N.W., Washington, DC 20049, to find the program nearest you. For the free booklet *Working Options,* request publication number D12403 from AARP Fulfillment at the above address.

• Register with a temporary employment agency. Senior workers are being actively recruited for a wider variety of positions, and temping is ideal for those who like flexible hours. Kelly Services, which has 850 offices in the United States and Canada, offers job opportunities ranging from engineering assignments to care and companionship for shut-ins. Adia Services, another major temp agency, also has an extensive placement program for retired workers.

Start Your Own Business

You've worked hard for XYZ company and it's not easy to leave the career, the structure, the interactions with colleagues, the feeling of contributing, or the paycheck. But you've had a dream of starting your own company, and time is running out—now may be the time to do it. Maybe you've reached a high level of success, but what you do isn't satisfying anymore. Although locked to your company by the golden handcuffs of a large salary, retirement benefits, expense accounts, perks, and prestige, you wonder if you can, if you *should,* seize your dream and start your own company.

In an interesting study by the Entrepreneurial Research Consortium, preliminary findings suggest that while 4 percent of American adults—about seven million people—are trying to start a business, as many as one-half will never actually open their doors. The gestation period for a new business tends to be longer than people realize or may be prepared for. The median amount of time that elapses before the "wannabes" quit trying is twenty months. Early research shows that people with high school diplomas are more likely to try to open a business, but college diplomas and advanced degrees make very little difference. In the past, men have been far more likely to try to start a business than women. Now pilot studies indicate in the twenty-five to forty-four age bracket, the prime years for starting a business, there is no gender gap. In fact, overall women are now starting businesses at twice the rate of men.

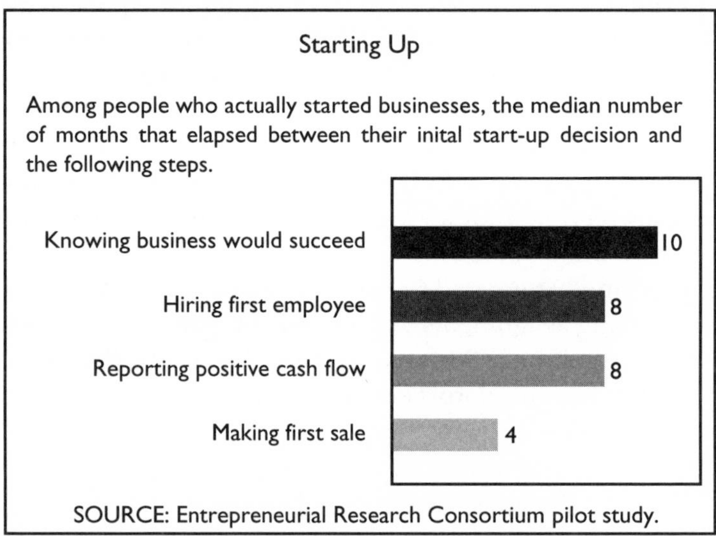

Starting Up
Among people who actually started businesses, the median number of months that elapsed between their inital start-up decision and the following steps.
Knowing business would succeed
10
Hiring first employee
8
Reporting positive cash flow
8
Making first sale
4
SOURCE: Entrepreneurial Research Consortium pilot study.

This chart shows that it takes the average entrepreneur four months to make the first sale, eight months to staunch losses and move into the black, eight months to hire the first employee, and ten months to feel confident that the business will succeed. No wonder the first months of starting a new business are stressful! But if you would like to leave the rat race and enter your own race and you're willing to devote the start-up time and effort to that new venture, here's how to turn your dream into reality.

Start by taking a vacation or sabbatical to experiment with and analyze how it would feel to actually live the dream and have your own company. Use the time to thoroughly research what this new career path would entail, how long it might take to turn a profit and to establish your credibility and visibility, and how much capital would be required.

Talk to others—lots of others—who are in the same or similar businesses. Analyze your weak points, including any bad habits that may interfere with your business's success. Look into getting additional education, training, and practice to increase your potential for success. Ask yourself—and a trusted friend or counselor (not a family member)—if you have what it takes to succeed in this endeavor.

Your family's financial needs, both short term and long term, will be critical in your decision. Consider living expenses, insurance, and savings and pension plans, and decide how you can make your finances work during the start-up period.

You'll have some fear; that fear is healthy. Don't be discouraged by the fears or concerns of your spouse, family, or friends. It will force you to deal realistically with financial problems and other hurdles.

Don't expect your new venture to flourish overnight. To succeed in business you need an idea, a plan, and financial backing. Most businesses fail because they were undercapitalized. A solid business plan can tie the idea and the financing together to create a successful business.

A business plan is a blueprint for your company that takes your business concept and turns it into a workable entity. It includes a description of your business, the market for your product, and your business structure, identifies your competition, and outlines your organization and personnel. It projects sales, expenses, and cash flow for three years, describes your marketing strategy, staffing, and equipment needs, and identifies the source and amount of funding you expect, the application of that funding, and a break-even analysis.

Your business plan will be a valuable tool when you seek capital funding, and it will also guide you as your business progresses. Revise your plan regularly as your business grows and develops, and keep accurate financial records so you have an up-to-the-minute record of where you stand and whether you are on target. There are many excellent software programs that will help address these questions and develop a business plan that you can update and change as needed. Some software programs you might explore include Business Plan Builder by JIAN ($99), Business Plan by Success, Inc. ($79), and Smart Business Plan by American Institute ($99). Periodically review your progress and reevaluate on the basis of your experience. Reassess your plan to make sure you're not overloading yourself, neglecting your family, or creating havoc with your finances.

If you must temporarily detour because things aren't going as planned, don't panic. Write a new plan for the next twelve months: Build on the strengths in your original business plan by deleting the weak points and learning from your experience.

Honey, I Want to Start My Own Business: A Planning Guide for Couples, by Azriela Jaffe (HarperCollins, 1996), offers tools, tips, exercises, ideas, testimonials, and other resources. Jaffe gets up close and personal with more than 130 entrepreneurial couples who share insightful triumphs as well as painful defeats in a variety of industries across the nation.

Know the Home Office Rules

Having a new endeavor or sideline business that you operate from your home can mean extra cash to supplement your income as well as tax benefits. When you have a business, some of the personal expenses that ordinarily aren't deductible become deductible business expenses.

Keep in mind, however, that the home office rules are strict. To qualify for tax deductions, you must reserve part of your home, preferably a separate room—not the kitchen table—exclusively for business and use it for business on a regular basis. It has to be the primary site of your part-time business, such as where you meet clients or customers. If you have a legitimate home office, you can deduct depreciation plus a prorata portion of the cost of running your home, reducing your taxable income from the business. Depreciation reduces the basis (tax cost) of your home, increasing the taxable gain when you sell the home. For example, if your home cost $150,000 and you claim $15,000 as depreciation, when you sell the home the IRS will treat it as though you only paid $135,000 for the home. That means that you will pay tax on an additional $15,000 of income from the sale.

Understand How to Handle Expenses

Think about all the necessities of doing business and what they cost. You can deduct all ordinary and necessary business expenses—salaries, postage, stationery, telephone, books and magazines, travel, entertainment, legal expenses, and so on. If you buy furniture, equipment, or machinery for your business, you can depreciate it over several years. Or you might want to consider "expensing" up to $18,000 of equipment—that is, deducting the whole expense in the first year rather than spreading the cost over several years.

Having my own business really gave us some good tax advantages. But there were other benefits too, as Courtney and Chase can tell you. They work with me, filing, sorting, getting mass mailings ready. Our accountant suggested I hire them for tax reasons, but having them has been a great help. (Marge G., age forty)

You can shelter some of your income from tax by hiring your children to work in the business. Their wages are deductible from your income as business expenses, and each child can earn over $6,000 a year tax-free. The first $4,150 (the 1997 amount—it increases each year) of a child's income is sheltered from tax by the standard deduction, and your child can put an additional $2,000 of salary into an IRA and shelter that from tax.

Caution: If you hire your child, the employment must be genuine and the salary must be reasonable, or the deduction will be disallowed. Since the IRS is always suspicious of family arrangements, document the child's hours worked and be prepared to prove that the child actually renders business services, such as filing, sorting, and other clerical duties, office cleaning, inventory taking, or working as an apprentice. On the personal side, kids, as much as we love them, may "flake out" at times, causing us some real grief as employers. If you have other employees, they may resent or be jealous of privileges they feel your child might be enjoying.

Limit Your Liability

If what you do in your business has the potential for someone to be injured economically or physically, you may decide to incorporate your business to limit your personal liability. There are many choices for structuring your business, and you will want to check with a competent business attorney as well as your personal accountant to determine what will best suit your needs. Either a C corporation (which is appropriate for profitable businesses) or an S corporation (in which profits and losses are passed through to the shareholders) will reduce your liability exposure, or you might want to consider the limited liability company, which is available in most states. The limited liability company gives you the benefit of limited liability, just like a regular corporation, but it is taxed like a partnership, with all profits and losses passing through to the tax return of the shareholder.

Consultant or Employee?

There is sometimes a fine line between being an employee and being an independent contractor. The distinction is important, whether you are working for someone or have someone working for you. Consultants are responsible for paying their own payroll taxes, including income tax withholding, state disability insurance, and Social Security taxes. An employer is responsible for withholding those taxes from employees, and for matching some of the taxes as well.

The Internal Revenue Service uses twenty common law factors to determine who is an independent contractor. Not all factors have to apply, and the courts have given different weight to each factor according to individual circumstances. Workers are independent contractors if they

1. are not required to follow specific instructions to do the job.
2. are not trained by the hiring company.
3. don't have to do the work themselves.
4. do work not essential to the continuation of the hiring company.
5. set their own work hours.
6. don't have a continuing relationship with the hiring company.
7. control their own assistants.
8. have time to pursue other work (don't work full time for one entity).
9. determine where they work.
10. control the order and sequence in which they do the work.
11. are hired for the final result and not required to give interim reports.
12. are paid by the job, not by the hour.
13. work for more than one company at a time.
14. pay their own business expenses.
15. furnish their own tools.
16. have significant investment in their own equipment, office furniture, machinery, and so forth.
17. make services available to the general public (they have a Yellow Pages ad, business cards, a business license, or a registered business name).
18. risk losing their own money.
19. cannot be fired so long as they meet contract specifications.
20. can't quit without liability (may be legally required to compensate the hiring firm for failure to complete a job).

Volunteering

Giving back through volunteerism can give you a new perspective on working. Dissatisfaction with your life and career can't always be cured by starting your own business or by taking a sabbatical so you can recharge. Volunteering may fill the void for a lot of people; by giving back, you can gain a renewed sense of purpose and fulfillment.

Whether it is driving for Meals on Wheels, leading a scout troop, or coaching a Little League baseball team, retirees represent the country's most abundant source of volunteers. Almost half of all people age sixty and over devote part of their free time to helping others, according to a study by Marriott Senior Living Services, the division of Marriott that operates its retirement communities. Indeed, there's no shortage of work to be done, and thousands of charitable organizations depend on retirees. You can volunteer at schools, churches, hospitals, and social service agencies in your community, or you can turn to programs such as the following that will match your skills and interest to groups and individuals who need you.

Retired and Senior Volunteer Program (RSVP). You can join more than 425,000 people age fifty-five and over across the country who volunteer through RSVP, a program that's administered by the Corporation for National and Community Service. It recruits volunteers in your community and refers them to schools, hospitals, social services agencies, and other local organizations needing volunteers. RSVP volunteers in every state perform tasks ranging from teaching English as a second language to serving as docents in a museum. Check your local phone directory for the phone number of the RSVP nearest you. If there is no listing, contact the program located in your state capital.

AARP Volunteer Talent Bank. AARP has a large database that matches volunteers with AARP's own service programs and those of a number of national organizations, such as the American Red Cross and Recording for the Blind. For an application, write to AARP Volunteer Talent Bank, 601 E Street N.W., Washington, DC 20049.

National Park Service uses volunteers, mostly retirees, for all kinds of tasks—working at information desks, maintaining trails, guiding tours. For information, write to the National Park Service, Division of Interpretation, P.O. Box 37127, Washington, DC 20013, or call (202) 523-5270.

Time dollars. One hundred communities in thirty states have embarked on an innovative program that uses time dollars. It's a simple concept: A senior volunteer earns credits by providing transportation, companionship, a hot meal, or some other service to an elderly recipient. When the volunteer needs similar help, he or she can cash in the credits for services from other volunteers in the program. Most volunteers bank their credits, but some donate them to elderly relatives or other recipients. Time Dollar uses a computer program to keep track of participants' accounts. For more information, write the Time Dollar Network, P.O. Box 42160, Washington, DC 20015.

Use Your Specific Skills to Help Others

You've spent years developing and honing your skills in your field. Most likely there is a nonprofit organization, a struggling young entrepreneur, or a newly privatized business in the former Eastern bloc that could benefit from your expertise. If you're interested in sharing your specific business knowledge, here are a number of programs to consider in the United States and overseas:

Service Corps of Retired Executives (SCORE). SCORE has 12,900 volunteers in local Small Business Administration offices all over the country. SCORE counselors advise small business owners on writing business plans, marketing new products, and exporting, for instance. They also conduct prebusiness workshops for would-be business owners. Women and minority counselors and those with computer skills are especially needed. Call 800-634-0245 for the office nearest you.

National Executive Service Corps (NESC). This national organization matches retired business managers and executives with social service agencies, schools, cultural and performing arts organizations, health-care agencies, environmental groups, and other nonprofits. Skills in strategic and business planning, management information systems, and finance are needed. A typical volunteer consultant might work two days a week on a project lasting four to six months. Volunteers ensure that more of the organization's resources go toward programs supporting its mission and less toward administration. Write the NESC at 257 Park Avenue South, New York, NY 10010, or call (212) 529-6660.

International Executive Service Corps (IESC). IESC matches the talents of both retired and working executives with the needs of businesses in developing countries. Volunteers are in demand in central Europe, eastern Europe, and the former Soviet Union for industry restructuring and privatization and investment banking. Projects generally run for a couple of months. IESC pays the travel expenses of volunteers and their spouses, while the company seeking help provides living quarters. The host company also provides an interpreter, so familiarity with the country's language is not required. Write to IESC Recruiting Department, P.O. Box 10005, Stamford, CT 06904.

Citizens Democracy Corps (CDC). CDC is similar to IESC, but its clients are primarily small- to medium-size businesses in eastern Europe and Russia. CDC seeks in particular volunteers who have run their own businesses and can help with accounting systems, financial planning, marketing, quality control, and production. As with IESC, the host client provides housing and an interpreter and CDC covers the volunteer's travel expenses. If the assignment is for two months or longer and

---

SMART TIP

TAX DEDUCTIONS FOR VOLUNTEERS

If you're a volunteer and you itemize deductions on your tax return, you can claim certain unreimbursed expenses as charitable contributions.

- **Transportation.** You can deduct twelve cents per mile if you drive your car for charity or to and from the site of your volunteer activity. You can also deduct parking fees and tolls, taxis, or public transportation.
- **Travel.** If you are a group's chosen representative at the organization's convention, your unreimbursed expenses for travel and transportation are deductible, including reasonable costs of meals and lodging.
- **Uniforms.** Cost and upkeep of required uniforms are deductible only if they cannot be worn as everyday clothes.
- **Supplies.** You can deduct the cost of supplies you buy for charitable work, such as stationery and stamps.

Certain things cannot be deducted—the value of your time or services contributed to a charity, the value of the use of your property, or the cost of meals, unless the charitable duty takes you out of town overnight. To back up deductions, save receipts, and keep an auto log with the date, purpose of the trip, starting point and destination, and number of miles driven.

---

your spouse plans to stay with you at least 75 percent of the time, CDC will also pay your spouse's travel expenses. If desired, CDC will try to arrange an assignment for the spouse as well. CDC has field offices in each of the six countries to which it sends volunteers—Poland, the Czech Republic, the Slovak Republic, Bulgaria, Romania, and Russia—to facilitate the projects and inspect the living quarters. To add your name to CDC's database of volunteers, call 800-394-1945 for an application.

After you've reviewed these antidotes to the rat race, discuss them with your spouse and determine which options to explore in more depth. Before taking any action, be sure you are clear on the real reason behind your desire to kiss the race good-bye. You may just need some time off for family, friends, and yourself. You may want to gain flexibility and autonomy by telecommuting, switching jobs, or starting your own business. Or maybe you just need to recharge your batteries by taking a study vacation or a sabbatical or by sharing your time, talents, expertise, and advice with others as a volunteer.

What we have explored in this chapter is the stuff that early retirement fantasies are made of—the options, the freedom from stress, the joy, the fun, the permission to experiment to find what might give you the most fulfillment as you journey through your next fifty years. But there are times when the unexpected, the unplanned for, happens, as we discuss in the next chapter.

9

Big Changes—Divorce, Death, Disability, and Remarriage

A realistic wag once said, "Only two things in life are certain—death and taxes." It is surprising he missed the third: change. Change is a constant, and during your next fifty years, chances are great that you'll face divorce, death, disability, remarriage, or any of a host of other life-changing events.

> I guess I'm struggling with the fact that it feels so unfair—Jim dying of a heart attack at fifty-seven. We had planned for our retirement together and looked forward to seeing our granddaughter grow, and to having other grandkids. Now there's a big hole where my life used to be. (Marguerite M., age fifty-three)

> My life is just unbearable at this moment. We've been married for twenty-seven years. Maybe I've been too dedicated to my work—I should have spent more time at home—but the affair she's having, and now the divorce, are painful. I'd thought about retiring maybe in a few years, but now I'm not sure I'll ever be able to. I've heard the horror stories from other guys who have gone through divorce—they say it's financially devastating. (Mike I., age fifty)

> I never thought I'd find someone to love again. Laurie was all I wanted before cancer took her. But this relationship feels good. Maggie really understands my children and they get along so well. We're really looking forward to the wedding. (Edward T., age fifty-one)

Retirement is a time to enjoy the fruits of your hard work, but sometimes the unexpected happens and it is not always a happy event, as Marguerite and Mike discovered. Death of a spouse and divorce can feel even more devastating when they occur in marriages of many years. But as Edward attests, there is life, and there can be joy, even after such traumatic events. It is all about how we respond to what life deals us, isn't it?

In this chapter we consider some contingency planning that you can do now to prepare for unexpected events later. We discuss steps you can take so that if a major change happens, it won't throw you. Putting plans in place, even something as simple as a list of where important papers are stored, can make the lives of those you love easier in the event of your death or your life easier in the event of your spouse's death.

According to Gail Sheehy in her book *New Passages,* how well we negotiate the passage from First Adulthood to Second Adulthood of life, the years after age forty-five, determines how well we will ultimately age and the quality of life we'll experience. Lifespan planning is important as you plan for your next fifty years.

Noting that people are taking longer to grow up and much longer to die, Sheehy suggests that recently we have seen all stages of adulthood shift by up to ten years. Baby boomers now in their forties reject the whole concept of middle age as we knew it in the time of our parents. A woman who reaches age fifty today—and remains free of cancer and heart disease—can expect to see her ninety-second birthday. Men too can expect a dramatically lengthened life span.

Middle age may be as obsolete a concept as we believe that retirement is. "Imagine the day you turn 45 as the infancy of another life," Sheehy writes. In our parents' time, forty-five to fifty was the beginning of decline. Now men and women who embrace a Second Adulthood can journey through entirely new passages that will lead them to more meaningful lives, with more spontaneity, playfulness, creativity, and satisfaction. But it is not an easy journey. We have no role models in parents or grandparents to follow. The roles of men and women have changed and we are all forging new territory.

As they think about retirement, besides redefining middle age, boomers must redefine success. That's not easy either. Baby boomers jam middle management ladders, find their careers peaking sooner than they expected, and face forced retirement. Many boomers are realizing that both sexes may have to work past sixty-five to provide security over longer lives.

According to Sheehy, during the "flaming 50's" women feel more "can do" in a work environment than men, who begin turning toward family. We believe this is true for several reasons. Time and energy to focus on other activities is freed up when the caretaking years end and the nest is empty. There is more media attention on and acceptance of successful—and older—women. Men who are successful will move from competing to connecting during this time, women from pleasing to mastery, and both must deal with aging, declining sexual potency, and menopause. Think about how this impacts your planning for retirement.

> Gerald was really ready to retire and spend more time with our grandkids Adam and Ashley. At first it seemed strange because he had always been so ambitious. Now that he had been CEO for a couple of years, it was as though he finally accepted that he had made it and now wanted to go back and capture the childhood years with Adam and Ashley that he missed when our kids were growing up. For me though it's different. I've just started this new business and I don't want to retire yet. (Micki D., age fifty-five)

Add to this scenario changes such as divorce, death, loss of job, disability, or even the happier aspect of marriage or remarriage, and your Second Adulthood can be a very complex time both emotionally and economically.

Divorce

We had dinner recently with a wonderful couple married fifty-four years. While joking about what an accomplishment this was, we heard what we've heard so often—their marriage had had its good and bad moments. Even long-term marriages are vulnerable and can be torn apart when children move out, careers plateau, aged parents die, or career options seem to dwindle. For those over fifty-five, the number of divorces is a third higher than it was twenty years ago. Divorce is never easy, and as you are nearing retirement or in retirement, it can be financially and emotionally devastating, for many reasons:

• Jobs are more difficult to find for older individuals. It may be essential to have two incomes to support two separate households, but ask any woman in her fifties or sixties who has not worked outside the home how easy it is to find a job. Men have an advantage, but it is still difficult to find new employment, as those who have been laid off can attest.

• Retirement plans may need to be divided, reducing retirement income for both. This is especially difficult when only one spouse has worked outside the home and the retirement plan is the couple's main income-producing asset. Retirement plans rarely provide enough income to support the same lifestyle a couple enjoyed while working. Dividing those benefits can result in a very meager income indeed.

• Maintaining two households and other duplicate expenses is costly. As we approach retirement, we usually think of downsizing a home to save costs. Paying rent or mortgage, utilities, and other household expenses on not one but two properties can be a real hardship.

• Friendships, social contacts, and loyalties have been developed and nurtured over many years. When a marriage ends, the inevitable losses in this area can be particularly painful as we approach the retirement years. Long-term marriages often mean long-term friends, the very kind we look forward to traveling, golfing, or just being with. Both men and women feel the loss of friendships and loyalties deeply.

Retirement itself is a major life change, so adding divorce can create enormous stress. If you suspect that divorce may be a change you'll face in the future, you will need to know some specifics about Social Security benefits after divorce, how divorce affects retirement plans and other assets, how to look for hidden assets, and how to work with attorneys to get through the process with the least amount of financial and emotional cost.

Consider what happened to Congresswoman Enid Waldholtz of Utah. She tearfully told the media that she had no knowledge of her husband's pattern of alleged financial fraud and deception because she had completely entrusted him with their family finances. While this may or may not be true, it is not very smart. And unfortunately, in our practice, we have heard many horror stories of women who trusted too much. Even smart, capable women like Waldholtz can be vulnerable if they don't pay attention. Ignorance is no excuse. Even if one spouse earns all of the money and handles the finances, husbands and wives share equal legal responsibility and liability.

In many two-income families, wives are often uninformed about crucial financial matters. When a husband is self-employed, this may be even more true. If you don't know enough about your family finances and you suspect your marriage is in trouble, here are some things you'll want to do now:

- Carefully review your tax returns for the last three years, paying special attention to income and deductions reported. Schedule A lists sources of interest and dividends. Are there any surprises?
- Identify the beneficiary and owner on insurance policies you and your spouse own. Remember that the owner has the right to change the beneficiary at any time.
- Make a list of bankers, stockbrokers, tax accountants, lawyers, and other financial advisers you and your spouse do business with. Do you feel comfortable asking questions or requesting information from all of them?
- Review the most recent account statements from banks, brokerages, and mutual fund companies. Do the account balances reflect what you would expect? Have any accounts been closed with assets transferred elsewhere? If so, find out why.
- If you own a house or other real estate, ask a lawyer about a title search if you suspect there may be a lien against the property.
- Contact one of the major credit bureaus and request a copy of your credit report periodically: TRW, 800-682-7654; Trans Union, 800-916-8800; Equifax, 800-685-1111. Review the report carefully, note any discrepancies, and take the steps necessary to correct them.
- Visit your local bookstore or library and pick up *Divorce and Money,* by Violet Woodhouse and Victoria F. Collins with M. C. Blakeman, or *Smart Ways to Save Money During and After Divorce,* by Ginita Wall and Victoria F. Collins. Both are from NOLO Press in Berkeley and can also be ordered by calling 800-992-6656. There are other excellent books that can serve as resources, but—you guessed it—we collaborated on these.

Dividing the Marital Pie

Besides the family residence, retirement plans such as defined contribution and defined benefit plans are the largest asset a couple may hold. And like the family home, there can be an enormous emotional attachment to this asset on the part of one or the other spouse.

> That money in my retirement plan is there because of my sweat and blood. It's my money and she's not going to walk out the door with any part of it during this divorce. (Tom M., age fifty-four)

> Who do you think took care of the kids and the home and his mother as well? Our family revolved around his schedule for all these years. Because of the entertaining and the other things I did as a corporate wife supporting his career, I had to give up my own. Of course I'm entitled to half of his retirement plan—I've earned it. (Stephanie M., age fifty-five)

Just how a divorcing couple's assets are divided depends largely on the state in which they live. States have their own laws on splitting the funds in various retirement plans. In community property states (Arizona, California, Idaho, Louisiana, Nevada, New Mexico, Texas, Washington, and Wisconsin), the funds accumulated in retirement plans during a marriage are shared equally. But in other states, called equitable distribution states, the courts have more discretion over the division, often to the detriment of the lower-paid spouse. But no matter how they are divided, your retirement plans probably won't be enough for each of you to finance the retirement you've planned.

Defined contribution plans

Here are some guidelines for dividing your defined contribution plans, such as 401(k)s, 403(b)s, and SIMPLEs if you're salaried, or Keoghs and SEPs if you're self-employed. (For more details on these plans, see chapter 5.)

If your plan and your spouse's plan are about equal in value, generally the courts will let each of you keep your plan intact. Or the judge may divide the total between you and instruct your employers in a court order which share belongs to each of you. Defined contribution plans are relatively easy to split because they consist of company stock or money invested in securities. If your 401(k) is to be divided in half, your employer will most likely set aside your spouse's share. Your future contributions will go entirely into your own account. As an alternative, the ex-spouse may withdraw his or her share as a lump sum and roll it over into an IRA or take it as cash. The money taken as cash is taxable as income, but the law imposes no 10 percent penalty on withdrawals by ex-spouses, even if they are younger than fifty-nine and a half years old.

Defined benefit plans

Defined benefit plans are another story entirely and are more difficult to value and to divide in divorce. (Again, see chapter 5 for more details.) If you must split a pension with your ex, some states use the fixed-date method to determine the value. Based on your salary and years of service, the benefits office will calculate what your pension would be if you were to retire on the day you expect your divorce to be final. For example, let's say $12,000 a year would be the amount you would qualify for on that date. A court might order your company to give your spouse $6,000 a year of your pension no matter how big your benefit actually turns out to be when you retire. Your spouse can start collecting the $6,000 when you reach the earliest age at which you can retire, even if you elect to continue working and delay receiving your share of the pension.

A more complicated way used by some states to determine pension value is called the "fractional method," also known as the "time-rule method." To get an idea of how this works, divide the number of months during which you were married *and* employed at your company by the total number of months you have worked for your company, married or not. Next, multiply the result by your estimated pension benefit on the date you plan to retire. Finally, multiply that amount by the percentage of your pension the court has awarded to your spouse. For example, you have been married ten years (120 months) and worked at your company for fifteen years (180 months). You expect a $20,000 pension when you retire at age sixty-five. Divide 120 by 180 and multiply the result (0.667) by $20,000, resulting in $13,333. If the court gives your spouse half of your benefit, he or she would get $6,667 a year.

The fractional method entails a gamble for you both, because you might opt to work beyond age sixty-five, thereby boosting your pension and your ex's share of it. On the other hand, you might take early retirement, and your pension and your ex's share would be smaller.

Whichever method you use, your ex can file for a share of your pension at the earliest retirement age that your company will allow. Doing so, however, locks in the amount your ex will receive even if you continue to work and your benefits keep growing.

What You Need to Know about Qualified Domestic Relations Orders (QDROs)

QDRO, pronounced "quadro," is not an alien from another planet, it stands for qualified domestic relations order. It will be an important document in your divorce if you have a qualified retirement plan that includes all the variations on defined contribution plans, defined benefit plans, and tax-sheltered annuities. The QDRO tells the plan administrator how the benefits are to be assigned to each party in a divorce. It is particularly important because if the QDRO doesn't say it, you don't get it, even if the plan says you are entitled to the money or benefits. An order about the division of your retirement benefits within the final document, such as a divorce settlement agreement, domestic relations order, or marital settlement agreement, may substitute for a QDRO, if the plan administrator determines that it qualifies. If your retirement assets are in deferred annuities, IRAs, SEP-IRAs, or a nonqualified deferred compensation plan, then you will not need a QDRO to divide these plans.

Requirements for a domestic relations order to be a QDRO are complex and depend on the plan's terms and conditions as well as the age of the participant. See an attorney or actuary who is familiar with them to be sure one is drafted properly when the final settlement agreement is being drawn.

What You Need to Know about Social Security If You Are Divorcing

A divorced spouse may have the same right as a married spouse to Social Security benefits, even if the insured worker has remarried. However, if the divorced spouse remarries, he or she may lose rights to benefits of the insured worker's record.

When workers start collecting retirement or disability payments, divorced spouses may receive benefits if

- they are sixty-two or older;
- they do not qualify on their own employment records for benefits that equal or exceed one-half of the worker's full amount; and
- they were married to the worker for at least ten years.

The benefits received by the divorced spouse do not reduce any benefits the worker or the worker's current spouse or children may be receiving.

Even if the worker is not actually receiving benefits, the divorced spouse can get retirement payments at age sixty-two if the worker is eligible for benefits and they have been divorced for at least two years.

Death of a Spouse

> I just can't think clearly now. My life feels so empty. I had relied on him for handling our finances and now I'm just not sure whom to trust or what to do. (Margaret K., age fifty-nine)

> I just wish I had asked her what she wanted done. We never really talked about her dying and now there's so much I need to know. It's incredible how little I really knew about our family finances. (Reynold T., age forty-six)

If your spouse dies unexpectedly, you may find yourself emotionally devastated and financially unprepared. You are vulnerable to the advice of well-intentioned friends and family as well as a whole cadre of financial advisers, insurance agents, and stockbrokers who may or may not have your best interests at heart. To help you through this difficult time, there are some things you can do to regain your financial peace of mind.

Develop Your Support Team

A support team that includes friends, family, a counselor or therapist, and trusted financial professionals can be a valuable resource in seeing you through this difficult time. They can help you gather the information you need, review documents, make decisions, follow up on paperwork, and just simply be there for you when you need to talk. Contact your church or synagogue for information on local grief support groups. Don't feel you have to go it alone. The AARP Widowed Persons Service ([202] 434-2260) will give you names and telephone numbers of support groups in your area offering job training and investment education. Ask them to send a free copy of *Final Details,* a brochure that tells you what you need to know about getting your affairs in order after your loss.

Another excellent resource is *On Your Own: A Widow's Passage to Emotional and Financial Well-Being,* by Alexandra Armstrong and Mary Donahue (Dearborn Financial Publishing, 1993). This book offers encouragement and advice for dealing with every psychological and financial issue of widowhood, and includes numerous helpful checklists, worksheets, and questionnaires.

Right now give some thought to whom you might include on your own support team. Part of the planning process *before* a spouse dies is to have a conversation such as, "If something were to happen to me, here are the names and addresses of some people who could be of real help." If you've not yet drawn up a list of your trusted advisers, we urge you to do so as soon as possible.

> Mark's death came as a total shock. But the year before, we visited a financial adviser who suggested we make a binder called the

Carson Family Manual. We put in all sorts of information—names and addresses of our accountants, banker, insurance people, financial adviser, attorney, everyone we could think of who could be helpful. There was a section for brokerage, checking accounts, and credit card information as well as copies of insurance policies. We also included a list of where all our assets were and the contents of our safe deposit box. And yes, where the keys were! I can't tell you what a relief it was to go to that binder after his death and to have everything in order. (Sarah C., age forty-seven)

Contact Your Life Insurance Company

If you are the beneficiary on a life insurance policy, there are three ways you can elect to receive the proceeds: in a lump-sum payment, as fixed payments over time, or as an annuity. Don't rely only on what your insurance agent recommends; evaluate your options carefully and seek an independent opinion. If you consider yourself capable of investing wisely, opting for a lump-sum payment probably makes sense. If insurance proceeds are payable to a trust, a lump-sum payout will occur automatically.

If you opt for the fixed-payment method, the insurance company will distribute the proceeds and interest in installments paid over a number of years. If you choose this method, be certain that you can change your mind and withdraw the entire amount at a later time.

The annuity option is similar in that it is over time, but it offers you far less flexibility. The insurance company agrees to pay a certain sum for life, usually monthly, with the amount of each payment based on the size of the policy and your age. Since annuities are payable for life, this option is useful where your resources and investment expertise are limited. Still, the annuity option plan offered by the life insurance company that issued the policy may not be the best deal for you. Do some comparison shopping. If you want to purchase an annuity from another company because it has better terms and payouts, be sure to have the insurance company transfer the funds directly to the other company so that you will avoid adverse tax consequences. Be sure to get professional advice from someone other than an annuity salesperson before you select this option. (See pages 82–83 for more on annuities.)

If you choose the lump-sum settlement, draft a short letter to the insurer saying, "On [date] my spouse [name] passed away. Please forward to me all life insurance proceeds payable to the beneficiary listed for any life insurance policy in effect as of the date listed above." You'll need to enclose a certified death certificate (order ten or more when you make the funeral arrangements).

Remember also that you can leave the insurance proceeds with the insurance company, earning interest, until you make the final decision as to which settlement option is best for you.

Contact Your Spouse's Employer

You can apply for pension benefits with a similar letter sent to every employer for whom your spouse worked. There may or may not be pension funds available. You will also want to check with your spouse's employer to see whether you are eligible to receive a last paycheck, payment for accrued vacation and sick leave, company life insurance proceeds, a pension benefit, deferred pay, profit share, death benefits, or accident insurance proceeds. All should be forwarded to you.

> I was pleasantly surprised not only at how helpful the people at Janet's firm were after she died but at how much the vacation, sick leave, and other benefits added up to. It was far more than I would have thought. (Michael T., age forty-six)

Don't Rush to Invest

You've just received the proceeds from the life insurance policy and are anxious to invest the funds to get them working. Take some time before making any investment decisions. There's nothing wrong with using a CD, treasury bill, or money market fund as a parking place while you decide just what you want to do. As you gain information on your expenses and sources of income, you'll be in a better position to know whether your investment objective will be growth, balanced income and growth, or current income. Seek out a financial adviser or investment counselor you can trust and ask him or her to run a retirement projection for you and provide some financial-planning advice so that you have as clear a picture as possible of what the future holds. Our recommendation here is, when in doubt, procrastinate.

> Right after Don's death, I was just overwhelmed with all there was to do. I really couldn't concentrate or think logically to make any investment decisions. I also didn't have a clue whether I would be moving or what income I'd need. Leaving the portfolio just as it was for six months or so gave me the time I needed to sort everything out. (Helen G., age fifty-three)

Contact Banks, Brokerage Houses, Credit Card Issuers

Any financial institutions where you and your spouse may have an account in both names must be notified of your spouse's death. You'll need a certified copy of the death certificate and a letter of instruction to have them change the accounts to your name only.

Be on the lookout for scam artists. This is an especially vulnerable time, and you may receive a notice asking for repayment of a loan your late spouse never took out. Or you may get a false notice of overdue premiums on life insurance policies or even receive merchandise COD that your spouse never ordered. To clients and to you, we recommend that unless you knew about the debt or the purchase in advance, *don't pay it.* Ask the estate executor or your lawyer or other professional adviser how to handle anything that seems unusual.

Make an Appointment with Social Security

When we hear the words *Social Security,* we think of retirement. But Social Security can also provide benefits to people much younger than retirement age and also to disabled workers and survivors of deceased workers, regardless of age.

Call or visit your local Social Security office to let them know of your spouse's death and to determine what benefits you can receive. As a widow or widower, you are entitled to receive 100 percent of your spouse's benefit if you wait until age sixty-six to collect. But you can receive reduced benefits as early as age sixty or at any age if you have children living with you under the age of sixteen. If you are disabled *and* widowed, you can get benefits as early as age fifty.

Here are the documents and information you will need in order to file for benefits:

- Your Social Security number and birth certificate.
- Your deceased spouse's W-2 forms or federal self-employment tax returns for the most recent year, and the death certificate.
- Your marriage certificate or divorce papers, if the application is being made as a divorced spouse.
- Your children's Social Security numbers and birth certificates, if they are under eighteen and unmarried or under nineteen and full-time students in secondary school.
- Your checkbook or savings passbook, if you want Social Security payments to be deposited directly.

> The lady at the Social Security office was pretty helpful after Martin died. I came prepared with all the information she needed and a certified copy of his death certificate. We got the benefits all squared away and I'll start receiving them soon. An extra bonus I didn't expect was that I get a one-time death benefit of $255, which I understand goes to either the surviving spouse or children. (Sandra L., age fifty-eight)

If You Are Disabled

Fact of life: Your chances of being disabled during your working years are four to five times greater than your chances of dying during the same period.

> You can't imagine the shock when I got the call that Ellie had been in an accident. We just never thought it could happen to us—and we don't know at this point when she will be well again or even able to go back to work. (David S., age forty-five)

The unexpected disability, in the form of an injury or illness that prevents you from working, can be devastating to your finances as well as your physical and emotional health. The impact of the disability will be felt by those who care about you as well—family, friends, and coworkers. When disability strikes, you must replace your income somehow or face losing your home, your lifestyle, your savings, your investments. Isn't it ironic that we buy life insurance to protect our families in case we die, but we put off buying disability insurance—even though there's a far greater likelihood of needing it? One reason is that though people know they're going to die, they don't know they're going to be disabled. Another reason is that disability insurance is relatively expensive and the options are limited, whereas there are many ways to reduce costs of life insurance, such as buying term insurance.

You can obtain disability insurance from a variety of sources, including Social Security, workers' compensation, group plans, and private policies. Social Security and workers' compensation are automatically provided if you become totally and permanently disabled, but they come nowhere near what you might need for adequate protection. Your disability coverage taken together should provide you with a maximum benefit equal to 60 percent of your current gross salary. If your disability benefits are tax-free to you, your disability income will approximate your current after-tax income from work.

SMART TIP

TAX-FREE BENEFITS

Consider reimbursing your employer for your own disability insurance premiums. If you do and you begin to draw benefits, they will be tax-free to you.

When comparing and selecting disability coverage, here are some factors to consider:

- Go for the broadest definition of disability you can afford. For example, some policies define disability as the inability to perform *any* of the duties required by your occupation. Under many definitions, including that of Social Security, disability means you are unable to perform *any occupation.* Under that definition, you get no payment as long as you can work at something, even if the job you can perform after being disabled is menial and low paid. Sometimes a split definition is used, strict for the first months or years of your disability and then broad for the duration of the benefit period.
- A waiting period of ninety days or more will save in premiums. The waiting period is the time between the start of the disability and the actual beginning of the payment of benefits. Example: Jim is forty-five years old and earns $55,000 a year. The premiums for a disability policy for him with a ninety-day waiting period are $1,500 a year versus $1,900 a year for a thirty-day waiting period. Jim chose the cheaper coverage because he has saved enough in a combination of money market funds and short-term bond funds to pay his expenses in the early months of disability.
- Check the length of the benefit period and make contingency plans if you have an income gap. Many policies stop paying at age sixty-

SMART TIP

HAVE A COLA

If you purchase your own disability insurance, consider adding a COLA or cost of living rider. It is often worth the extra cost, especially if you're young.

five or sooner, so you may need savings to see you through until other retirement funds kick in.

Congratulations—You're Getting Married

Marriage, whether for the first time or second (or more), can be wonderful. Keep in mind you are not just merging hearts into one, but checkbooks, tax returns, estate plans, and bank and brokerage accounts as well. Don't let the excitement of starting a new life together make you throw caution to the winds. If you are approaching retirement or already enjoying it and have marriage plans, here's what you must know or do.

Holding Title to Property After Marriage

Something that sounds so simple—how you hold title on your assets—can cause major problems later on. Consider carefully the ownership, as spelled out by the title, on assets that you and your soon-to-be-spouse own, such as bank accounts or a house, so that those assets will go to your intended beneficiaries when you or your new spouse die. For example, if you own assets with your spouse as joint tenants, your children from a former marriage may get nothing on your death, even if your will leaves everything to them. Why? Because, in general, joint tenancy *overrides* a will or trust. Joint tenancy with right of survivorship is a legal way of owning property that is convenient and often works well for small estates, because it avoids probate and gives the surviving family member or spouse immediate access to the property. But it can create problems, as Catherine's children found after she died. The ski condo she purchased with Sam was held in joint tenancy. Although she and Sam had agreed it would go to her three children to use as a family vacation place, it went instead to Sam, who immediately sold it, much to their dismay. To ensure that the condo would go to her children, Catherine could have bought it herself and passed it by will to her children, or she and Sam could have bought it together and put it into a trust that would pass to her children as heirs.

Since how you take title may also impact how assets will be divided if the marriage doesn't work out, you will want to consult with a competent estate-planning attorney.

Drafting New Wills

A new marriage should be immediately followed by new wills. If you don't draft a new will, the law will probably assume that you intended to leave a sizable share or all of your estate to your spouse but just never got around to doing so, although that may not be your intention at all.

Think through the provisions of your new will or trust, especially if you intend to leave assets to kids from a former marriage. When you die, do you want the partner you love to have to move out right away because your children inherited the house, or would you instead allow your spouse some time to live there and plan the next move? How comfortable would it be if your spouse had to rent from your children? Who would take care of expenses during that time? And what about the furnishings in the residence—to whom do they go?

If you have young children, you'll need to think about who should be named as the guardian to raise them. Estate planners estimate that 80 to 90 percent of parents with young children have no formal instructions specifying who will care for the children in the event of their death—never mind who will manage the children's finances. Because of this, state courts are overloaded with battles over custody and money and the children's future can be in limbo for months or even years. Nowadays, with divorce and remarriage so prevalent, there is a trend toward more complex guardianship arrangements. When a stepparent has adopted the children and the biological parent has had little involvement in the children's lives, it can be difficult, and the courts work very slowly when there are no written instructions from the deceased parent. Absent clear guardianship instructions, economics can affect the outcome. It is not always the family member with the most affection for the child who receives custody, but the one with the most money. Because this is so important, we urge you to address this issue with your attorney so that your wishes are clearly spelled out.

Signing a Premarital Agreement

Discuss a premarital agreement with your soon-to-be spouse and with your attorney and, if appropriate, take steps to prepare one.

> It felt so unromantic when Christine said she wanted a premarital agreement. It almost felt like an insult to me at first. When she explained her rationale—how important it was for her to be sure that whatever money she had went to her children and that my income was substantial while hers was not—I understood her feel-

ings. Chris's bitter divorce made such an impact that she had to feel she was protected, and it had nothing to do with her love for me or confidence in our marriage. (Marc N., age forty-two)

As Marc found, premarital agreements are particularly popular among previously married partners who want to avoid the repeat of a financially chaotic marital breakup and want to protect their children's financial stake. Premarital agreements define each partner's separate properties brought into the marriage and describe their financial intentions after they wed. You can prepare such an agreement with the advice and assistance of your lawyer, but be sure that each of you has your own attorney review the agreement before you sign it.

Do premarital agreements hold up? The courts tend to honor premarital agreements as long as both parties to the contract are open and honest about their assets and liabilities and both have had the benefit of advice from their own attorneys. While most states will allow spouses to give up or limit their interests in their partner's estate, fewer states uphold agreements that limit or forbid alimony in the event of divorce.

If you are already married and have no premarital agreement, you can create a postmarital agreement. Not very romantic either, these documents are often less stressful to execute and define what will happen to your property in the event of a divorce. Especially useful for business as well as personal reasons, these agreements can be used to make clear which spouse has rights to certain property, such as a vacation home or a family business. They can also be used to update or renegotiate a premarital agreement that was signed previously.

Be sure to get the advice of a competent family law or estate-planning attorney if you think a premarital or postmarital agreement would be appropriate in your situation.

Selling or Buying a Home Together

If you or your intended spouse are near or over the age of fifty-five, you'll want to plan your timing carefully for tax reasons if you are buying or selling a home. You may be able to exclude some or all of the gain from being taxed when you sell the home you own. Under current law, you can exclude up to $125,000 of the gain from taxes if you meet certain requirements.

First, you need to be at least fifty-five. Second, you must have owned and used the home as your principal residence for a total of at least three years during the five-year period ending on the date of sale. Third, you need to make a *special election* on a form that is attached to your income tax return. That is, you need to state to the IRS that you are intending to take advantage of the $125,000 exclusion of gain on the sale of this home.

Since you only get to use this exclusion once under the law, you want to pick the right time to use it. If both of you own a home and you wait to sell either or both houses until *after* the marriage, as a married couple, you only get one $125,000 exclusion, not two. If, instead, each of you met the requirements and completed the sale of your houses *before* your wedding date, you could each exclude $125,000 in gain.

There is only one exclusion per married couple, so if one of them had used the exclusion before they married each other, neither of them could use it again after they married. This would be an incentive for the spouse who had not yet used the exclusion to sell his or her house *before* the wedding date and use the exclusion. To make things worse, if you use your $125,000 exclusion during your marriage and later divorce, no further exclusion is available to *either* of you or to any *future* spouses.

There are special rules that apply if one of you has been incapacitated, hospitalized, in a nursing home, or temporarily absent for periods, if you are married but filing a separate income tax return, or if you are a widow or widower whose deceased spouse already used the exemption before the marriage.

Since this is truly a one-time exclusion, save it for the biggest gain you'll ever have. If you bought your home for $300,000 and sold it for $320,000, it would not make sense to use the exclusion to exclude the $20,000 gain from taxes, as you will lose the balance of the $125,000 maximum amount.

Revisit Your Beneficiaries

Consider what happened in Barry's situation. Many years ago he signed a beneficiary designation naming his two grown children from a prior marriage as the beneficiaries on his retirement plan. Barry married Cassandra and they agreed to keep their assets separate, including retirement plan assets. Soon after the marriage, Barry signed a new will leaving everything to his children. But when he died, Cassandra received all of the retirement benefits. Why? Under federal law, Cassandra was the sole beneficiary of the retirement plans because she never signed a necessary *waiver* form after the marriage concerning retirement plan benefits. If your spouse does not sign the waiver, what happens may be different from what you intended. This is especially significant if the retirement plan is a major asset in your estate. Talk to your attorney about steps you can take to avoid this result.

Review Your Retirement Plans

It is important to do all you can to avoid unnecessary estate taxes on your retirement plans and be able to defer income taxes on these assets for as long as possible. Retirement plan distributions, whether the distribution is in the form of a lump sum or an annuity, could be subject to an estate tax and an income tax when one of you dies, depending on the size of your estate and whom you designate as the beneficiary.

There are, however, ways to avoid estate tax and to delay immediate income tax when you die, even for estates over $600,000. The key is to coordinate your will or trust and beneficiary designations to take advantage of the tax deferral strategies that are available. Whether retirement plan payouts, such as those from company plans, Keogh plans, or IRAs, qualify for this special tax deferral is somewhat tricky to determine.

Your spouse must be named as the primary beneficiary, either directly or through a QTIP trust which is specifically written to qualify as a designated beneficiary trust. (See more on QTIP trusts on pages 229–30.) You will certainly want to check this out while you and your spouse are both alive so you don't pay unnecessary estate and income taxes at the death of your spouse. The survivor may be left with much less than you had intended unless you do some advance planning. We suggest you consult with your attorney to take steps now to avoid this problem.

Other Considerations Before Marriage or Remarriage

- Find out whether your Social Security benefits will be affected by your marriage. For example, a divorced person claiming benefits on an ex-spouse's working record could lose those benefits by remarrying.
- Get advice on any potential liability you might have for your soon-to-be spouse's past debts, and devise ways to protect your assets. If your intended has large debts or a poor credit history, you may end up financially liable and without credit.
- Determine the effect of adding your new spouse to the title on the home you brought into the marriage. If your spouse's business venture goes belly-up, will the house be sold? If you divorce, how will the house

be divided? Will your house be sold due to a debt incurred by your spouse before marriage that was never paid off?

• Determine whether you will be forced to use your assets to pay for your spouse's nursing home costs and medical bills, even if you've signed a marital agreement saying you'll each pay your own way. Consult with an attorney to ease your concerns.

• Protect your inheritance for your children with a qualified terminable interest property (QTIP) trust, which gives you a measure of control over assets even from the grave. This trust benefits your spouse (even if your spouse remarries) in that he or she can receive income from your assets. At the same time, it gives you the final say as to the ultimate beneficiaries (your children for example) once your surviving spouse passes away. Whether you are in your first marriage or a remarriage, this allows you to meet the obligation you might feel to provide for your surviving spouse without penalizing your children. As beneficiaries they will receive whatever is left in the trust after your spouse passes away.

• Consider a qualified domestic trust (QDOT) if you are married and you or your spouse are permanent residents but not U.S. citizens. A QDOT is a special trust that allows a noncitizen surviving spouse to delay paying death tax upon the first spouse's death. Depending on the assets in the trust and the timing of distributions from the trust, the death tax may be paid during the survivor's lifetime or at the survivor's death.

• Review with your attorney how beneficiary designations on life insurance, annuities, IRAs, 401(k)s, and other retirement plans should read after a marriage. The best planning in a will or trust will be worthless unless you hold title to your assets in a way that complements your intended plan. Otherwise assets may pass outside the will or trust to unintended beneficiaries. Remember the case of Catherine and Sam and their vacation condo and Barry and Cassandra and his retirement plan? Your spouse may need to sign a special waiver, as Cassandra should have done, so that certain retirement benefits can go to someone else, such as your children from a prior marriage.

• Plan for your stepchildren. If you are remarrying and you or your future spouse have children from a former marriage, talk to your attorney about how your will or trust should deal with stepchildren. If you don't confront this issue, upon your death, state law may give stepchildren and your children equal shares in your estate. Even if that's what you want to happen, don't leave your family arguing over what you intended and paying attorney's fees to sort things out.

• Be sure that your will or trust specifies who will pay estate taxes. Otherwise it could be that your spouse or a child will receive an asset outside the will or trust free of tax, leaving the beneficiaries under the will or trust to pay the death tax on that asset. This could result in an unfair depletion of assets passing under the will or trust. It may be preferable to provide that each beneficiary, whether inheriting under your will or trust or receiving an asset through a beneficiary designation, pays his or her fair share of estate tax according to how much was received.

Why Seniors Don't Marry

Fact of life: About 885,000 older people live with partners to whom they are not married because they would lose pension and other retirement income from their former spouses if they remarried.

Although remarriage might seem romantically appealing, as we age it is sometimes more appealing financially to simply live together. That's because the financial security most retirees depend on can be eroded by the simple act of marriage. Here are four reasons *not* to get married:

Pensions can be affected. Remarriage can mean you forfeit your deceased spouse's benefits. Even though unmarried partners receive no survivor benefits, the retiree can take a lump-sum distribution and buy an annuity and name the partner as beneficiary.

Social Security benefits can be reduced. Two singles living together can each have an income of $25,000 before their benefits are subject to tax. A married couple filing jointly is limited to $32,000. More of their benefits would be taxed if they were to marry.

Home ownership can be tricky. As you learned earlier, if you are fifty-five or older, you can escape taxes on $125,000 of profits from the sale of your house. If you and your spouse are both over fifty-five, you may think that you have a $250,000 combined exemption, but that is not so. There is only one exemption per married couple, so one way to double up on the exemption is not to get married.

Medicaid may cost an arm and a leg. Though states vary in their eligibility rules, a married couple may have to deplete a significant portion of their jointly owned assets before Medicaid will pay for long-term nursing home care for the sick spouse. The assets of the healthy partner of an unmarried couple are not counted in the eligibility criteria. The only exception is property you transfer to your partner in the three-year period before you apply for Medicaid and after you enter a nursing home.

A great resource for knowing more about finances for unmarried couples of any age is *The Living Together Kit,* by Toni Ihara and Ralph Warner (NOLO Press, 1995).

Divorce, the death of a spouse, and disability are all changes that have both economic and emotional impacts that are dramatic and long-lived. Just how well you negotiate through these changes—and happier ones such as remarriage—says a lot about how well you've planned and how secure you'll be during your next fifty years.

If you have already experienced any of the major life changes covered in this chapter, you know that they have influenced your decisions concerning where and how you will live during your next fifty years. Let's now explore what you need to consider as you make some choices about your destination for retirement and the style of living that you would like to enjoy.

PART IV

MAKING THE MOST OF RETIREMENT

10

• • • • • • • • • •

Choosing Your Retirement Destination and Style

They say the three most important criteria when buying a home are location, location, and location. *Where* you choose to retire has a tremendous influence on how satisfying your retirement will be, and three factors—finances, family, and friends—will play a significant role in where you ultimately choose to retire. Once you've decided to retire, it is time to replace your retirement dreams with concrete plans for the future. Maybe you've always wanted to live abroad. Now is the time to consider it seriously. Experiment and enjoy knowing that the decisions you make when you first retire may change as your needs change.

> When we first retired, all Jim could think of was golf and all I could think of was travel. We figured if we moved to South Carolina we'd have the money for what we both wanted. After awhile, we got our fill and longed to move back to where the children and grandchildren are. We're now in a retirement villa six miles from where they live in California, and it's great—we can see them a couple of times a week after work and on weekends too. (Angela A., age fifty-eight)

By answering the following questions, you will have a better sense of whether you should move or stay put and, more important, how to set your priorities for choosing your retirement destination.

- Do you find your current lifestyle too complex, cluttered, hectic, and busy?

- Is simplifying your life a priority for you?
- Does staying at home sound like a great vacation and good chance to renew and reconnect with your life and yourself?
- Does taking time off mean doing what you want to do—play golf, hike, walk, shop, write, read, catch up?
- How close do you want to be to family and friends?
- If you are grandparents, do you want to be close enough to get together with your children for long weekends and special occasions, but not so close that you get locked into being called on to baby-sit frequently?
- Is the next place you choose to live the place you'll likely live till you die?
- If you move away from family and friends, how will you feel about being isolated if your spouse dies?
- Do you want to continue living in the state in which you currently reside?
- Are there other states in which you could reside that are more financially friendly?
- How important to you are tax considerations in deciding where to live?
- Which states have the best cultural and leisure activities for you?
- Do you want to live abroad? To what extent is the desire to live abroad based on love of travel, family or friends abroad, or concern about protecting assets?

Where Do You Want to Live?

Picture this: You are walking on a white sand beach with the aqua ocean lapping at your ankles. The sun is setting in the distance and soon you'll be feasting on lobster and champagne as you overlook the crystal blue sea. Or this: Your cabin sits amid beautiful trees just below the chair lift—a short walk in the winter to great skiing, in the summer and fall to breathtaking hikes.

Is this the stuff only travel magazines are made of, or could this fantasy be a possibility for you? The challenge is to choose the place that will fulfill your fantasy *and* meet your requirements. While the lure of a fresh start in a faraway place is appealing, keep in mind that putting down new roots involves energy, money, and time, as well as some risk, at a stage in your life when what you may really want is some R and R closer to home.

Or you may really long for a move that will lift you out of your rut and get you involved in new friendships, hobbies, and activities. According to Eva Kahana, a gerontologist and chair of the Department of Sociology at Case Western Reserve University in Cleveland, daring to plan for the future helps older people improve the quality of their lives. This is probably true for most of us. When we plan for the future we feel optimistic and enthusiastic about what we dream and plan. We often unconsciously take better care of ourselves so that we can reach the fantasy in our mind's eye.

Once you are ready for retirement, chances are that your children will be on their own. Perhaps the house that previously provided for everyone's needs is now too big, and you and your spouse are overburdened with maintenance chores. On the other hand, you may like the community, have many good friends and neighbors, and be accustomed to the comforts that your dwelling provides. List the benefits of remaining in your present housing, and also list the benefits of moving. For example, do the places you are considering living have opportunities for part-time work and easy access to consumer services such as banks, restaurants, good shopping malls? Do they have high-quality medical care and low crime?

Many magazines, including *Worth* magazine and *Money* magazine, regularly evaluate taxes, quality of life, education, and health care in different states or cities. In a recent survey by *Worth* magazine, Wyoming came first in terms of giving citizens the best services for their tax dollars. Alaska was the runner-up and New York was last. The rankings focused on five main areas—education, welfare, health and hospitals, highways, and law enforcement—and analyzed such factors as the percent of income that goes to taxes, students per teacher, percent of high school graduates, percent of two-year-olds fully immunized, percent of highway miles rated first class, and percent of violent crimes with arrests. There were extra points for state benefits and fiscal discipline.

Though your emphasis should be on your individual needs, not on what a magazine editor thinks is important, these lists provide up-to-date information in a format that will help you decide what is important. For Hank and Eloise, a low crime rate was a major factor in where they chose to live, while for Marlene and Tom, the closeness and quality of health-care facilities ranked at the top of their list. For Edie, a recent widow, proximity to her children and grandchildren and easy access to symphony, art museums, and other cultural events were key factors. What is important to these folks might not fit your needs to a tee, but you'll find it helpful to eliminate what you don't want so you can zero in on what you do want.

From time to time, other states or cities will be listed as most desirable as different criteria are used in the survey. As you review lists of the most desirable places to live, ask yourself what is really important to you. Who knows—a state or city you might not have considered could turn out to be somewhere you would enjoy for at least part of your retirement years.

How does the state where you currently live compare with other states on education, welfare, health and hospitals, highways, crime prevention, clean air, cultural activities, and other factors you consider important? You may find that with a short move, you can relocate to a better environment.

Mistakes People Make in Deciding Where to Retire

Here are five of the most common mistakes people make in picking their retirement locales. As you weigh your choices, review this list to be sure you are making the best move for you.

Underestimating the cost of the move. A relocation can easily cost \$40,000 to \$50,000 today, if you factor in the costs of buying and selling a home, a car or two, and new appliances, plus improvements to your new home. Taxes are also an important consideration. Before you decide where to move, investigate how state income taxes and property taxes compare with those you pay now. Call your accountant or the state's department of taxation for more information. Although moving expenses were tax deductible when you were employed, they probably won't be in retirement. That's because a deduction for moving expenses is allowed only if you are working full time in your new job, and most people in retirement work no more than part time.

Going where your friends are. Don't let friends exert too much influence on your decision where to move. Many retirees move to communities where their friends have already relocated. But don't ignore factors such as employment and cost of living, just to follow your friends. While having a network of friends can be important to your future happiness in your new locale, it is not the only factor to consider. Also, friends won't be lost forever if you end up in different communities: You have an excuse to visit one another. Here are two perspectives:

> Quite frankly, the compelling reason for us to move to Tucson was that our golfing friends were all headed that way. Nothing else really mattered as much in making our decision to move. We figured we could cope with the weather, and the other things, like cultural and educational opportunities, crime, government, [and] shopping convenience, would be OK for us if we had our friends close by. (Janet J., age fifty-one)

> The biggest mistake we made was to move to Florida because our friends were there. The humidity is unbearable and we're finding that activities with friends get old fast when you do them every day. When we were working, we really looked forward to getting together for golf, dinner out, and other things. Now, with unlimited time, we really want more to do. (Ed Y., age fifty-five)

There are those for whom proximity to friends and family is far more important than taxes, cultural events, and closeness to the shopping malls. Make sure you know your own needs and priorities and be willing to reconsider and move if you become unhappy with where you are living.

Moving to a destination you've enjoyed on vacation. Unfortunately, this is one of the most common mistakes retirees make in relocating. They expect their experiences after moving to that dream vacation spot to be an extension of their holidays. Perhaps you've walked the beach at Cabo San Lucas and thought, If only this could go on forever. Everything is perfect. But when you're on vacation, you are not likely to see the downsides. Before deciding to move to a new area, you should spend a week or two there during the off-season. Is the weather tolerable? Are sufficient conveniences, services, and activities available to you during those months? Follow events for six months subscribing to the local newspaper. Is there enough to do in the off-season? Are taxes stable? What about crime? Has the local infrastructure kept up with growth? Are there enough people in the area who share your interests and could become friends?

Downsizing your living space. Many retirees, in an effort to simplify life, buy a house or condo that turns out to be too small to live and entertain in comfortably. Even if it is just you and your spouse, consider moving to a house or apartment that has at least three bedrooms if you can afford it. You'll want space for visiting children, grandchildren, and friends, and you may need extra closet space, a workroom, or even an office, should you want to continue working for extra income.

Ignoring weather problems. While extremely warm or cold weather may *seem* manageable, the climate changes may be more than you bargained for. That is one reason why one of every three people who moves to Florida to retire later moves from there. The hot climate and not being able to generate an adequate income can be big disappointments. As you consider the year-round climate of the new location you are investigating, ask yourself: Do I want this weather all year? If it's a temperate climate like California or Arizona, will I miss the change of seasons? Can I handle high humidity or severe cold? Is this climate good for my health? What about air quality and smog? Are these factors that will affect me?

Consider a College Town

College towns are a great environment for retirement. They tend to be beautiful, stimulating, and restful, and the cost of living is usually not too high. These locations tend to show up on list after list of desirable places to live:

Ashland, Oregon
Boulder, Colorado
Chapel Hill, North Carolina
Chico, California
Columbia, Missouri
Gainesville, Florida
Oxford, Mississippi
San Luis Obispo, California
South Hadley, Massachusetts

Let's consider four of these favored places in more depth: Boulder, San Luis Obispo, Ashland, and Chapel Hill.

Boulder. Boulder, at the base of the breathtaking Flatiron Mountains, is a definite favorite. Home to the University of Colorado, Boulder offers a rich and diverse cultural atmosphere. Here you can enjoy the Shakespeare Festival, one of the top three in the country, along with the nationally acclaimed Bach Festival and the Colorado Dance Festival. Summers find residents enjoying the Chataugua Auditorium's film series, dance, music, and dramatic presentations. Classes designed for seniors run the range from gourmet cooking to computers, sailing to archaeology. But Boulder has a downside: Its cost of living is about 13 percent above the national average, and its housing costs are 49 percent above the national average, due to a spectacular rise in home prices during the last five years.

San Luis Obispo. With a population of forty-two thousand, San Luis Obispo is home to California Polytechnic State University. The town is culturally and intellectually rich, the setting is scenic, and retirees can enjoy some of California's best weather. The school sponsors lectures and concerts, many of which are free to seniors. You can visit the Mozart Festival in late July and early August and the Wine Festival at harvest time in September, and the beaches, just fourteen miles away, are enjoyable anytime.

Ashland. Home of Southern Oregon State College, Ashland, population seventeen thousand, is a unique town nestled among gently rolling hills. It enjoys a very low crime rate, intellectual stimulation, and the beauty of the nearby Cascade Range. Ashland is also the home of a nationally acclaimed Shakespeare festival that has been changed from an annual event to a year-round production in three theaters, one of which is open-air. Downtown, and in the nearby towns of Jacksonville and Medford, you'll find a wide selection of restaurants and shops. The area also offers great hunting, fishing, and skiing.

Chapel Hill. Chapel Hill, North Carolina, with a population of forty-three thousand, is part of a research triangle that also includes Raleigh and Durham. This town houses the University of North Carolina and lies within miles of two other major universities, five four-year colleges, and eight two-year colleges. More Ph.D.s have retired here than to any other city in the United States. Research Triangle Park, the largest research park of its kind in the country, draws scientists from all over the world. The town and university campus are beautiful, and the people here are extremely friendly. Senior citizens can audit university classes on a space-available basis, and fees are minimal for continuing education courses.

The Taxing Aspects of Where You Retire

When it comes to federal income taxes, it doesn't matter where in the country you live—everyone is taxed the same. But state taxes, including income tax, sales tax, property tax, excise taxes, gasoline tax, and licensing fees, can be vastly different depending on where you choose to live. Most people select a retirement community because of friends, relatives, or lifestyle—a warm climate, a slower pace, and so forth. Few people decide to retire to a particular state solely for tax reasons. But you can combine easy living and tax benefits if you do a little planning. Consider the case of Jim and Susan.

Jim Cooper was president of a small company located in southern California. He and his wife Susan loved to ski, hike, and enjoy the outdoors, but hated to pay taxes. When Jim retired, he and Susan thought a move to the mountains—Incline Village in Nevada—would fit their needs perfectly. They wanted their new home to be near the outdoor activities they loved, and they wanted to save on income taxes. California's taxes are onerous for high-income, high-net-worth individuals, and Nevada blesses its residents with no state income tax. Although Jim and Susan will still owe money to California for any income earned there, all of their unearned income, such as interest dividends, capital gains, and pensions, will go untaxed under Nevada law and will not be taxed by California, since they are not California residents.

Changing Your Domicile

Jim and Susan found that changing domiciles entailed several steps that took time, but were manageable once they understood the rationale. If you are considering switching states, keep in mind that the specific rules for each state are tricky. Talk to a tax professional to ensure that you follow the rules to the letter and don't trip up on your trip out. Here is what they did and what you will need to do to change your state of residence or domicile:

- Spend a greater portion of each year in your new domicile state—that is, more than 50 percent of your time.
- Execute and file a declaration of domicile with the appropriate office in your new domicile state.
- Sell your home in your old state.
- Register and vote in your new state.
- File all tax forms at the IRS Service Center in your new state.
- Register cars, boats, and so forth in your new state.
- Sign a new will in your new state.
- Obtain a driver's license in the new state and surrender your old license to your previous state.
- File a final resident tax return in the old state.
- Make sure that your principal bank or securities accounts are located in your new state.

- Establish advisers—for example, attorney, trust officer, and accountant—in your new state.

Remember that "domicile" means your permanent home for an indefinite period of time. It is where you intend to reside now, with no plans to change in the future. You may have several residences, but only one domicile. Give careful thought to which state will be your domicile, keeping in mind that your property rights in divorce or succession will be determined by the state in which you reside. For example, Matthew learned that California, a community property state, imposed a different set of rules on his divorce settlement from what it would have been in his former state of Virginia, which divides property equitably rather than equally. And all of his property was subject to California divorce laws, even though it had been acquired during his years in Virginia.

Retiring to a Tax-Friendly State

Become familiar with all of the various taxes in the state to which you are planning to move. Income tax is important, but it is not the only consideration. Is there a sales tax? Sales taxes take a big bite out of the income you spend on goods and services in all states except Delaware, Montana, New Hampshire, and Oregon. California boasts the highest sales tax in the country. Find out what the sales tax rate is for the state and city you are considering, and what goods and services are taxed. If drugs, food, and services are free of tax, you'll save money over the long run. Compute the income, sales, and property taxes you would pay in a typical year on your anticipated income and expenditures for each locale you are considering. Adding all taxes together will give you a clear picture of whether you are moving to a tax-friendly or tax-fierce state.

Estate taxes

Every state has some form of death or succession tax, and probate fees vary from one state to another. Not only do the tax rates differ, but differing rules can create vastly different taxes depending on the state in which you are a resident. For example, some states do not have a marital deduction that allows you to leave any amount of assets to a spouse without incurring estate taxes. Be sure to consider carefully the estate tax laws, rates, and assets subject to tax. If you have a large estate, changing where you live in retirement could significantly affect the estate taxes your heirs will pay on your death.

The least expensive states in which to retire for estate tax purposes are those that have an estate "pick-up tax" equal to the credit the federal government gives for state death taxes. Because the state pick-up tax does not exceed the federal credit, the state tax does not increase the total estate taxes due when you die. Pick-up tax credits run from 0.8 percent of the federal taxable estate to 16 percent, depending on the size of your estate.

States that impose a pick-up tax are Alabama, Alaska, Arizona, Arkansas, California, Colorado, District of Columbia, Florida, Georgia, Hawaii, Idaho, Illinois, Maine, Minnesota, Missouri, Nevada, New Mexico, North Dakota, Oregon, Rhode Island, South Carolina, Texas, Utah, Vermont, Virginia, Washington, West Virginia, Wisconsin, and Wyoming.

High-tax states exceed the maximum credit. New York, for example, imposes an estate tax that runs as high as 21 percent of the federal taxable estate, exceeding the federal credit amount by 5 percent.

Gift taxes

If gifting to children and grandchildren on a regular basis is one of your pleasures, a state gift tax could take the fun out of your gifts. Six states have a gift tax: Connecticut, Delaware, Louisiana, New York, North Carolina, and Tennessee. Does the state you want to move to impose one? If so, what is the rate and is there a minimum exempt amount?

Generation-skipping tax

A generation-skipping tax is imposed on gifts and bequests that bypass a generation of heirs. For example, Manfred wants to give some stock to his grandson, Manfred III. The stock is considered a generation-skipping gift because it bypasses Manfred Jr.'s generation. The government is deprived of the tax in the parent's generation, so it taxes the original gift made by Manfred himself to make up for this. Some states impose a generation-skipping tax in addition to the federal generation-skipping tax on gifts over $1 million. States that impose a generation-skipping tax are Alabama, Arizona, California, Colorado, Florida, Illinois, Missouri, Nevada, Rhode Island, South Carolina, Texas, Virginia, and Washington. If you are planning to make very large gifts directly to your grandchildren, you might not want to live in one of these states.

Income tax

There are seven states that do not have an income tax. They are Alaska, Florida, Nevada, South Dakota, Texas, Washington, and Wyoming. On the other end of the scale, the states with the highest state income taxes include California, Hawaii, Montana, and Oklahoma. Adding local income taxes makes New York a high income tax state as well. But some states that don't impose an income tax have other taxes. For example, Florida imposes an intangibles tax on stocks, bonds, and certain other investments. Local municipalities and counties may impose their own income taxes, so relocating from one place to another within the state can affect your net income.

Property taxes

All states impose property taxes, but Alaska imposes no property tax on those over sixty-five. Taxes on the value of real estate are set by the

---

SMART TIP

THE BEST AND THE WORST FOR STATE TAXES

Consider the total impact of taxes, including property, sales, and income taxes. Here is a ranking of the ten highest and ten lowest states with respect to state and local tax burdens for a retired couple, both age sixty-five, living in the capital cities of each state and the District of Columbia.

How the States Rank

States with the Lowest Taxes	*States with the Highest Taxes*
1. Alaska	1. Wisconsin
2. Delaware	2. Iowa
3. Montana	3. New Jersey
4. Hawaii	4. Massachusetts
5. Wyoming	5. District of Columbia
6. Mississippi	6. Rhode Island
7. Virginia	7. Maryland
8. Oregon	8. Idaho
9. Louisiana	9. New York
10. South Carolina	10. Minnesota

SOURCE: *Kiplinger's* magazine.

---

county or township in which the real estate is located. Since these rates and assessments vary widely, you'll want to check these out thoroughly before buying a new residence. The lowest property tax rates are in Alabama, Arizona, Hawaii, Louisiana, New Mexico, and West Virginia. For California residents, Proposition 13, which permits only minuscule increases in property taxes each year for longtime home owners, has kept their property taxes low as well. Of less concern but still important are taxes on transferring property or recording deeds. Real property transfer or deed-recording taxes are imposed by virtually every state at rates generally between 1 and 2 percent. Remember to add these to your cost of moving too.

Retiring Abroad

The lure of exotic places is strong for many retirees. The Social Security Administration sends more than 360,000 checks to destinations outside the United States each month, including Costa Rica, Mexico, Canada, Great Britain, Greece, Germany, Italy, and Israel. Every month fifty-six thousand of those checks go to Mexico alone. But as Mexico has become more industrialized and more expensive, Americans have moved farther south—Costa Rica, Belize, and Guatemala. About seventeen thousand retired Americans make their primary homes in Central America and the Caribbean.

Living abroad has many advantages, and retiring abroad can save you big bucks. Jane Parker, coauthor of *Adventures Abroad,* estimates that in some cases a couple can enjoy foreign retirement living at one-third to one-half of what it costs to live in the States. According to her study, comfortable living in Mexico could cost $1,000 to $1,200 a month. Living in Portugal costs $1,800 to $2,000 a month, and Costa Rica costs somewhere between those figures. For this you get a one-thousand- to twenty-five-hundred-square-foot home in a middle-class neighborhood, enjoy fresh food from open air markets and local delicacies from restaurants, and attend plays and concerts for less than ten dollars each.

Other locations you may want to consider are Canada's Maritime Provinces (New Brunswick, Nova Scotia, and Prince Edward Island), Honduras, Ireland, Portugal, and Uruguay. These locations have beauty and charm, and offer affordable and comfortable living.

State Department data further illustrates that many Americans choose to live in other countries. For a variety of reasons, including

U.S. POPULATION ABROAD AS OF OCTOBER 15, 1992

Area	Resident U.S. Citizens*	Area	Resident U.S. Citizens*
Argentina	13†	Italy	104†
Australia	62	Jerusalem	43
Canada	296	Mexico	539
Costa Rica	23	Netherlands	19
Dominican Republic	97	Panama	36
Egypt	17	Portugal	26
France	59	Saudi Arabia	40
Germany	354	South Korea	30
Greece	32	Spain	79
Hong Kong	24	Switzerland	27
Ireland	46	United Kingdom	255
Israel	112	Venezuela	24

*Totals represent abroad estimates and may include some non-U.S. citizens as well as dual nationals.

†Figures are in thousands.

SOURCE: U.S. Department of State, unpublished data, 1993. Data are taken from the annual noncombatant personal evacuation requirements report, which is used solely to estimate the number of potential U.S. citizen evacuees from a given country in a crisis.

proximity to family and reasonable cost of living, Americans are moving abroad in large numbers, as the chart above shows.

If you are considering moving abroad, you might want to call Boston-based Lifestyle Explorations at (508) 371-4814 for a free packet of information. They pinpoint locations that are especially attractive for American retirees.

Evaluating Locations Abroad

Before you decide to retire abroad, consider the same factors you would in evaluating locations in the United States, including affordable cost of living, low incidence of crime, comfortable climate, good health care, and accessibility to cultural and consumer amenities. In addition, investigate how stable the country and the currency are. How sophisticated are the communications systems, including phone, fax, and mail? What about safety in banking and financial institutions?

Before deciding where to move, make a trial run. If possible, rent a home in that location for six months to a year. If a week at a time in your proposed destination is all you can manage, visit at different times during the year. The longer you visit, the more accurately you'll assess the local attitude toward Americans and whether the culture is compatible with your personal tastes. Be sure to check the tax laws. Must you pay taxes to your new country, to the United States, or to both? Will that cause your taxes to increase?

Valuable resources are IRS publication 593: *Tax Highlights for U.S. Citizens and Residents Going Abroad* and IRS publication 901: *U.S. Tax Treaties.* You can order both by calling 800-829-3676.

SMART TIP

CHANGING PLACES

A good way to examine life in another country is by living there as the residents do, not in a hotel room. Try exchanging time in your home for someone's home in the country that interests you. To find a family with whom to trade, join a home-swap agency. You can trade your home on your own, advertising in the local paper of the community where you'd like to consider living, but using one of these organizations can be easier.

HomeLink
P.O. Box 650
Key West, FL 33041
800-638-3841

Cost: Seventy dollars for an annual directory, including a listing of your home, plus monthly updates for homes of sixteen thousand members worldwide.

Intervac U.S.
P.O. Box 590504
San Francisco, CA 94159
800-756-HOME

Cost: Sixty-five dollars a year (sixty dollars for seniors sixty-two and over). The directory is published in four installments, with ten thousand listings in thirty countries.

Buying a Home Abroad

Americans considering a home abroad should exercise caution and do lots of research. There are many rules and regulations for living and buying property in each country. Generally, real estate commissions are likely to be higher than the usual 6 percent we customarily pay in the United States, and closing costs can run 15 percent of the sale price, compared to 1 to 3 percent here. Many foreign countries also impose a transfer tax or stamp tax, which will set you back a few hundred dollars.

Whether purchasing an inexpensive villa or a castle abroad, be sure to ask what you will own. Homes bought in the United States are usually fee simple, which means you own the home and the land. Foreign purchases may be something less than a full fee simple, especially in Great Britain and Austria. You may own the house but only lease the land. For example, if you are interested in the more fashionable London neighborhoods, you will most likely be buying your home with a long-term lease. In Belgravia and other West End sections of London, the land is owned by the Duke of Westminster and his family, so when you buy a home there you are renting the land from him. A low price on a home in such places might not signify a bargain but instead mean that the lease is short-lived. Although renewals of leaseholds may be automatic in some places, future costs and their effect on property value is an unknown you must face.

Some countries limit where foreigners can buy. Switzerland, for example, restricts real estate sales by requiring foreigners to get a permit, and only a limited number of permits are issued. In Greece, Americans whose parents are Greek are not restricted, but other Americans are limited in where they can purchase a home. A similar situation exists in Mexico, but there, laws may be more easily relaxed.

Applying for a mortgage in the country of your choice can be challenging. The rules of financing may be quite foreign indeed. In many cases lenders will finance a smaller percentage of the sale price than in America—say 50 percent—and seller financing is often unknown. Mortgage types differ too. For example, in England there are no fixed-rate mortgages, and all mortgages float with interest rate changes. In Spain and Italy, mortgages for foreigners are nonexistent, so you must buy for cash or ask the seller to consider making a private mortgage loan to you.

Although home prices in some countries can be quite reasonable, there may be significant other costs, such as real estate taxes and other charges. If you buy a home in Italy, for example, your property taxes will be quite high, but buy a similar home in France and you'll find that your home's appreciation goes untaxed. In Greece, unless your parents are Greek, you'll pay a "transfer of title" fee, which can be substantial. Spend plenty of time in your new home country learning as much as you can from real estate agents, bankers, lawyers, and other home owners before you decide to purchase property.

Check with the American chamber of commerce in the country where you are considering buying a home. Generally, foreign embassies, consulates, and tourism offices in America are not helpful with foreign real estate purchases, although they can provide you with copious information about other aspects of life in various countries.

If you decide to sell your foreign real estate and return to the United States, your profit may be locked in the foreign country. If your home is in Spain, you would be allowed to take out of the country only your original purchase price plus what local authorities consider a fair profit. Your opinion of fair and theirs may be entirely different. In addition, your profits may be reduced by a foreign capital gains tax, and you may be taxed on cash proceeds taken out of the country.

It Could Be Taxing to Live Abroad

Since we're talking taxes, keep in mind that U.S. citizens residing abroad are still liable to the United States for income taxes, even on some foreign earnings. You can currently exclude up to $80,000 for income you've earned from working abroad, but not from income from foreign investments. Retirees working abroad are liable to their host country for taxes, but the United States gives you credit for any foreign taxes you pay. In many countries your Social Security benefits are fully taxable. As a result, you may pay more taxes by living abroad.

Estate Planning and Investment Planning When Living Abroad

If you retire abroad, you will need to do some special estate planning, particularly if you purchase a home. Consult with an attorney familiar with the laws of the foreign land where you own real estate. Get advice on how to minimize the estate tax bite, which in some countries can reach 50 percent, and to ensure that your property passes to the heirs you intended. You might even need two wills, one for your U.S. property and one for foreign assets.

If you are living abroad, make sure your retirement investments are still appropriate. Consider the following:

• Given fluctuations in currency values, what portion of your investments should you convert to local currency? There is no right answer, but the prudent retiree should probably convert only a small portion of investments to foreign currency, as U.S. dollars are one of the more stable currencies in the world. Consider the experiences of these two retirees.

> When we moved to Mexico, little did we know that the value of the peso would decline by more than 75 percent! Having converted our retirement funds to pesos years ago, we couldn't afford to return to the United States to live, which is what we'd hoped to do. (Edwin A., age fifty-eight)

> In 1985 we retired to a lovely town in Provence. Our dollar bought ten francs at that time, but three years later it was worth only five and a half francs. It made a serious dent in our lifestyle to have our income and retirement savings in U.S. dollars. (Margot E., age fifty-five)

• Will your investments in municipal bonds continue to be tax-free, or will they be taxed in a foreign country? Consider reallocating your funds from municipal bonds to corporate bonds if you will be taxed on interest in your new host country. If there is no tax advantage for you, corporate bonds make more sense because they pay a higher rate of interest.

• Should you lower the volatility in your portfolio? Most individuals near or at retirement age look for ways to lower the volatility or risk in their portfolios whether they live in the United States or abroad. This is because they may need to draw an income stream from their investments and do not want to be penalized by needing to sell stocks during a market downturn. Whether abroad or at home, you will want to use the same strategies to reduce risk in your portfolio. These include diversification, reducing your equity exposure and increasing your bonds, and incorporating foreign investments via mutual funds.

> Living abroad as we do, I can't easily trade in my securities account back home on a timely basis, so high-tech and other volatile stocks aren't the place to invest. A good rule seems to be: The more exotic the place you're living, the more boring your investments back home should be. (Eric N., age fifty-four)

• Should you open a brokerage account and make investments in your host country?

> When we saw what the Chilean stock market had done the last eight years, we knew we wanted to invest. We did our homework and selected five stocks and invested about $40,000. Needless to say, the stock market didn't continue its past performance, but we do think our investments are good for the long term. What surprised us the most about all of this was the lack of written information and statements on our accounts—so different from our U.S. brokers, who deluge us with information, ads, and statements. (Marta M., age fifty-eight)

Where to Get Information

The following are some sources for information about possible retirement locales.

• *Places Rated Almanac* software (Prentice Hall Computer Publishing; $39.95). You can view on-screen the best and worst attributes of 343 metropolitan areas in the United States and Canada. This software allows you to give additional weight to the individual factors, such as climate or cost of living, that are most important to you.

• *Where to Retire* magazine (Vacation Publications; $9.95 for four quarterly issues). Each issue highlights several locales that appeal to retirees. Recent issues have covered Asheville, North Carolina; Vero Beach, Florida; and St. George, Utah, for example. To subscribe, call (800) 338-4962, ext. 252.

• *The World's Top Retirement Havens* (Agora Books). Each chapter focuses on a different country and covers everything from immigration procedures to buying versus renting to where to stay while you are looking.

• *Retirement Places Rated* (Prentice Hall; $16.95), by David Savageau, a relocation consultant. This book ranks more than 150 areas based on cost of living and taxes, housing, climate, crime, recreational amenities, health-care services, and public transportation.

• *International Living* (Agora; $58 for a year's subscription) is a monthly publication with valuable information on retiring abroad. The September issue each year has a Global Retirement Index listing the top twenty-four retirement destinations in the world. Contact (410) 223-2605 for information.

Choosing Your Retirement Style

Once you've decided whether to stay put in your current state of residence or put down new roots elsewhere, you must choose between a home, condo, apartment, or retirement or care facility. Your choices can be categorized into four groups: independent-living, assisted-living, personal-care, and custodial-care arrangements.

Independent Living

Many younger, healthier retirees prefer independent living. They may live in the general community, as they have for years, or move to a retirement community that is almost like a cruise ship on land. A retirement community or village is constructed exclusively for retired people to free them from the noise and commotion of living among young families. The physical arrangements and types of services provided vary widely. Most retirement communities provide excellent recreational facilities, including golf courses, tennis courts, and swimming pools, as well as libraries, club rooms, and auditoriums. Some even offer a shopping center and hospital on the grounds with full-time doctors and nursing staff. A retirement community is likely to be at least forty to eighty miles away from a large city, at which distance land costs drop sharply. Property taxes may be lower because the communities do not have the large education expenses of areas with many children.

Available housing within retirement communities includes single-family detached homes, duplexes, townhouses, condos, and high-rise buildings, ranging in size from one to three bedrooms. You can rent or purchase units. Nonprofit organizations such as churches, unions, fraternal societies, veterans' organizations, civic associations, and teachers' organizations sponsor some retirement facilities. Business corporations sponsor others as investments.

> What I like [about my retirement community] is that it is really a self-contained place that meets all my needs. The recreational and social facilities are excellent and they have planned activities for the residents that could keep a person busy all the time. Monthly maintenance costs are low and I feel safe because there are security guards protecting the entrances and grounds. I can also get good medical attention whenever I need it, and that's a relief not only to me but to my children as well. (Mary W., age sixty-three)

Not all retirement communities are alike, and there are disadvantages to consider as well.

> Quite frankly, this is more costly than we had anticipated. We paid close to $100,000 to begin with as the initial entrance cost and now the monthly maintenance fee keeps rising. (Janelle D., age sixty-two)

> We're just not enjoying the lifestyle here as much as we thought. The location feels a bit isolated and there aren't the cultural or social advantages that we had living in a big city like San Francisco. We're living in fairly close quarters with our neighbors. Our social contacts are limited to a group of retirees, and frankly, some of them have become pretty boring. (Stuart T., age fifty-nine)

Assisted Living

Victoria Collins tells of the concept of assisted living from personal experience: It was a bad case of the flu shortly before Christmas one year that started the two-year decline in her mother's health. Living alone in a townhouse since Dad died, Mother would have died from dehydration had we not happened to call to say hello and then realized she needed an ambulance. After being rushed to the hospital, she spent several weeks recuperating. It became clear to us that she could no longer live alone, so we began to explore what options were available. We moved Mother from independent living to a family-living situation with my sister in Spokane, but then we discovered assisted living.

At one end of the spectrum is independent living; at the opposite end is custodial care in an institution such as a nursing home. In the middle is a new industry called assisted living. This includes congregate-housing facilities, assisted-living facilities, continuing-care retirement communities, and life-care communities. These facilities allow you to choose the levels of care you want. You can live independently if you are able, but services, even a nursing home, are available if needed. Some facilities have a menu of services from which to choose. For example, Mother needed help with bathing and walking to the dining room and to other activities but did not require assistance with dressing or eating. At the facility where she lived she paid for only the help she needed and could request more or less, as her health and abilities dictated. Mother enjoyed her time in the assisted-living facility and we as a family felt a real sense of relief. Looking back though on the process and the decisions we made along the way, my only wish is that we had considered this option sooner rather than later. As loving and caring as my sister was, it was not the same as Mother being in a comfortable, secure environment with friends her own age and activities and meals designed especially for them.

In some assisted-living communities, residents are required to pay an up-front fee or an endowment or fee over time. Such fees may be refundable, in whole or in part. They're not direct real estate investments, so residents have no potential for appreciation.

Some communities charge entrance fees that may be based on age and health. Younger people may pay a higher entrance fee, while healthy people may have a lower monthly bill because they don't require assistance with daily-living activities such as mobility, eating, hygiene, dressing, and so forth. The healthier you are, and the more likely you are to outlive your life expectancy, the more attractive a nonrefundable entrance fee will be. With a nonrefundable entrance fee, chances are you will get more housing for your money.

In a newer community you may get a partial refund on initial fees. If you decide to move, you may receive 50 percent to 90 percent of the entrance fee back. If you live there until death, the refund will go to your heirs. If you are married, flexibility is particularly important. Often, after one spouse dies, the survivor may want to move into a smaller unit or find alternative housing. With refundable fees you don't feel locked into a given community and the refundable fees will allow you to leave a larger inheritance. However, be aware that refundable fees may be 10 to 25 percent higher than nonrefundable fees at comparable facilities.

When evaluating facilities, ask these questions:

- What if you are unhappy and want to leave?
- What happens if you or your spouse dies?
- What are your options if the facility deteriorates (perhaps after a change in management)?
- How stable are monthly fees likely to be?

Look for the same contract items that you would in considering a long-term-care insurance policy. For example:

- If nursing home care is included, does it cover custodial care (the most common form) or only skilled care, related to the treatment of a certain condition?

- Who will decide what level of care is needed?
- Is there a time limit on this care—will you have to leave after six months or a year?
- If there is no custodial-care facility on the premises, is there an arrangement with a nursing home, or will residents have to find a facility themselves?
- Is the purchase of long-term-care insurance required, and if so, at what cost?

Answer each of these questions to evaluate the retirement facilities you are considering.

Personal Care and Custodial Care

These options are for someone who needs a higher level of service and is unable to function on his or her own. Personal care refers to someone who is hired to attend to the individual either at home or in the home of a family member, while custodial care generally means a setting like a home that houses six patients or small facility specifically designed and staffed for protective supervision and twenty-four-hour care. Someone who has Alzheimer's may require supervision and assistance but may not need medical treatment, whereas a patient with a broken hip needs medical care but not necessarily full-time supervision.

Here are some other terms you may encounter:

Board-and-care home. This is similar to assisted living except on a smaller scale and with more personalized services. The home or building is generally licensed by the state and the manager supervises the residents' well-being.

Continuing-care retirement community. This type of housing development is planned, designed, and operated to provide a full range of accommodations and services for older adults. Within the complex may be units for independent living, congregate housing, assisted living, and nursing home care.

Life-care community. Usually a large entrance fee is required in this kind of facility, which is similar to a continuing-care retirement community except that the resident and the community have a legal agreement or life-care contract that guarantees nursing services or health-related services and room and board for the duration of the resident's life or for a specified term.

Cooperative housing. In this type of facility the tenants own shares of stock in the complex but not the individual units. They share the costs of maintaining the complex in exchange for the right to occupy their living units.

Elder cottage housing opportunity (ECHO) housing. A relatively new approach to an old idea, these are separate, self-contained, removable units that are placed on the same property as the home of a family member or friend.

For more information on retirement-housing options for yourself or a parent, check the phone book under the government listings for headings such as "Senior Citizens Affairs"; "Aging, Department of"; or "Aging, Office on." You can also call Eldercare Locator toll-free, 800-677-1116.

Retiring in Style

Chances are the three Fs—finances, family, and friends—will determine where you will retire and just how satisfying your retirement will be. In this chapter we covered the broad spectrum from the five big mistakes people make in selecting a retirement destination to considering whether the state you will live in is tax-friendly or tax-fierce. Moving from the States and living out your fantasy to retire abroad requires even more thoughtful planning and research. Long vacations and house swapping in your retirement destination can give you valuable information before you take the step of buying a home in another state or country.

Once you've decided just where you want to retire (at least for now), you have several choices of the specific types of housing. You may be more comfortable in an independent setting like a condo or apartment or in a community setting like a retirement villa or village. You may be healthy and active or you may need an assisted-living facility. The great thing is we have more choices now for our retirement destination than ever before in history. And because this book is about your next fifty years, consider that you may live in several different places in the course of your life span. Each place will add a different dimension and a new richness to your life.

No matter where you live, however, there are two important financial-planning issues you'll need to address. How well prepared you are with respect to insurance and estate planning can save you lots of money and your heirs lots of grief.

11

• • • • • • • • • •

Beyond Saving—Insurance and Estate Planning

Insurance—Your Retirement Parachute

No matter how carefully you plan your retirement, no matter how diligently you save, a catastrophic loss can destroy everything you have carefully stashed for your future. Conventional wisdom says that retired folks no longer need insurance—they have Medicare to protect their health and no longer need life insurance to protect their family. Don't believe it—today's retirees often need both health and life insurance, and their retirement planning is inadequate without it. Most retirees should consider long-term-care insurance as well.

Fact of life: About half of those between twenty-five and forty-four feel they won't have enough money to cover medical costs during retirement.

Health Insurance

If you are not yet sixty-five, you will need private health coverage until you turn sixty-five and are entitled to Medicare coverage. If you are employed, your family is probably covered under a group medical insurance plan. Group health insurance coverage through your employer generally provides the best insurance premium rates. If you don't have such coverage available to you, plans are available through a variety of sources, including insurance companies, health maintenance organizations (HMOs), and preferred provider organizations (PPOs), such as Blue Cross/Blue Shield. HMOs provide all of your medical needs for a set fee and are generally your best bet. If an HMO isn't available in your area, Blue Cross/Blue Shield is generally your best bet. Be careful though, because some of "the Blues" have been ailing financially in recent years. Before you buy insurance, check the financial health of Blue Cross/Blue Shield in your area in *Best Insurance Reports,* a publication that rates insurance companies, available in most large libraries.

SMART TIP

COMPARE POLICIES BASED ON YOUR FAMILY'S NEEDS

To compare insurance policies, analyze your family's needs carefully. Review a typical year of medical care for your family, estimating the coinsurance and deductible costs you would pay under each policy you are considering. Add the cost of the insurance itself, and you can determine the most economical policy.

If you are not covered under a group plan and are looking for individual or family coverage, consider a large annual deductible to reduce the monthly cost of the insurance. Raising the deductible from $100 a year to $1,500 or more will reduce your premiums tremendously. If you are rarely ill, you will be way ahead financially. In addition, if you are self-employed you can set up a medical savings account (MSA) to which you can contribute 65 percent to 75 percent of the deductible under the high-deductible plan.

It is very important to have a high upward limit, at least $1 million, so that you are protected against financial devastation if you or a member of your family becomes seriously ill or injured. To save insurance costs, you may want to consider a less costly major medical policy, which allows you to assume the cost of routine medical care but insures you against the greater risk of major illnesses and injuries.

If you leave a job where you had group coverage, you may be eligible to continue that coverage for eighteen months after you leave your employment under the provisions of legislation known as COBRA (Consolidated Omnibus Budget Reconciliation Act). This may not be your best value, though, as other coverage may be less expensive. In addition, if you develop an illness during the eighteen months you are covered under COBRA, you may not be eligible for coverage at reasonable rates once the eighteen months is up. In general, you are better off establishing enduring medical insurance rather than opting for short-term COBRA coverage.

Medicare

All the saving and planning in the world won't help you if a catastrophe strikes. That was the reasoning behind Medicare, which came into being in 1975. Through a national catastrophic health insurance plan for older Americans, it was hoped that they could live with dignity and not end up in poverty. However, the one thing the system didn't count on was senior citizens living so long! At the time Medicare was instigated, and benefits pegged to age sixty-five, it was anticipated that most Americans would live for just a few more years after that. Surprise! People are living longer and medical expenses are continuing longer. And Medicare spending has gone up and up, escalating enormously every year.

Medicare has been the source of much debate lately and will continue to be controversial in the future. The critics of Medicare say it is too costly, especially with more and more Americans becoming covered at sixty-five. The supporters of Medicare say that its coverage is very important for the elderly, because everyone is eligible regardless of preexisting conditions or illnesses. The strongest proponents of Medicare are those covered under Medicare currently, all of whom are eligible to vote. For that reason, changes to the Medicare system will be cautious and gradual.

> When I turned sixty-five this year, I was surprised to learn that I had to pay for Medicare insurance. What did they do with the payroll deductions that they took from me all those years? (Phyllis G., age sixty-five)

Under the current system, you are eligible for Medicare at age sixty-five, even if you continue working. Part A Medicare is hospital insurance and Part B is medical insurance for such expenses as doctors' fees and outpatient services. Part A is free if you've paid Social Security taxes for ten years or are married to someone who has. All others must pay a monthly premium of $200 or so. Part B coverage, which covers outpatient doctor visits and lab fees, is optional and costs about fifty dollars a month. You will need Part B coverage only if you are not covered by an employer's health plan. Part B premiums are deducted from your Social Security benefits if you are receiving them. Otherwise you must pay the premiums each month.

Medicare covers all hospital expenses for sixty days, but you must pay a hefty deductible before your coverage begins. Unfortunately, unlike private plans, the deductible applies per hospitalization and is not a yearly amount, so if you are hospitalized several times during the year, it can be quite expensive. After sixty days, you must share in the expense, and once your hospital stay exceeds 150 days, you are on your own.

Part B medical insurance, which pays for doctors' visits and other outpatient care, has an annual deductible of one hundred dollars plus a copayment of 20 percent. It doesn't pay for long-term nursing care, dental care, prescriptions, eyeglasses, hearing aids, or expenses outside the United States. Not all doctors participate in Medicare, so if you see one who doesn't, your actual payment may be higher; a nonparticipating doctor can charge Medicare recipients 15 percent more than the Medicare-approved fee schedule. A sixty-page Medicare handbook is yours for the asking. Just call 800-772-1213.

Medigap Insurance

> I'd always heard that once you got older the insurance agents would leave you alone. But now AARP and everyone else is trying to sell me insurance to pay what Medicare won't. (Felix V., age sixty-six)

Many people purchase what is known as "Medigap" insurance, to cover the deductibles and coinsurance amounts under Part B and to provide the services and supplies that Medicare does not. There are ten standard Medigap policies that have been authorized by the government. Those ten policies, lettered A through J, range from limited, less expensive coverage to deluxe coverage for a deluxe premium. Following is a rundown of the provisions of the policies.

Plan A covers the copayments for hospitalization under Medicare Part A and the copayment for doctors' visits under Part B, but it does not cover the hospitalization deductible or the Part B $100 annual deductible. On the other end of the scale, Plan J covers the hospital deductible and the doctors' visit deductible, plus it provides one hundred days of skilled-nursing care, foreign emergency care, custodial care, preventative care, and half of prescription drug costs up to $3,000 a year, subject to a $250 annual deductible.

A popular alternative to the standard Medigap plans are coordinated-care plans, or HMOs, which cover all of your health-care needs for a low monthly fee. Once you sign up with a coordinated-care plan, you no longer need to fill out the Medicare reimbursement forms or shell out hefty copayments and deductibles. All of your health care is covered for a nominal fee per visit, and your prescriptions may be covered as well. The major drawback of coordinated-care plans is that your health care is overseen by the plan and you must visit their doctors, specialists, druggists, and hospitals.

Life Insurance

> I've always had a thing about insurance—I felt it was being sold to me and I didn't really need it. Now I can see there's a pretty good reason to have it. (Gerald F., age fifty-nine)

You need life insurance to pay estate taxes and to ensure that those who depend on you can continue their lifestyle after you are gone. Although it might be beneficial to get a life insurance checkup periodically, be sure that your life insurance professional has your best interests in mind. Some don't. Be particularly wary if you are encouraged to use the dividends on an existing policy to buy a new policy. You would be better off using those dividends to reduce your existing policy's premium than to buy a new policy that creates cash value very slowly.

Likewise, don't cash in your existing policy to buy a new one before getting a second opinion. Life insurance agents receive a hefty commission when they sell new policies, so it is tempting for them to encourage you to use the surrender value of one policy to pay for a new one. For a forty-dollar fee, the Consumer Federation of America Insurance Group will compare your current policy with the new one you are considering. Call them at (202) 387-6121.

Never buy life insurance to pay your mortgage when you die, unless you have serious health problems that make other insurance unobtainable. Credit life policies are invariably more expensive than the same amount of declining term insurance, which does not build up cash value and has lesser face amounts each year.

A new feature of some life insurance policies is the before-death option. This "living insurance" allows you to receive a monthly payment of 2 percent of the policy's cash value if you are in a nursing home. Living insurance policies are often more expensive than regular insurance policies, so compare prices carefully. Some insurance policies now have an accelerated death benefit clause that allows you to receive a lump-sum payment of your death benefit if you are terminally ill or permanently confined to a nursing home and have six months or less to live.

SMART TIP

TURN DOWN NO-TURNDOWN LIFE INSURANCE

Beware of the no-turndown life insurance policies advertised on television. The policies are very expensive and are best suited for those who are extremely elderly or terminally ill. With most of those policies, in order to receive the full face value you must have been a policy holder for a number of years. For example, if you die after holding the policy for just one year, your beneficiary would receive only 15 to 25 percent of the payout; during the second year, a typical payout might be 30 to 50 percent. If you are healthy, you will also find that the premium is very, very high. In addition, the death benefit is often only $10,000 or so, and the policy does not build up cash value, so all of your premiums are lost if you drop the policy.

Another insurance to avoid is dread disease insurance, which covers only one illness or just a few. You are far better off with a comprehensive medical policy that covers every illness, since you have no way of knowing your future health.

You Can Use Life Insurance to Increase Retirement Benefits

> When Dad was ready to retire, an insurance salesman tried to talk him into something called pension maximization. But it would have required Mom to give up her right to pension income after Dad died, and she didn't want to do that. (Stan C., age forty-four)

One way to increase retirement benefits is to forego the joint and survivor annuity option on your retirement plan. This is called pension maximization, and here's how it works:

Under a normal joint and survivor annuity, the couple will receive a benefit while the employed spouse is alive, and upon his or her death the survivor will receive a survivor benefit, generally about 50 percent of the previous monthly payment. If the spouse waives his or her right to survivor benefits, the benefit paid while the employed spouse is alive will be greater, but no benefit will be paid after his or her death.

Obviously, that would be a hardship for the surviving spouse unless there is some other source of funds. That's where a life insurance policy would be useful.

You may find that you can purchase a life insurance policy on the employed spouse that will provide benefits when he or she dies, and that the premiums for such a policy will be less than the step-down in benefits. For example, if the additional benefits you'd receive would be $500 a month and the insurance premium would be only $300 a month, pension maximization makes sense. But if the reverse is true, pension maximization is obviously not beneficial.

SMART TIP

INSURE BEFORE YOU SURRENDER

Before you agree to waive survivor benefits in favor of a higher pension and purchase a life insurance policy, be sure the amount of life insurance is great enough to fund the survivor's needs. Be certain also that by giving up pension benefits for your spouse, you are not giving up cost-of-living adjustments or medical benefits for him or her that will be difficult to duplicate in any insurance scenario.

Long-Term-Care (Nursing Home) Insurance

Under Medicare, you will be eligible for twenty days of skilled nursing home coverage if you enter within thirty days after a three-day hospital stay. But Medicare doesn't cover long-term care. For that reason, more and more seniors, almost 3.5 million in 1995 according to a survey, are buying long-term-care insurance. The number of policies issued has increased more than 25 percent a year for the past eight years. Not only is the need for the insurance increasing, but premiums are decreasing, which makes long-term-care insurance more affordable. These two trends are likely to continue as our population grays. As modern medicine makes longer lives possible, chronic illness affects more and more of us. For some people, that chronic illness will force them into nursing homes. A third of the population eighty-five and older is in a nursing home of some sort, in part because of increasing inability of family members to care for their elderly ill.

Nursing home coverage, referred to as long-term care, can be very expensive and may not be essential. It is estimated that two out of every five people over sixty-five will spend time in a nursing home, but half will stay six months or less and most of the rest will spend less than three years there. If you have the money and want the coverage, here is what to look for:

- A policy that does not require a hospital stay before entering the care facility. Only 46 percent of nursing home residents were hospitalized prior to entering the nursing home.
- The right to collect no matter what skill level of care you are receiving.
- A policy that pays at least eighty dollars a day for three years. Only 11 percent of nursing home residents stay more than three years.
- Inflation protection, so that the coverage increases as nursing home costs go up.
- Coverage for mental diseases such as Alzheimer's.
- Home-health-care and adult-day-care coverage.
- Noncancelable coverage rather than just "guaranteed renewable," which still gives the company the right to cancel your policy or raise your costs.

Estate Planning—It's More than Writing a Will

> I guess I knew that I was really growing up when I learned to say "When I die" rather than "If I die." (Glenn C., age fifty-two)

It's never easy to think about death, whether it's your own or that of a loved one. That's the reason so many of us procrastinate when it comes to estate planning.

Realizing that we are not immortal can come as a shock. Imagining the death of a spouse can make us aware of the pain, grief, feelings of abandonment, and even anger that might come with such a loss. Often the spouse who has been less involved in family finances may experience tremendous fear about how he or she would cope without the other. This is when feelings of inadequacy can surface uncomfortably.

It is important to acknowledge that all of these feelings are very normal. But do not let them hold you back from putting in place an estate plan that assures that your wishes will be met when you are not around.

Begin by talking openly and honestly with your spouse and hearing what he or she has to say as well. Consult with a competent estate-planning attorney who can tell you what your options are and the best ways to accomplish what you want.

When it comes to estate planning, most people are confused. They cope with that confusion by making plans that are either too simple or too complex. Erring on the simple side, they leave everything to their spouse, with no regard for saving income taxes or probate costs and estate taxes. Those whose wills are too complex leave things mired in a cobweb of trusts that are difficult to interpret and impossible to live with.

Estate planning does not have to be difficult. As a matter of fact, even if you have done nothing, some of your estate planning has been done for you. For example, any assets that you own in joint tenancy with another, such as your home, will pass to the surviving tenant upon your death. Anything that you own in beneficiary form, such as life insurance, retirement plans, and IRAs, will pass to the beneficiary that you have named. So even if you don't have a will, the disposition of those assets has been taken care of. Even if you do have a will, it will not govern those assets in joint names with survivorship rights or in beneficiary form.

Writing Your Will

> Everything I have is going to go to Rosemary when I die, because she's my wife. So why do I need a will? (Leonard S., age fifty-one)

Wills can be either simple or complex. With the most simple will, you name an executor for your estate and a guardian for your children, and leave everything to your beneficiary, often your spouse—hence the nickname "I Love You" will. The simple will has two advantages: It is easy to write and understand, and if you leave everything to your spouse, there will be no estate taxes due immediately. That is because, in addition to a $600,000 exemption, the estate laws allow an unlimited marital deduction for anything you leave to a spouse. However, if your surviving spouse dies with more than $600,000 of net estate, then his or her estate will have to pay estate taxes, which range between 35 and 55 percent. Because these tax rates are so high, and because they are applied to money on which you already paid income tax during your life, the estate tax is considered very cruel by many. Administrative and probate costs are heaped on top of estate taxes too, so even less money passes to your heirs. For those reasons, many people go to extraordinary lengths to save estate taxes and administrative expenses.

If your estate is under $600,000 and fairly straightforward, you may be able to write your will yourself. A number of computer software kits are available, including *Willmaker* (NOLO Press), *Willbuilder* (Sybar Software), *Expert Will* (Expert Software), *It's Legal* (Parsons Technology), *Home Lawyer* (Mecca Software), *Personal Law Firm* (Bloc Publishing), and *WillPower* (Jacobi and Meyers).

Making Gifts

If you are planning to make gifts to your heirs to reduce your estate, consider giving away property that increases in value each year. In that way it will increase in their estate rather than in yours. If it increases in your estate it will only cause your estate to pay more taxes when you die. By giving it to them it will increase in their estate, not bulking up yours.

You may also want to give away property that does not create income, that would be hard to liquidate, and that you rarely use. For example, gifting a portion of your artwork or jewelry will transfer assets from your estate without reducing your income or lifetime enjoyment.

If your property has gone up in value, you might consider one advantage of *not* giving it away. Under current law, when you die, the appreciated property will get a step up in cost basis to its value on the day of your death. That cost basis represents the amount that is not taxable, so your heirs can sell the property at that value without paying any capital gains tax. However, if you have appreciated assets that you plan to sell while you are alive, you may wish to transfer them to family members in a lower tax bracket than yours, as they will pay less tax on the sale. And if you have investment property that has lost value over the years, you should sell it and claim the investment loss. If you keep it until your death, the property's cost basis will step down to its value on the date of your death and the tax loss will be lost.

Charitable Gifts Save Taxes

You may not be able to have your cake and eat it too, but you can give money to a charity and yet keep some benefits. Many charities have a pooled income fund from which they will pay you income for life in exchange for your gift. You make a gift to the charity, for which you'll receive an income tax deduction equal to the value of the gift less the value of the lifetime income you'll be receiving. The gift will be out of your taxable estate, so it won't be taxed when you die, and if you donate securities or real estate that has gone up in value, your gift will be based on the current value and you will not have to pay capital gains tax on the untaxed appreciation of the property while you held it. The income you receive will depend on the income that the fund earns during your lifetime.

The pooled income approach is an excellent way of getting income from non-income-paying securities or real estate that has appreciated. To obtain income in any other way, you would have to sell the appreciated property and pay capital gains tax on the increase in value. By donating it to a charity, you will get a hefty charitable deduction, escape the capital gains tax, and receive income for life.

SMART TIP

REPLACE GIFTS WITH INSURANCE

If you wish to make a gift to charity and yet don't want to diminish your estate, purchase a life insurance policy that will pay your heirs an amount equivalent to your gift to charity.

Probate

> There are all those books written about how to avoid probate. If probate is so bad, why don't they just do away with it? (Lucille T., age forty-eight)

The probate system exists to make sure that all of your debts and taxes are paid when you die and that your assets are distributed according to your wishes or the laws of your state, if you die without a will. Probate can take time, so it takes longer for your heirs to get their assets, but the terms of the will can take place immediately. Once you die, the executor of your will is required to begin the proceeding by notifying the probate court of your death.

Probate can be avoided in a number of ways. In most states, small estates or estates in which everything is left to the surviving spouse are not subject to probate or are subject only to a simplified probate that is not very expensive. The probate court will not have jurisdiction over anything held in joint tenancy with right of survivorship or in beneficiary form, nor will the court have jurisdiction over assets placed in trust. If your estate can bypass probate for any of these reasons, you may wish to put your assets in a living trust to sidestep probate. Any assets titled in the name of your living trust will not go through probate and will therefore not be subject to probate fees. You may want to have a pour-over clause in your will that transfers, or "pours over," any assets that are in your name into the trust when you die.

Living Trusts

A living trust is revocable, so you can put assets into it, take them out, or change beneficiaries during your lifetime. Any assets not titled in the name of your living trust will be governed by the terms of your will. For that reason it is important to coordinate the terms of your trust and the terms of your will, and to be sure that you title assets in the name of the living trust if you want them to be subject to the terms of that trust and to avoid probate (though they won't escape estate taxes).

Once you have set up your living trust, you must fund it. Funding the trust is the most important part of setting up a trust, because the trust is useful only if you have changed your property title to reflect the living trust as the owner. Otherwise the trust won't control it and you will have wasted your money.

You may decide to let your attorney take care of titling the assets, but if you want to reduce costs, you can retitle most of the assets yourself. Your attorney can give you an example of a letter you can send to your bank, financial adviser, mutual fund companies, insurance companies, and others. In that letter, you will tell them in what name the assets should be retitled and give them your authority to make the change. To begin the retitling process, make a list of every asset you own that needs to be retitled, and then list the date on which you sent the letter requesting the retitling and the date on which you received confirmation that the retitling was complete. Create this kind of list even if your attorney is taking care of the details for you—it is far easier for you to be sure that the retitling is done correctly than for your heirs to sue the attorney for malpractice.

Generally, real estate is transferred by the use of a deed. Although the format varies from state to state, the deed will tell how the property is currently titled, it will tell how it should be titled in the future, and it will provide a legal description of the property. The deed will need to be signed, notarized, and recorded where the property is located. You may contact the county recorder's office for detailed information, or have a title company or an attorney in that state handle the transaction for you. Some states may charge a fee for transferring the property.

Retitling your home should not cause any problems with your mortgage company, but you should notify the mortgage holder of your actions. Also be sure to notify the insurance company that title is now in the name of the living trust, so that your policy can be changed accordingly.

To name the trust as the owner or beneficiary of your life insurance, contact your insurance agent for the proper papers. The designated beneficiary for employer-provided life insurance can be changed by contacting the employee benefits department.

Notes that are owed to you can be assigned by you to the trust by an assignment that you have notarized and attached to the original note. The assignment does not require the signature of the other party, but if the original note was recorded, as a mortgage might be, then you will probably want to record the assignment as well.

To change checking and savings accounts and CDs, you will need to sign new signature cards at the bank. You can continue to sign the signature card and the checks with your usual signature, and print your own name, address, and telephone number on the checks, without any indication of the trust.

To change the name on your brokerage account, the broker will probably need a copy of the trust document, a letter of instruction, and a signature guarantee that they can provide. If you hold stock certificates, you will need to sign a stock power assigning the securities to the trust and send it to the transfer agent for the company (any brokerage house can provide this information for you). If you have lost the stock certificate, you will need to sign an affidavit of lost certificate before the transfer can be made.

To change ownership of savings bonds, call the Federal Reserve Bank at 800-245-2804 and request the proper forms.

Most states will allow you to change the title for your vehicles to the name of the trust, but some states will impose a transfer tax if you do so. If your state imposes such a tax, you may want to wait until you purchase your next car and title it in the name of the trust. If you change the title to your vehicle, be sure to notify the insurance company.

For valuable personal property that is not titled, your attorney can prepare a bill of sale or an assignment to effect the transfer.

If you have an interest in a limited partnership, the general partner can provide you the form you need to assign your interest to the trust.

You can make your living trust the beneficiary of your retirement plans, but if you are married, you may not want to. If your living trust is the beneficiary of your plan, then the plan will have to be liquidated upon your death, and income taxes will have to be paid at that time. But if your spouse is the beneficiary, your spouse will be able to roll over the proceeds into his or her own IRA, thus delaying the payment of taxes until the money is actually withdrawn. A good solution is to name your spouse as your first beneficiary and the living trust as your second. To change the beneficiary of your employer-sponsored plan, simply contact the employee benefits department. To change the beneficiary of your IRA, SEP, or Keogh plan, contact the custodial institution where the account is located.

Other Trusts

> I know that a living trust won't save estate taxes. Do I need to set up some sort of trust that does? (Eileen K., age forty-nine)

If your estate, or your combined estate with your spouse, is over $600,000, you may want to do some estate planning by using trusts. Here's how it works. Let's say that you and your spouse have a $1 million estate. If you live in a community property state, your spouse will probably be the owner of half of the estate, or $500,000, and you will own the other half. Thus, when you die, your will can govern only your half of the estate. If you live in a non–community property state, then your will should govern whatever portion of the property that you own. If you leave your entire estate to your spouse, when she dies, her estate will be $1 million, and the estate will owe taxes on the excess over $600,000. Those taxes are approximately $150,000. However, if you leave your half of the estate in trust for your children, when your spouse dies, she will have an estate of only $500,000, which will not be subject to taxes because it is below the $600,000 exemption amount. That type of trust, called a bypass trust, provides that the income from the trust will go to your spouse, and she can also tap any principal she needs for her health, education, support, or maintenance. The beneficiaries won't receive anything until she dies. You can leave up to $600,000 tax-free in a bypass trust, and the rest of your estate can be left outright to your spouse.

> I love Carolyn and I want her to be financially secure after I die, but I want my money ultimately to go to my children, not to hers. (Edward L., age fifty-two)

If you do not want your present spouse to be the primary beneficiary of your estate, you can use a QTIP trust. For example, if you are in a second marriage and you would like your assets to support your current spouse but ultimately go to your children, a qualified terminable interest property trust is perfect for you. You will still use the bypass trust, but instead of leaving the rest of your estate to your spouse, you can leave it in a QTIP trust. That trust will generally provide that the income from the trust will go to your surviving spouse, with property going to your children. The only difference between the QTIP trust and the bypass trust is that it will be taxable in your spouse's estate when she dies.

Life Insurance Trusts

Another type of trust you might find useful is the life insurance trust. Remember that the face value of life insurance is ordinarily a taxable part of your estate. That is true if you are the owner of the policy or your estate is the beneficiary of the policy. However, if a third party is the owner of the policy, then the proceeds won't be a part of your estate. So make a life insurance trust the owner of the policy, and each year you can fund the trust with annual gifts to pay the premiums.

Be careful, though. If you transfer existing life insurance policies into a trust and you die within three years of the transfer, the proceeds

---

SMART TIP

DON'T OWN LIFE INSURANCE

If you own your own life insurance policy, you may have a problem. The proceeds will be a part of your taxable estate, and if the value of your estate is over $600,000, the excess will be subject to federal estate taxes of 37 to 55 percent.

There are two solutions:

1. You can transfer the existing policies to someone else, such as a child, and continue making the premium payments as a gift to the new owner of the policy. But if you die within three years of transferring the policy, the proceeds will be taxed in your estate.
2. You can set up a trust to own your life insurance policies. Your insurance trust can make provisions for payout of death benefits to a group of beneficiaries, and it can also pay the taxes on your estate.

---

of the life insurance will be a part of your taxable estate. Here is how it works. Assume that your estate will be taxable, and so you decide to purchase a life insurance policy to pay the taxes. If the taxes will be $200,000, you will need a policy for $200,000. But if you purchase it with yourself as the owner or your estate as the beneficiary, you've just compounded your problems, because you have now increased your estate by another $200,000, which will increase the taxes by $100,000 or so. That means you'll need even more insurance!

To get off that financial merry-go-round, purchase the policy in the name of a life insurance trust and make the trust the beneficiary. Each year you can gift the trust up to $10,000 to pay the premiums, and when you die, the trust will receive the proceeds. But wait! Your estate will need the proceeds to pay estate taxes. That's easy enough to accomplish: Just have the life insurance trust purchase some of the assets from the estate for the cash. The life insurance trust can then distribute the assets to your beneficiary, and your estate has the cash with which to pay the taxes.

Now that you have all of the pieces of your retirement puzzle in place—retirement plans, continuing career options, lifestyle choices, insurance, and estate planning—it is time to begin your countdown to retirement.

12

Countdown to Retirement

> I never knew that getting ready for retirement would be so much work. I always thought I'd just retire, and that would be that. (Joe P., age sixty-two)

Most of us grew up thinking that retirees lived on a pension check that came directly from the company for which they worked all their lives. That pension check came month after month, year after year. But these days, many employer plans give you a choice of whether to leave the money with the company, take it as a lump sum, or transfer it to your IRA. With the erosion of many company plans, you may find that you have to save additional money for retirement in savings accounts, mutual funds, and stocks and bonds. As you approach retirement, you must make a myriad of decisions regarding investing the money, housing, continuing your career part time, insurance, and estate planning.

Whether you are going to work part time in retirement or you plan a full-blown retirement, the closer you get to your retirement date, the more concentrated must be your planning for your next fifty years. Not only must you review your retirement plans and rearrange your funds, you'll also need to adjust and monitor your other investments. It's time to pay close attention to your Social Security record, to plan for continuing medical insurance, to decide where you are going to live and what to do with your house. If you plan to continue to work in retirement, you must lay a firm foundation for your future career. The chart on pages 234–35 shows you what you should do if your retirement is five years or more away and the steps you should take as your retirement date gets closer. In the pages that follow, we discuss these tips more fully.

Five Years or More to Retirement

If you are five years or further from retirement, you have time to get your house in order and to plan carefully for your future. Your financial life may be complicated by kids in college and parents needing help, so you may need to postpone retirement until those expenses lessen. As you plan for retirement, prepare *two* budgets—one for today's expenses and a projected one for your retirement years. As you move toward retirement, your current expenses should dwindle to your projected retirement levels.

> Randy and I are talking about retiring in seven years. We sat down and figured out what our expenses will be, and we are right on track for having enough money for the $5,000 a month we projected we'd need. The problem is, we're now spending over $8,000 a month, so I'm not so sure our retirement budget is realistic. I think we'd better practice living on $5,000 a month to see how it feels, or else delay retirement so we can sock some more away. (Candy S., age forty-six)

Before you can project your retirement expenses, you must decide where you are going to live. Will you keep your current house or sell it? If you keep it, should you remodel to make it livable for years into the future? If so, now is the time to borrow the money for remodeling, while you are employed and will qualify for a loan. Remodeling early will also give you adequate time to pay for the expenses so you won't be stuck with the loan payments after you retire.

Just as important as saving money for retirement is investing it wisely. Don't be too conservative with the money that you won't need for ten years or longer, or you'll have difficulty outpacing inflation. You won't draw out all of the money to spend it on the day you retire, so remember, you are still a long-term investor even though your retirement may be only five years away.

Project your retirement income by talking to your employee benefits office at work to see what benefits you can expect to receive at your targeted retirement date. Find out what medical benefits you will receive,

COUNTDOWN TO RETIREMENT

Category	Now to Five Years Before Retirement	Two Years Before Retirement	Three Months Before Retirement	In Retirement
Cash flow	Write out two budgets—one with current expenses, the other with expected expenses in retirement. Plan to pay off debts by retirement.	Update your current and future budgets. Get debts paid off, except mortgage.	Consider paying off mortgage. Delete career expenses and add any new retiree expenses.	Fine-tune your cash flow plan every year so that your projected spending matches your actual spending.
Investments	Use computer programs to project retirement needs and investment returns. Discuss with a financial planner your goals and how to adjust your asset mix to meet them.	Adjust the balance between growth and income investments to reduce your market risk and increase income.	Keep at least 50% in equities to offset inflation. Include international funds for diversification.	Keep at least 30% of your money in stocks to offset inflation and provide growth.
Defined-benefit retirement plan	Ask your benefits office to project your pension in monthly and lump-sum payments.	Evaluate how best to take your pension; if as a lump-sum, decide how to invest it.	Make plans for a trustee-to-trustee rollover into an IRA. Purchase the investments you have chosen for your lump sum.	Invest your lump sum immediately to avoid the tax consequences.
401(k), Keogh, or other tax-deferred retirement plans	Put the maximum in your plan. Wait as long as possible to tap the money so earnings grow tax-deferred.	Keep contributing the maximum. If you will take a lump sum, ask an accountant how to minimize taxes.	Decide how to take your money. At $59^1/_2$, you may start penalty-free lump-sum withdrawals.	At $70^1/_2$, you may have to start minimum withdrawals from all tax-deferred retirement plans.

Category	Now to Five Years Before Retirement	Two Years Before Retirement	Three Months Before Retirement	In Retirement
Social Security	Check your earnings by sending Form 7004 to your local Social Security office. Be sure your employers contributed the right amounts.	Double-check your account by sending your local Social Security office another Form 7004.	Decide when after age 62 to start receiving Social Security.	At age 70, there is no limit on the income you can earn without reducing your Social Security benefits.
Medical insurance	Check into long-term–care coverage. Ask your benefits office what your medical benefits will be in retirement.	If you need individual coverage, start shopping for it now.	Apply for the coverage one month prior to retiring.	Medicare starts at 65. Six months before then, shop for Medigap insurance.
Emergency fund	Put amount equal to three months' expenses in a money market fund.	Set up (or renew) a home-equity line of credit that you can tap in case of an emergency.	Your cash and home-equity line of credit should amount to one full year of expenses.	Keep one year's expenses in the fund; tap it only when you must.
House—Sell vs. keep	Decide whether to keep your present house or sell it. If you sell, decide whether to buy another or rent.	If you plan to move after retiring, visit potential locations during vacations.	If you are selling, put your house on the market three to six months before retirement.	Do not sell your house until you are 55 unless you are buying another. Take the one-time capital-gains tax exemption on the sale.
House—Repairs and improvements	Renovate now; it's easier to borrow if you're employed.	Budget now for any big-ticket repairs you may need after you retire.		
Career	Decide if you are going to work in retirement. If so, begin preparing for your second career.	Establish network. Check out potential jobs. To see if you like a career, try it on weekends and vacations.	Set up home office. Begin your new career.	Continue networking for clients and referral sources. Establish goals and business plans.

and then investigate the cost of additional medical insurance that you may need to make up the gap in Medicare coverage. This is a good time to look into long-term-care insurance, which will protect you if you have to enter a nursing home. The earlier you take out long-term-care insurance, the lower the premiums you can expect to pay.

Send Form 7004 to the Social Security Administration so you can check to be sure that they have credited your account with the proper earnings over the years. If any of the information is wrong—$0 wages reported in a year you were employed, for example, or only partial wages for a year you changed jobs midway in the year (maybe wages for only one job were posted)—contact them right away and correct your record.

Two Years Before Retirement

Not much time is left, so financially, it's time to straighten up and fly right. If debts are a problem for you, reduce expenses so you can make extra payments toward that debt. Make a two-year plan to become debt-free so you don't enter retirement with a slew of credit card debt hanging over your head. If you need to buy a new car or replace the carpet or appliances, do it now so that you can pay for the bulk of those items from your income before retirement.

Adjust your investments to reduce the risk on money that you will need in two to five years. To do this, move a portion of your portfolio out of growth stocks and invest in income stocks, bonds, and mutual funds. Keep in mind, though, that you'll not need all funds liquid at any one time. Because inflation erodes the value of fixed-income investments over time, you'll want to move funds from growth to income investments slowly, on an as-needed basis. For example, you may decide that you need enough safe, liquid investments to support one to two years of expenses. Perhaps you'll want to move the money first into an intermediate-term bond fund and later into a series of CDs that will mature every six months, providing you with enough cash for the next six months' expenses.

Ask your employee benefits department to update the figures on how much your retirement stash will be worth when you retire, and decide whether you will take your pension in monthly installments or as a lump sum. You will probably want to consult a financial planner or an accountant who is experienced in helping people make these decisions, to be sure that you make the decision that best minimizes your future taxes.

Check again on your Social Security record by filing another Form 7004. If you found errors the last time you checked, make sure they have been corrected and that all new earnings have been posted to your account.

A projection of your retirement income is very important at this stage. Recompute what you expect to receive from retirement plans and investments, and recompute your retirement expenses. If you plan to fill in the gap with continued employment, begin exploring in earnest your options for employment in retirement. If you are thinking of a new part-time career that you've never tried before, explore it by actually working in the field on weekends or vacations, even if it is as an unpaid apprentice. If you will need additional education or skills updated, enroll in the course work now. Network with others in the field so that you will be able to connect with those who can use your services when the time comes.

Three Months Before Retirement

Excited? You're almost there! Start thinking retired. No, we don't mean you should go fishing rather than to work, but rather, you should move financially toward your new lifestyle. If you've been employed in an office, resist the temptation to update your fall wardrobe of suits and fancy dresses. You won't need those clothes in retirement. If you will be leaving work entirely or changing careers, don't renew your professional publications. If you plan to take courses at the local university or to travel, send off for the college catalogs and talk to a travel agent.

Begin the paperwork to finalize your retirement plans. If you will be receiving payments from your employer, be sure that you have completed the correct forms for the employee benefits office. If you will roll the money into an IRA, establish that IRA account in advance and decide how the funds will be invested when you receive them.

File another Form 7004 to ensure your Social Security earnings record is correct. If you expect to begin receiving them immediately, apply for your Social Security benefits. Remember that if you intend to work more than minimally, your benefits will be reduced, so you might be better off delaying benefits until you are seventy and can collect them without reduction for earned income.

Keep enough money in liquid investments (savings, CDs, and short-term bonds) to fund the income you will need for the next year or so. Review the allocations recommended in chapter 4, and invest the rest of your money partly as recommended in "Two Years to Retirement" and the balance as recommended for the longer term in "Ten Years to Retirement." The younger you are, the greater the percentage of your portfolio you should have invested with the long term in mind.

If you are selling your home, it's time to put it on the market. If buying a new home or moving to a new location, scout out your new surroundings and begin the house-hunting process.

If your employer will continue to provide medical insurance to you as a retirement benefit, that's great. Otherwise it is time to decide on medical coverage and complete the application process.

By now your debts should be paid off. To reduce your expenses, if your mortgage is not large, consider paying it off from funds you have saved or will receive at retirement. Sure, you'll eliminate a tax deduction for the mortgage interest when you pay off the mortgage, but remember that your tax savings amount to only about one-third of the payment you make, so by paying off the mortgage, even though your taxes will increase, you'll cut your overall expenses considerably.

SMART TIP

SHOULD YOU PAY OFF YOUR MORTGAGE?

Compare the interest rate you are paying on your mortgage with the rate of return on your long-term investments. If your mortgage interest rate is higher than the rate of return on your investments, use the money to pay off your mortgage and reduce your expenses.

Money Management in Retirement

Retirement isn't just an event, it's a way of life. You'll never be able to retire from smart money management. After retirement, you'll need to budget just as diligently as you did before. Adjust your budget every year to accommodate the activities you expect to enjoy, and adjust your investments to keep them within the asset allocation parameters you have set for your portfolio. Be sure to keep at least one year's income needs available at all times. Don't convert your entire portfolio to liquid assets, though, or you'll run out of money before your time runs out.

If you have retired early, you will probably continue to work part time, or perhaps you will take a break from working and go back into the workforce for a while later on. Either way, continue to update your skills so that you will be able to make the most of your employment.

Age Matters

Your age is critical in planning for income in retirement. If you retire early at fifty-five or younger, your retirement income options are limited, but if you wait until sixty-five you'll have a greater latitude for income sources. Delay your retirement past seventy and you'll have to draw some retirement income even if you don't need it. Here are the ages that are important in designing your retirement income.

Age Fifty-five

Profit-sharing plans, Keoghs, 401(k) plans. Once you are retired from work, you can begin receiving payments from these plans without penalty.

IRAs. You can begin receiving "annuitized" payments from an IRA at any age, as long as they continue until age fifty-nine and a half and are for at least five years. (See page 116.)

Personal residence. This is your opportunity to scale down your living quarters. Once you are fifty-five, you can exclude from taxation up to $125,000 of profit from selling your home.

Age Fifty-nine and a Half

IRAs, SEPs, and Keogh plans. You can begin receiving payments from these plans without penalty, even if you continue working.

Age Sixty-two

Social Security. You can receive reduced benefits if you retire early (but you aren't eligible for Medicare until you reach sixty-five or older).

Age Sixty-five

Social Security. You can receive full benefits (age sixty-six to sixty-seven for those born after 1942).

Medicare. You are eligible for Medicare at sixty-five, even if you have not yet retired.

Age Seventy and a Half

IRAs, Keoghs, SEPs. You must begin taking minimum benefits by April of the year after you turn seventy and a half to avoid penalty.

Social Security—The Government Giveth, Then Taketh

Your Social Security income will depend on several factors, including your earnings during your lifetime and the number of years over which those earnings were spread. But you will find that your current earnings have an impact as well. You sacrifice one dollar of benefits for every three dollars you earn in retirement if your income is over $13,500, and if you are under sixty-five, you lose one dollar for each two dollars you earn over $8,640. But there's good news if you are seventy or older: You can earn as much as you like and still collect your full Social Security benefits.

Most people assume you must begin collecting Social Security benefits once you are sixty-five to sixty-seven, but that isn't the case. If you wait until you are older, you will receive an additional 8 percent per year for every year you delay beyond age sixty-five. (If you were born before 1943, the percentage for each year is smaller.) That means that you'll benefit twofold by working until you are seventy rather than sixty-five. Not only will you receive the additional percentage each year, but your wage base will increase as well, and so your regular benefits will be higher.

Of course, the opposite is true if you retire earlier than sixty-five—your earning years will be less and so will your benefits. They will be reduced by 20 to 30 percent if you retire at age sixty-two, depending on what year you were born.

Retirement Income Choices

You'll need to make some decisions regarding the income you will receive from your retirement plan. You have three choices when it comes to receiving retirement income:

1. Receive regular monthly payments from your pension and pay taxes on the payments as you receive them.
2. Transfer the money from a pension into an IRA, from which you will periodically take payments and pay taxes on those payments.
3. Take the pension in a lump sum and pay taxes all at once, using five-year forward averaging, if received before the year 2000.

Under options one or three, your employer will withhold 20 percent of the payment for tax withholding. That withholding will be claimed as a tax payment on your income tax return, just as the withholding on your wages is.

Paying Estimated Tax

Be aware that even though the payments you receive from your IRA will not have withholding taken out, they are still taxable. The government requires that the taxes you owe on the IRA income and other income for which there is no withholding at the source be paid in quarterly estimated tax payments. These payments are due on April 15, June 15, September 15, and January 15 of the following year. Alternatively, if you are still employed, you can ask your employer to increase the withholding from your paycheck to cover the additional taxes due. Simply file a new W-4 withholding allowance form with your employer directing that additional taxes be withheld from each paycheck.

SMART TIP

HOW TO COMPUTE ESTIMATED TAX PAYMENTS

To compute the amount of estimated tax payments or extra withholding required, jot your estimate of this year's income and deductions in the margin of a copy of last year's income tax return. Using the tax rates for the current year (see the instructions for Form 1040-ES for estimated tax payments), calculate the taxes on your estimated taxable income. Subtract from that amount your estimate of withholding for the year and estimated tax payments already made. The result is the additional taxes you will owe for the year. Divide that amount by the remaining estimated tax installment dates or by the number of pay periods remaining for the year. That figure is the amount of estimated tax you must pay for each remaining installment of estimated tax, or the amount of extra withholding you should request of your employer.

Although making accurate calculations is important, the IRS does allow you a 10 percent leeway. But if you fail to pay at least 90 percent of the income taxes you will owe for the year through withholding and estimated tax payments, you will incur a tax penalty for failure to pay estimated income taxes, unless you rate an exception because your withholding plus estimated tax payments for the year equals your total tax for the prior year.

You may have to pay state income taxes on your income as well as federal income tax, if you live in one of the states that imposes a state income tax. Several states have no income taxes, including Alaska, Florida, Nevada, South Dakota, Texas, Washington, and Wyoming. Many states that impose a personal income tax exempt all or part of your private pension income from that tax. Those states include Arkansas, Colorado, Delaware, Georgia, Hawaii, Louisiana, Maryland, Michigan, Minnesota, Mississippi, Montana, New Jersey, New York, Pennsylvania, South Carolina, Tennessee, Utah, Virginia, and West Virginia. Even if you live in one of the states that fully taxes private pension income, you may escape state tax if your retirement income is from a federal or state government pension. That's because most states exempt at least part of federal and state government pensions from taxation. In addition, only half of the states tax Social Security benefits.

What's Taxed, and What's Not

> My grandmother was surprised to hear that in America, people pay taxes all their lives. In the old country, once you were seventy you didn't have to pay taxes anymore. (Celeste F., age thirty-eight)

Taxes are a fact of life, even during retirement. Retiring from work doesn't mean you retire from paying taxes, but you may not be paying as much in taxes after you retire as you pay right now. Some of your Social Security income will go untaxed, as will the income from certain investments, such as municipal bonds. If you made contributions to pension plans for which you did not get a tax deduction, when those contributions are returned to you in the form of plan benefits, they will be tax-free. The same is true of the return of your original contributions to an annuity.

Salary income, of course, is taxable. Income you receive from working for yourself is also taxable, and the taxes hurt much more than those you pay on salary income. The tax pinch is greater because you owe both income taxes and self-employment tax on that income. In addition, you have to fork it over to the government voluntarily, rather than it being extracted automatically, as it is when you receive paychecks.

Your Social Security benefits will be taxed if your total income exceeds $32,000 if you are married or $25,000 if you are single. You will pay tax on one-half of the amount of Social Security benefits you receive, but if your income is over $44,000 ($34,000 if single), 85 percent of your Social Security benefits will be taxable.

The withdrawals you made from your IRA accounts will be taxable unless you have made contributions to nondeductible IRAs. In that case a portion of each withdrawal you make will be tax-free. If you are under fifty-nine and a half, you will also have to pay a 10 percent penalty tax on all IRA withdrawals, unless you annuitize the payments (see page 116).

Pension income is also taxable to you, whether you receive it in monthly payments or in one lump sum. The only way to escape income taxes is to take the lump sum and immediately deposit it into an IRA. If you decide to take a lump sum and pay all of the taxes at once, you can use a method called five-year forward averaging to figure your tax, so long as you receive the payments before the year 2000. That method lets you calculate your tax as though you had received it over a five-year period, thus lowering the tax rate. The five years is hypothetical, though—you must pay all of the taxes in the year you take the lump sum. But be aware that taking the lump sum and paying taxes on it all at once will reduce the funds you have invested for your retirement. It is generally best to roll the money into an IRA and delay the taxation as long as you can.

SMART TIP

LUMP-SUM ROLLOVERS

If you receive a lump sum when you leave a job but you intend to become employed again, don't mingle the funds you receive from your old employer with any other IRA funds, or you won't be able to roll them into your new employer's plan. Once you roll the money into your new employer's plan, you may be able to borrow from the plan if it allows loans. You can never borrow money from an IRA.

Excise Taxes

As though income taxes weren't enough, you are subject to a 15 percent excise tax if your combined payout from all of your retirement plans is over $155,000 a year. You will also pay an excise tax if you receive a lump-sum distribution from your retirement plan of $775,000 or more and you don't roll it into an IRA. (These excise taxes are suspended for distributions received in 1997, 1998, and 1999.) Just keeping the money in the plan until you die won't work either; there is an excise tax imposed if your plan is worth $775,000 or more when you die. Most employer plans require that you begin taking distributions when you retire, and under federal tax laws you must begin taking minimum payments by the time you are seventy and a half. Those payments are calculated actuarially, depending on your age and the age of your beneficiary.

Minimum Required Distributions from Retirement Plans

When you turn seventy and a half, you must begin taking payments from your retirement plans, whether or not you need the money, unless you continue to be employed. The amount of the payment is calculated based on your life expectancy according to IRS tables at the time of the distribution, and there is a 50 percent excise tax if you fail to take the payments.

Your annual distribution is calculated by dividing the balance in the account at the beginning of the year by the life expectancy of the owner, or the combined life expectancies of the owner and the designated beneficiary. If you are trying to defer the taxation of the money for as long as possible, you may choose to use the joint lives of yourself and a younger beneficiary. For beneficiaries other than your spouse, the payments will be calculated as though the beneficiary were no more than ten years younger than you are, no matter what the beneficiary's age.

For example, Harvey is seventy and his daughter Eleanor, age thirty-six, is his beneficiary. Harvey has accumulated $1 million in retirement plans, and he must now begin taking minimum payments. For the purpose of this calculation, his daughter's age will be presumed to be sixty, so their combined life expectancy is 26.2 years. That means Harvey must take an annual distribution of $38,168 ($1 million divided by 26.2 years).

If Eleanor were Harvey's thirty-six-year-old spouse instead of his daughter, he could use her actual age for calculation of the joint lives. That results in a joint life expectancy of 40.6 years, so Harvey would be required to take an annual distribution of only $24,630 ($1 million divided by 40.6 years).

If you die before you begin receiving payments from the retirement plan or before you reach the required minimum distribution date, the balance in the account must be distributed within five years after your death or over the beneficiary's life.

Investing in Retirement

Don't invest conservatively for income, thinking you'll preserve the principal and live off the income only. You are far wiser to stratify your investments so that at least 50 percent of your money is in stocks or equity mutual funds. Over the long run those assets will outperform bonds, though the dividend rate is far less than the interest rate on bonds. Anytime you are investing you have three goals: preservation of principal, growth of principal, and income. The more you seek one, the more you have to give up of the others, so a balanced approach is generally best.

> I think I'll be OK if I keep my principal intact and spend only the income that it generates. (Quentin R., age fifty-nine)

Many clients who come to us feel as Quentin does. That strategy seems safe to them, but unfortunately, the strategy has problems. To generate enough income, you will tend to invest in assets that produce higher income, sacrificing the growth of principal. Without principal growth, and with continuing inflation, the income generated from your investments will not keep up with inflation. That means that you will probably end up with a lower standard of living over the next fifty years than the one you enjoy today.

A modern variation of the strategy of keeping your principal intact is to spend your total return from the investments, preserving your principal. For example, if your $500,000 retirement portfolio is up 15 percent one year, you'll be able to draw $75,000 for your living expenses. But if your portfolio earns only 5 percent the next year, you'll have only $25,000 with which to cover your expenses. Sure, you'll keep the dollar value of your principal intact, but because your total return will be high in some years and low or even nonexistent in others, you will be eating caviar one year and pork and beans the next.

If you are intent on preserving your capital, you might try this strategy: Allocate your investments in a diversified portfolio that will maximize returns and minimize risk (see chapter 4), and then withdraw 8 to 10 percent each year. In some years your portfolio will decrease, and in some years it will increase. Assuming that your long-term return is at least 8 to 10 percent, over time you will find that your capital stays intact or even grows.

Here's an example, based on the S&P 500 total return for the years 1973 through 1996. In the chart on page 246, we have assumed that the retiree withdrew 10 percent of the account balance each year. In years in which the S&P 500 declined, the retiree drew less, and in years in which it grew, the retiree withdrew more. Over the years, the retiree was able to draw out more than was in the account to begin with, and still ended up with more than he started with.

Year	*Account Balance*	*Withdrawal at 10%*	*S&P 500 Total Return*
1973	$100,000	$10,000	−14.7%
1974	75,300	7,530	−26.5
1975	47,816	4,782	37.2
1976	60,821	6,082	23.8
1977	69,215	6,921	−7.2
1978	57,310	5,731	6.6
1979	55,361	5,536	18.4
1980	60,012	6,001	32.4
1981	73,454	7,345	−4.9
1982	62,509	6,251	21.4
1983	69,636	6,964	22.5
1984	78,340	7,834	6.3
1985	75,441	7,544	31.0
1986	91,284	9,128	18.7
1987	99,226	9,923	5.2
1988	94,463	9,446	16.6
1989	100,698	10,070	31.7
1990	122,549	12,255	−3.1
1991	106,495	10,650	30.5
1992	128,326	12,833	7.7
1993	125,375	12,537	10.1
1994	125,500	12,550	1.3
1995	114,582	11,458	37.5
1996	146,092	14,609	23.0
		$213,980	

Most people who espouse these strategies are not really concerned about preserving their capital for their heirs; they're just afraid that they might outlive their capital, so they want to keep it intact. It's the same principle as having a fifty-dollar bill in your wallet. As soon as you break it, even if it's only to pay for a package of gum, the rest of it seems to disappear and you are left with nothing. As long as you don't tap any of it, you know you'll always have that fifty dollars.

But no one lives forever, and so the trick is to make your money last as long as you might. That means you can increase your spending without ever running out of money. For example, if you increase your spending so that your money is exhausted by the time you are 110, the chances are excellent that you will not exhaust the money during your lifetime, unless you live to be 115 or 120.

If you are spending both income and principal each year, each year you will be liquidating some of your investments. If you find that the market has slumped, which is called a bear market, it is important to have enough money set aside so that you can wait until prices begin to rise again. Most bear markets last only a year or two, so if you keep enough money in a money market fund or in short-term bonds or CDs, you'll be able to ride out a bear market. As you draw money from the money market fund, replenish it by periodically selling shares in your stock and bond funds. You will probably do this as a regular part of your asset rebalancing.

Rebalancing Investments in Retirement

Once you reach retirement age, rebalancing your portfolio may be tricky, particularly if many of your assets are invested in IRAs. For example, if you have several IRAs with different mutual fund companies, it can get complicated to withdraw money from one IRA and transfer it to another. You must do this correctly and within the appropriate amount of time to avoid being taxed on the distribution. There are two ways to accomplish the rebalancing hassle-free. One way is to put most or all of your IRA investments with the same family of mutual funds. In that way you will be able to transfer from fund to fund within the same family. The other way of handling the problem is to have the mutual fund take care of it. You will ask the mutual fund to which you want to transfer money to withdraw the money from the transferring mutual fund. Once you have instructed the mutual fund that will receive the money to take care of the matter, they will do so without further input from you. For example, let's say that you want to transfer $5,000 from Fidelity Magellan fund to Vanguard Intermediate Bond fund. You merely tell Vanguard to take care of the matter. They will provide you the necessary form.

If your money is in both taxable accounts and IRAs, be careful when rebalancing. Each time you make a sale in a taxable account and transfer the money to another account, you will end up with a taxable transaction. If the money has been there for some time, you probably paid far less for it than you sold it for. The profit is taxable, and that could result in a large capital gain for you. This is true even if you transfer within the same family of funds.

There are two ways to rebalance and not incur capital gains taxes. If you are planning to invest additional funds, don't make any transfers. Instead, invest the new money in the account that needs to be shored up. If you are not investing new money, evaluate your portfolio as a whole, including both taxable and IRA investments. Then do the rebalancing from fund to fund within the IRAs, leaving the rest of your portfolio intact.

For example, assume you want to end up with equal amounts in each of four funds. Your current investments are as follows:

	IRA	*Non-IRA*	*Total*
Intermediate Bond Fund	$40,000	$50,000	$90,000
Growth Stock Fund	80,000	50,000	130,000
Income Fund	60,000	50,000	110,000
International Stock Fund	70,000		70,000
	$250,000	$150,000	$400,000

To rebalance so that each account equals $100,000, you must add $10,000 to the bond fund and $30,000 to the international stock fund, selling $30,000 of the growth stock fund and $10,000 of the income fund. Make these transfers within the IRA accounts and you will not incur any taxes on the sale, since all transactions within IRA accounts are not taxable.

If you need money to live on during the coming six months to a year, also consider rebalancing by selling assets needed to fund your expenses for the forthcoming year. That money can be transferred to a savings account and will be available for your use. Since you would have had to sell assets anyway to fund your living expenses, your taxes won't be any higher than they would have been without rebalancing.

For example, if you will need $40,000 for living expenses during the coming year, transfer that from your investments to your money market fund and you will end up with $360,000 invested. To rebalance your portfolio so that you have $90,000 in each account, withdraw $40,000 from the non-IRA funds that have the least amount of gain, probably the bond fund. Then make transfers within the IRA funds so that you end up with $90,000 in each type of fund.

Reverse Mortgages

Many retirees find that their income falls short of their needs after a number of years because of inflation. But inflation has a good side too. They may discover that the value of their homes continues to grow year after year. So they are richer on paper while poorer in their pocket. That is why the reverse mortgage was created.

A reverse mortgage is a handy way of getting payments from your house after all those years of making payments. To qualify for a reverse mortgage, your home should be free of debt or your mortgage should be very low. Your income level is not an issue, but your age is. The older you are, the more you can borrow, since your life expectancy will be less, and that determines the loan term. Under a reverse mortgage, you can borrow a lump sum or receive monthly payments for as long as you live in the house. Once you die or sell the house, the loan will need to be repaid.

The amount that you receive is based on a formula that includes your life expectancy, the home's market value, and any underlying indebtedness. When your home is sold, the loan will be repaid along with interest. If you apply for a reverse mortgage, expect to pay closing costs of several thousand dollars. So that you can compare the options offered by various lenders, each lender is required to tell you the total costs you will incur if you live in your home for two years, your actuarial life expectancies, or 40 percent longer than your life expectancy. This information will help you shop for the best deal.

What if after your death, your heirs sell your property and the total amount due the lender exceeds the amount that comes out of the property? Too bad for the lender. With a reverse mortgage, you and your heirs are guaranteed that the loan will never cost more than the value of your home. Because of that provision, you can expect to pay an insurance premium that will protect the lender against such a loss.

A word of caution: If you move to a nursing home, the consequences can be devastating. Unless you have specified provisions to the contrary, the loan will probably come due immediately, which means that your home will have to be sold in order to pay back the loan.

To get a list of reverse-mortgage lenders throughout the country, send a self-addressed, stamped envelope to Reverse Mortgage Locator,

National Center for Home Equity Conversion, 7373 147th Street W., Suite 115, Apple Valley, MN 55124.

Ten Steps to Keep Your Nest Egg Growing

When you are about to retire, you will likely find that your nest egg represents more money than you've had at any other time in your life. Over the course of your retirement you'll have to make many financial decisions, and making wrong choices could mean hefty tax consequences or a significant loss over time. Here are ten steps you can take to keep your nest egg growing during retirement.

1. **Think long term.** If you still have ten or more years to provide for your retirement needs, invest at least a portion of your assets in longer-term, growth-oriented investments, such as stock mutual funds. Subtract your age from one hundred to compute the minimum percentage of growth-oriented investments you should own.

2. **Send your pension to your IRA.** Uncle Sam will take 20 percent of a lump-sum distribution as withholding if you take your distribution in cash, before you even see the check. To defer taxes, have the pension plan administrator send the money directly to your IRA. There will be no withholding, and you can draw money from your IRA as you need it and defer paying taxes on the rest.

3. **Anticipate the rising cost of living.** Inflation won't retire when you do. When you were working, periodic raises made up for inflation, but now you'll have to depend on the growth of your nest egg to keep up with increasing costs. Stocks historically have been one of the best weapons for fighting the effects of inflation.

4. **Don't put all of your eggs in one investment basket.** To minimize risk, maintain a diversified investment mix, shifting periodically among stocks, bonds, and CDs as your needs change. A family of mutual funds will allow you to transfer money from one fund to another with ease, to maintain the diversity you need.

5. **Don't tap your retirement income too soon.** Some retirees go on a spending spree as soon as they retire, and they regret it later. Delay withdrawing money for as long as you can. The longer you can build up your retirement assets tax-deferred, the better.

6. Put off taking Social Security benefits. Two-thirds of retirees begin taking reduced Social Security benefits before they are sixty-five to sixty-seven years old. But early benefits can be costly over time, particularly if you live to be more than eighty. If you wait until you are sixty-five to sixty-seven to receive benefits, you'll get at least 20 percent more each year than if you do so at sixty-two.

7. Don't rely on Medicare for long-term care. Convalescent expenses can smash your nest egg. Medicare coverage for nursing homes is limited to 150 days and is paid only if admission to a nursing home follows a hospital stay. Evaluate your family medical history, adult-care facilities, and home-health-care costs in your area to determine your need for long-term-care insurance.

8. Assume that taxes will be with you in retirement. Unless you plan to reduce substantially your standard of living in retirement, it's likely you'll still face a considerable tax burden. Consider tax-advantaged investments such as municipal bond funds to reduce your taxable investment income.

9. Put your estate plan in order. It is likely you need more than a simple will to protect your estate. Consider living trusts to avoid probate and variable annuities or life insurance to pass assets automatically to your heirs. Charitable trusts can also reduce estate taxes when you die.

10. Get regular investment checkups. Financial checkups are just as important as medical checkups, to make sure that your portfolio is functioning properly and working hard enough to meet your goals. Periodic checkups can prevent future financial problems.

A Final Word

As you journey through your next fifty years, you can be sure that the rules of retirement will change many times. Your retirement won't be like your parents', but then baby boomers have always blazed new trails, haven't they? You may retire early or keep on working. You may decide to build a large nest egg now so that you can stop saving, let your nest egg grow, and spend everything you make in the meantime. Or you may decide to save very little now and take frequent sabbaticals instead of prolonged retirement, returning to the workplace each time with renewed energy. Perhaps you will even opt for a traditional retirement in your mid- to late sixties, having saved a tidy sum to get you through to age one hundred or beyond.

Worksheet 12.1

WHAT IS TRUE FOR YOU?

	T	F
1. I've done a retirement projection and determined the amount of investment and savings necessary to produce the income stream I want.	_____	_____
2. I'll most likely change my investment mix to 60 to 80 percent in bonds when I retire.	_____	_____
3. The years until retirement as well as the years after retirement until death are included in my planning.	_____	_____
4. I rarely consider the worst case scenario when I make investments.	_____	_____
5. I'm sure I have the right mix of growth and fixed-income investments in my 401(k).	_____	_____
6. When I change jobs or retire, the funds I receive from my 401(k) will help pay down my current debt, thereby reducing my expenses and income needs during retirement.	_____	_____
7. The 401(k) plan I have at work is excellent and gives me the opportunity to save.	_____	_____
8. Borrowing from my 401(k) plan makes sense because I am earning the interest someone else would on the loan.	_____	_____
9. The maximum contribution I am allowed to make to my retirement plan is what I aim for.	_____	_____
10. In my 401(k), I buy as much of my company's stock as I can.	_____	_____
11. I've given a lot of thought to the capital gains exclusion and how that impacts me when I sell my home.	_____	_____
12. Buying more stocks on margin in my IRA makes sense if I'm confident about the market's potential.	_____	_____
13. I believe my parents are in good shape financially and do not need my help.	_____	_____
14. It's important to support my grown children and other family members financially.	_____	_____
15. We'll tap into our personal stock and bond accounts before we begin to use our retirement accounts.	_____	_____

No matter what your decision regarding retirement—and you can change that decision next week or next year—the important thing is to start planning in earnest. Now that you've finished this book, let's have a reality check. Take a moment to answer the questions on Worksheet 12.1, page 252, marking the first response that comes to mind.

Now check your answers. If the odd-numbered questions were true for you and the even numbered false, you are off to a great start. If some of your answers were marked differently, that does not necessarily mean you are wrong. Please think about the rationale behind the question and perhaps refer to the section of the book where we discuss that issue. The questions you've just answered can serve as a barometer to indicate the kinds of conditions you're likely to encounter ahead.

As we wrote this book, we thought about retirement a great deal. We talked to our clients and to each other about retirement and we realized that each person's version of retirement is a little different. Some of us get so much satisfaction from what we do, we hope we'll never have to retire. Others, even though they enjoy their current occupation, look forward to time in which they can expand their horizons, learn new skills, travel and think and write and draw and just plain *live.* And others are simply working to live and can hardly wait to kiss the rat race good-bye forever.

As we've talked with people about retirement, we have formulated some important advice we'd like to pass on to you:

Match your wealthspan to your lifespan. Easier said than done, you're thinking. We agree, but that's the essence of what we have tried to get across here. Investing appropriately for growth first, income second; taking full advantage of all retirement plans you have; and not borrowing against or otherwise consuming 401(k) distributions are just a few ways you'll increase your wealthspan.

Complete your life before you retire. Another way to say this is, forget the boxes. We have tended to compartmentalize education, work, and leisure as different phases of our lives. It's time to include all three as much as possible in your current lifestyle. Postponing pleasures until you retire is not the best way to live. Do what you can now to complete your life and to increase your enjoyment before you retire.

Ease your way into retirement. Change your attitude toward your life today, and you will bring the essence of retirement into your current life. In that way, you can integrate that retirement attitude into your everyday life, and that will give you a completely new viewpoint.

Think of retirement as a journey, not an event. You will find that retirement ceases to be an event to anticipate and becomes rather a journey through the final fifty years of your life. As you journey deeper into retirement, you will find more avenues to explore, roads to take you had not anticipated, and opportunities to delve into corners of life you had never expected.

We are following our own advice as we ease our way into retirement. Having retired at age forty from a large, stressful CPA practice, Ginita chose to return to work as a financial adviser specializing in life transitions. Still an active professional, Ginita sees giving up the major portion of her consulting practice one day yet continuing to counsel individuals experiencing transitions, perhaps on a volunteer basis. But she says she'll never give up the writing career she dreamed of for her retirement years. Fortunately, she began a few years ago to complete her life by integrating her writing and her retirement dreams into her current activities.

Victoria, satisfied and happy in her career, realizes at times that the pace is too hectic to allow for any personal space. When the pressures of a demanding job increase, so do her fantasies of a sabbatical or even just a day or two off. With children and grandchildren important as well as a love of travel, she is learning how to integrate all into her schedule through delegation and working smarter, not harder. Someday she may want to leave her position as an investment counselor, but for now she has captured a great deal of the essential quality she was seeking in retirement.

It is time for you to think carefully about your retirement and to distinguish your true retirement dreams from your ideas of traditional retirement. Deconstruct your retirement, then reinvent your retirement. Whether you decide to continue working, take a lengthy sabbatical, or retire completely, be sure that the time between now and retirement is as fulfilling as it can be. Work toward your retirement attitude as you plan for your retirement.

Whether your retirement is near or far away, always remember that your retirement dreams are possible with a little planning. And the more you save, the greater will be your options.

Wherever your next fifty years may lead you, we hope this book will be a guide.

Additional Resources

Glossary of Investment Terms
Recommended Reading
Retirement-Planning Software
Where to Find It: Asset Location Inventory

• • • • • • • • •

Glossary of Investment Terms

Accrued Interest. Interest due on a bond that has not yet been paid. If you buy a bond halfway between interest payment dates, for example, you must pay the seller for the interest accrued but not yet received. You get the money back, tax-free, when you receive the interest payment for the entire period.

American Depository Receipt (ADR). An easy way to add foreign stocks to your portfolio, these certificates are traded on the New York Stock Exchange and represent ownership of a specific number of shares of a foreign company.

Annuity. A tax-favored investment that generates a series of regular payments guaranteed to continue for a specific time (usually the recipient's lifetime) in exchange for a single payment or a series of payments. With a deferred annuity, payments begin sometime in the future. With an immediate annuity, payments begin immediately. A fixed annuity pays a fixed income stream for the life of the contract. With a variable annuity, the payments may change according to how successfully the money is invested.

Beta. A measure of risk or how volatile the price of an individual stock or mutual fund is compared with the market as a whole. A stock or fund with a beta higher than one is expected to move up or down more rapidly than the market average. A beta below one indicates less price fluctuation than the market in general.

Bid/Asked. The price a buyer is willing to pay for a security is the bid; the price the seller will take is the ask. The difference, known as the spread, is the broker's share of the transaction. On small, thinly traded stocks, you can expect larger spreads.

Blue Chip. A stock that is issued by a well-known, respected company, has a good record of earnings and dividend payments, and is widely held by investors.

Bond. A security that pays interest for a specified time, usually several years, and then repays the bondholder the face amount of the bond. Bonds issued by corporations are backed by corporate assets, and in case of default, bondholders have a legal claim on those assets. When government agencies issue bonds, they may or may not be collateralized.

Bond Rating. An analysis by an independent firm (such as Standard & Poor's or Moody's) of a bond issuer's ability to honor its promise to pay interest on schedule and repay the bond principal when due.

Book Value. One of the indicators investors use in evaluating a stock. The value of a company's net assets (total assets minus all liabilities) divided by total outstanding shares gives you the stock's book value per share. If a stock is selling a low multiple of book value relative to similar companies, it may be a bargain.

Capital Gain or Loss. The profit or loss that results when investments such as stocks, bonds, mutual funds, and real estate are sold—the difference between the price paid and the selling price. When the asset has been held for more than one year, the gain or loss is said to be long term. When assets have been held one year or less, the result is said to be short term.

Certificate of Deposit (CD). A savings instrument issued by a commercial bank, savings and loan, savings bank, or credit union. CDs are issued for a specified period of time, usually for a fixed interest rate. Terms generally range from six months to five years, and there is usually a penalty for early withdrawal.

Closed-End Fund. A type of mutual fund or investment company that issues a set number of shares and trades like other stocks on one of the stock exchanges. You may buy these funds at a discount or at a premium.

Common Stock. Ownership in a U.S. corporation is most often through common stock. Owners of common stock are entitled to all of the risks and rewards that go with owning a piece of the company. *See also* PREFERRED STOCK.

Convertible Bond. This special type of bond can be exchanged, or converted, into a set number of common stock shares of the issuing company. The choice of when to convert is up to the bond owner. The appeal of a convertible bond is that it gives you a chance to cash in if the stock price of the company soars.

Discount Broker. A brokerage firm that executes orders to buy and sell stocks, bonds, and mutual funds at lower transaction costs but provides little if anything in the way of research or other investment assistance.

Dividend. A share of company earnings paid out quarterly to stockholders, usually in cash but sometimes in the form of additional shares of stock.

Dividend Reinvestment Plan. Also called DRIPs, these are programs under which the company automatically reinvests a shareholder's cash dividends in additional shares of common stock, often with no brokerage charge to the shareholder. Great for small investors or to build a nest egg over time.

Dollar-Cost Averaging. This strategy calls for investing a set amount of money on a regular schedule, regardless of the share price at the time. In the long run, dollar-cost averaging results in your buying more shares at low prices than you do at high prices.

Earnings per Share. A company's profits after taxes, bond interest, and preferred stock payments have been subtracted, divided by the number of shares of common stock outstanding.

Ex-Dividend. The period between the declaration of a dividend by a company or a mutual fund and the actual payment of the dividend. On the ex-dividend date, the price of the stock or fund will fall by the amount of the dividend, so new investors don't get the benefit of it. Companies and funds that have "gone ex-dividend" are marked by an X in the newspaper listings.

Fixed-Income Investment. A catch-all description for investments in bonds, CDs, and similar instruments that pay a fixed amount of interest.

Foreign Stock. Shares of companies based outside the United States. Stocks of many British, German, and Japanese companies trade in the form of American depository receipts on the U.S. stock exchanges and can make good additions to a diversified investment portfolio. Foreign stocks can also be purchased conveniently and cost effectively through international mutual funds.

401(k) Plan. An employer-sponsored retirement plan that permits employees to divert part of their pay into the plan and avoid current taxes on that income. Money directed to the plan may be partially matched by the employer, and investment earnings within the plan accumulate tax-free until they are withdrawn, presumably at retirement. The 401(k) is named for the section of the federal tax code that authorizes it. The 403(b) plan is similar, but set up for public employees and employees of nonprofit organizations.

Full-Service Broker. A brokerage firm that maintains a research department and other services designed to supply its individual and institutional customers with investment advice. Commission rates are higher than those of discount brokers.

Ginnie Mae. A dual-purpose acronym that stands for both the Government National Mortgage Association (GNMA) and the mortgage-backed securities that this government agency packages, guarantees, and sells to investors.

Guaranteed Investment Contract (GIC). An investment product issued by an insurance company that works like a giant CD but without federal deposit insurance. The contracts generally run one to seven years. Managers of 401(k) plans often put many GICs together into a fund and offer this investment to plan participants.

Individual Retirement Account (IRA). A tax-sheltered account ideal for retirement investing because it permits investment earnings to accumulate untaxed until they are withdrawn. The individual contribution limit is $2,000 a year, and penalties usually apply for withdrawals before age fifty-nine and a half. All or part of the contribution may be tax deductible.

Initial Public Offering (IPO). The first public sale of stock by a company to investors. Such offerings are generally high-risk investments not suitable for most retirement portfolios.

Institutional Investors. Pension plans, mutual funds, banks, insurance companies, and other institutions that buy and sell large quantities of stocks and bonds. Institutional investors account for 70 percent or more of market volume on an average day.

Junk Bond. A high-risk, high-yield bond rated BB or lower by Standard & Poor's, Ba or lower by Moody's, or not rated at all by any agency. Junk bonds are generally issued by relatively unknown or financially weak companies.

Keogh Plan. A tax-sheltered retirement plan for the self-employed. Up to 20 percent of self-employment income can be diverted into a Keogh, and contributions can be deducted from taxable income. Earnings in the account grow tax-free until the money is withdrawn, and there are restrictions on tapping the account before age fifty-nine and a half.

Liquidity. The ability to quickly convert an investment to cash without suffering a noticeable loss in value. Stocks and bonds of widely traded companies are considered highly liquid. Real estate and limited partnerships are illiquid.

Load. There are two basic types: front end and back end. A front-end load is a fee (sales commission) charged when you purchase a mutual fund, insurance policy, or other investment product. A back-end load is a commission charged to mutual fund investors who sell their shares in the fund before owning them for a specified time, often five years. True *no-load* mutual funds charge neither fee.

Margin Buying. Financing the purchase of securities partly with money borrowed from the brokerage firm. Regulations permit buying stock up to 50 percent "on margin," meaning an investor can borrow up to half the purchase price of an investment.

Money Market Fund. A mutual fund that invests in short-term corporate and government debt and passes the interest payments on to shareholders. A key feature of money market funds is that share value doesn't change, making them an ideal place to earn current market interest with a high degree of liquidity.

Mutual Fund. A professionally managed pool of stocks and bonds or other investments divided into shares and sold to investors. Minimum purchase is often $500 or less. An *open-end* mutual fund continues issuing shares as investors send more money and stands ready to buy back shares at any time. The market price of the fund's shares, called the net-asset value, fluctuates daily with the market price of the securities in its portfolio. A *closed-end* fund issues a specified number of shares, and those shares then trade in the stock market just like other stocks. The price may be higher (called selling at a "premium") than the net-asset value of the stocks or bonds in the fund's portfolio, or it may be lower (a "discount").

NASDAQ. (Pronounced Naz-dak.) The acronym for the National Association of Securities Dealers Automated Quotations System, a computerized price-reporting system used by brokers to track over-the-counter stocks. Basically the Nasdaq system is the over-the-counter market. The largest and most actively traded stocks are listed in the Nasdaq National Market System.

Opportunity Cost. The cost of passing up one investment in favor of another. If the investment you choose outperforms the one you passed up, your opportunity cost is zero. If the one you passed up does better, however, your opportunity cost is the difference between the two choices.

Over-the-Counter (OTC) Market. Where stocks and bonds that aren't listed on the New York Stock Exchange (NYSE) or American Stock Exchange (ASE) are bought and sold. The OTC market is a high-speed computerized network called Nasdaq, which is run by the National Association of Securities Dealers. *See* NASDAQ.

Par. The face value of a stock or bond. Also called par value.

Penny Stocks. Generally, these are stocks selling for less than five dollars a share and traded over the counter. Penny stocks are usually issued by tiny, unknown companies and are lightly traded, making them more prone to price manipulation than larger, better-established issues. They are very high risk and not appropriate for a retirement nest egg.

Preferred Stock. A class of stock that pays a specified dividend set when it is issued. Preferred stocks generally pay less income than do bonds of the same company and don't have the price-appreciation potential of common stock. They appeal mainly to corporations, which get a tax break on their dividend income.

Price-Earnings Ratio (P/E). The price of a stock divided by either its latest annual earnings per share (a "trailing" P/E) or its predicted earnings (an "anticipated" or "forward" P/E). The P/E is an important indicator of investor sentiment about a stock because it suggests how much investors are willing to pay for a dollar of earnings. Stock listings in the *Wall Street Journal* include the P/E. A P/E above the market average indicates a stock that investors feel has strong growth potential and that sentiment has already pushed the price of the stock up.

Price-Sales Ratio (PSR). The stock's price divided by its company's latest annual sales per share. It is favored by some investors as a measure of a stock's relative value. The lower the PSR, according to this school of thought, the better the value.

Prospectus. A detailed document that describes the operations of a mutual fund, a stock offering, insurance annuity, limited partnership, or other investment. The prospectus reveals financial data about the company, background of its officers, and other information needed by investors to make an informed decision. It is required by federal securities laws.

Real Estate Investment Trust (REIT). A closed-end investment company that buys real estate properties or mortgages and passes virtually all of the profits on to its shareholders. REIT shares trade like stock on the New York Stock Exchange and other stock exchanges and offer a convenient way for small investors to add a real estate component to their investment portfolio.

Registered Representative. The formal name for a stockbroker, so called because he or she must be registered with the National Association of Securities Dealers as qualified to handle securities trades.

Return on Equity (ROE). A key measure of a corporation's investment results. ROE is calculated by dividing the total value of shareholders' equity—that is, the market value of common stock and preferred stock—into the company's net income after taxes.

Spread. Basically, this is a stockbroker's markup on a stock or bond. It is the difference between the bid and asked prices of a security.

10-K. A detailed financial report that must be filed with the Securities and Exchange Commission (SEC) each year by all companies whose shares are publicly traded. It is much more detailed than a typical annual report and can be obtained from the company or from the SEC.

Total Return. An investment performance measurement that combines two components: any change in the price of the shares, and any dividends or other distributions paid to shareholders over the period being measured. For example, the total return on a utility stock that rose 4 percent over a year and that paid a dividend of 6 percent (calculated as a percentage of your original investment) would be 10 percent.

12b-1-Fees. Fees charged by some mutual funds to cover the costs of promotion and marketing. Such fees reduce a fund's overall return to investors.

Yield. In general, the annual cash return earned by a stock, bond, mutual fund, real estate investment trust, or other investment. A stock yield is its annual dividend calculated as a percentage of the share price. For example, a stock priced at fifty dollars per share and paying an annual dividend of three dollars per share would have a yield of 6 percent. Bond yields can take several forms. *Coupon yield* is the interest rate paid on the face value of the bond (usually $1,000). *Current yield* is the interest rate based on the actual purchase price of the bond, which may be higher or lower. *Yield to maturity* is the rate that takes into account the current yield and the difference between the purchase price and the face value, with the difference assumed to be amortized over the remaining life of the bond.

Zero-Coupon Bond. A type of bond that pays interest only when the bond matures. Zeros sell at a deep discount to face value. For example, a $10,000 zero yielding 7.5 percent and maturing in twenty years would sell initially for about $2,350, with the investor receiving the full $10,000 twenty years later.

Recommended Reading

BOOKS

Chapter 1

Craig S. Karpel, *The Retirement Myth: What You Must Know to Prosper in the Coming Meltdown of Job Security, Pension Plans, Social Security, the Stock Market, Housing Prices, and More* (New York: HarperCollins, 1995).

Chapter 2

Victoria Felton-Collins with Suzanne Brown, *Couples and Money: Why Money Interferes with Love and What to Do About It* (New York: Bantam Books, 1990).

Chapter 3

Michael J. Gelb, *Thinking for a Change: Discovering the Power to Create, Communicate and Lead* (New York: Harmony Books, 1995).

Carol Keeffe, *How to Get What You Want in Life with the Money You Already Have* (Boston: Little, Brown, 1995).

Barbara Sher, *I Could Do Anything . . . If Only I Knew What It Was: How to Discover What You Really Want and How to Get It* (New York: Dell, 1994).

Chapter 4

Nancy Dunnan, *Dun and Bradstreet Guide to Your Investments* (New York: HarperCollins, 1996).

Thomas Gardner and David Gardner, *The Motley Fool Investment Guide* (New York: Simon & Schuster, 1996).

Janet Lowe, *Value Investing Made Easy: Benjamin Graham's Classic Investment Strategy Explained for Everyone* (New York: McGraw-Hill, 1996).

Martin J. Pring, *Investment Psychology Explained: Classic Strategies to Beat the Markets* (New York: John Wiley and Sons, 1993).

Ginita Wall, *The Way to Invest: A Five-Step Blueprint for Growing Your Money Through Mutual Funds with as Little as $50 Per Month* (New York: Henry Holt, 1995).

John F. Wasek, *The Investment Club Book* (New York: Warner Books, 1995).

Chapter 5

Lynn Brenner, *Building Your Nest Egg with Your 401(k)* (Washington, D.C.: Investors Press, 1995).

Karen Ferguson and Kate Blackwell, *The Pension Book* (New York: Arcade, 1995).

Peter Gaudio and Virginia S. Nicols, *Your Retirement Benefits* (New York: John Wiley and Sons, 1992).

Robert K. Otterbourg, *Kiplinger's Retire and Thrive: Remarkable People Share Their Creative, Productive and Profitable Retirement Strategies* (Washington, D.C.: Kiplinger Books, 1995).

Chapter 6

J. Robin Powell, *The Working Woman's Guide to Managing Stress* (Englewood Cliffs, N.J.: Prentice Hall, 1994).

Carole Sinclair, *When Women Retire: The Problems They Face and How to Solve Them* (New York: Crown Books, 1994).

Deborah J. Swiss, *Women Breaking Through: Overcoming the Final 10 Obstacles at Work* (Princeton, N.J.: Peterson's/Pacesetter Books, 1996).

Chapter 7

John Howells, *Retirement on a Shoestring* (Oakland, Calif.: Gateway Books, 1995).

Brett Machtig, *Wealth in a Decade: System for Creating Wealth, Living Off Your Investments and Attaining a Financially Secure Life* (Burr Ridge, Ill.: Irwin, 1997).

Ginita Wall, *The Way to Save: A 10-Step Blueprint for Lifetime Security* (New York: Henry Holt, 1993).

Chapter 8

Richard Nelson Bolles, *What Color Is Your Parachute?* (Berkeley, Calif.: Ten Speed Press, 1996).

Peter C. Brown, *Jumping the Job Track: Security, Satisfaction, & Success as An Independent Consultant* (New York: Crown, 1994).

Hope Deligozima, James Scott, and David Sharp, *Six Months Off: How to Plan, Negotiate and Take the Break You Need Without Burning Bridges or Going Broke* (New York: Henry Holt, 1996).

Joe Dominguez and Vicki Robin, *Your Money or Your Life* (New York: Penguin, 1992).

Paul Edwards and Sarah Edwards, *Finding Your Perfect Work: The New Career Guide to Making a Living, Creating a Life* (New York: G. P. Putnam's Sons, 1996).

Duane Elgin, *Voluntary Simplicity* (New York: Quill, 1993).

Mary Hunt, *The Cheapskate Monthly Money Makeover: Break Free from Money Worries Forever, Without Sacrificing Your Quality of Life* (New York: St. Martin's Press, 1995).

Azriela Jaffe, *Honey, I Want to Start My Own Business: A Planning Guide for Couples* (New York: HarperCollins, 1996).

Richard Poe, *Wave 3: The New Era in Network Marketing* (Rocklin, Calif.: Prima, 1995).

Bill Radin, *Breakaway Careers: The Self-Employment Resource for Freelancers, Consultants and Corporate Refugees* (Franklin Lakes, N.J.: Career Press, 1994).

Arthur Robertson and William Proctor, *Work a 4-Hour Day: Achieving Business Efficiency on Your Own Terms* (New York: Avon Books, 1994).

Ellen St. James, *Living the Simple Life* (New York: Hyperion Press, 1996).

Grace W. Weinstein, *Financial Savvy for the Self-Employed* (New York: Henry Holt, 1995).

Chapter 9

Alexandra Armstrong and Mary Donahue, *On Your Own: A Widow's Passage to Emotional and Financial Well-Being* (Chicago, Ill.: Dearborn Financial Publishing, 1993).

Patricia Scheff Estess, *Money Advice for Your Successful Remarriage* (Cincinnati, Ohio: Betterway Books, 1996).

Toni Ihara and Ralph Warner, *The Living Together Kit* (Berkeley, Calif.: NOLO Press, 1995).

Eva Shaw, *What to Do When a Loved One Dies* (Irvine, Calif.: Dickens Press, 1994).

Gail Sheehy, *New Passages: Mapping Your Life Across Time* (New York: Random House, 1995).

Ginita Wall and Victoria F. Collins, *Smart Ways to Save Money During and After Divorce* (Berkeley, Calif.: NOLO Press, 1994).

Violet Woodhouse and Victoria Felton-Collins with M. C. Blakeman, *Divorce and Money* (Berkeley, Calif.: NOLO Press, 1995).

Chapter 10

Seri Lise Doub, ed., *The World's Top Retirement Havens* (Baltimore: Agora, Inc., 1995).

Gary W. Eldred, *The 106 Common Mistakes Homebuyers Make (and How to Avoid Them)* (New York: John Wiley and Sons, 1994).

Seymour Goldberg, *J. K. Lasser's How to Pay Less Tax on Your Retirement Savings* (New York: Macmillan, 1995).

Joan Rattner Heilman, *Unbelievably Good Deals and Great Adventures That You Absolutely Can't Get Unless You're Over 50* (Chicago, Ill.: Contemporary Books, 1996).

William Molloy, *The Complete Home Buyer's Bible* (New York: John Wiley and Sons, 1996).

Wanda Urbanska and Frank Levering, *Moving to a Small Town: A Guidebook for Moving from Urban to Rural America* (New York: Simon & Schuster, 1996).

Chapter 11

Ben Baldwin, *The Complete Book of Insurance* (Burr Ridge, Ill.: Irwin, 1996).

Adriane G. Berg, *Gifting to People You Love: The Complete Family Guide to Making Gifts, Bequests, and Investments for Children* (New York: Newmarket, 1996).

Gerald M. Condon and Jeffrey L. Condon, *Beyond the Grave: The Right Way and the*

Wrong Way of Leaving Money to Your Children (and Others) (New York: Harper Business, 1995).

Harvey J. Platt, *Your Living Trust and Estate Plan: How to Maximize Your Family's Assets and Protect Your Loved Ones* (New York: Allworth Press, 1995).

Martin M. Shenkman, *The Complete Book of Trusts* (New York: John Wiley and Sons, 1993).

Chapter 12

Sia Arnason, Ellen Rosenzweig, and Andrew Koski, *The Legal Rights of the Elderly* (New York: Practising Law Institute, 1995).

Anthony Gallea, *The Lump Sum Handbook: Investment and Tax Strategies for a Secure Retirement* (Englewood Cliffs, N.J.: Prentice Hall, 1993).

Nancy Levitin, *Retirement Rights: The Benefits of Growing Older* (New York: Avon Books, 1994).

Suze Orman, *You've Earned It, Don't Lose It: Mistakes You Can't Afford to Make When You Retire* (New York: Newmarket, 1994).

Jack B. Root and Douglas L. Mortensen, *The 7 Secrets of Financial Success: How to Apply Time-Tested Principles to Create, Manage and Build Personal Wealth* (Homewood, Ill.: Irwin, 1996).

PAMPHLETS AND BOOKLETS

Before the Other Shoe Drops, by Penny Fall, is a twelve-page worksheet available for $3 from Penny Fall at Washington College, 300 Washington Avenue, Chestertown, MD 21620. All profits go to Washington College's annual fund.

These booklets are available from the Social Security Administration: *Understanding Social Security, How Work Affects Social Security Benefits,* and *How Your Retirement Benefit Is Figured.* To obtain these publications, call the Social Security Administration at 800-772-1213.

MAGAZINES

Retire with Money, from the editors of *Money* magazine, is a monthly newsletter that provides strategies and information that can help you maximize your wealth and live well in retirement. To subscribe, call 800-284-5300. Cost is $49.95 a year.

Tomorrow, from Bottomline. Monthly newsletter on a variety of topics for retirees or those considering retirement. Excellent quick-read format. Phone 800-753-8096. Cost is $49 a year.

• • • • • • • • • •

Retirement-Planning Software

While no computer can see the future, a computer can certainly help you plan for it. Today there are many excellent software packages for retirement planning.

In each case you will be asked to enter information on how much you're saving now, how much money you expect to need during each year of retirement, and so forth, and the program will ultimately tell you whether you are on track or falling short of your goals, and by how much. The programs provide guidance on recommended investment portfolios, based on your time horizon and risk tolerance.

These programs all require the use of many assumptions, some of which are difficult to estimate accurately. You will see that by simply changing the inflation rate a little or lowering your rate of return expectations, your end result will differ dramatically. Use all retirement-planning programs with caution!

Vanguard Retirement Manager is available in both Windows 3.1 and Mac versions and costs $29. This program lets the retired investor calculate how long the nest egg will last as one varies the size of withdrawals and future returns, and it helps one decide when to start collecting Social Security. To order, call 800-950-1971.

Fidelity's Thinkware is available on the Internet at www.Fidelity.com at location "Site News." Fidelity's software is certainly educational, but its sales pitch is somewhat stronger than Vanguard's. Offers five different sample portfolio mixes. For information on system requirements and to order, call 800-457-1768.

T. Rowe Price's Retirement Planning Kit costs $15, shipping included, and is available only in DOS. This is the only software to address the issue of whether to take your tax-deferred retirement money out in a lump sum versus over time, which almost always lowers your tax bill. (The other programs assume you take the money out over time.) For information on system requirements and to order, call 800-541-4041.

Price Waterhouse Retirement Planning System, $45 ("Lite" version is $19), is one of the easiest and most thorough planners. Call 800-752-6234.

Rich and Retired, by Data Tech, $59.95, is an extremely comprehensive program. The program scores high on ease of use, with various aids, including a Help Genie—an explanatory box offering additional information or instruction—on many screens. Call 800-556-7526.

Quicken Financial Planner, by Intuit, about $40, is a Windows-based product. This program is very easy to use. If you already use Quicken, Intuit's electronic-checkbook program, you can pull data out of Quicken directly into the planner. Call 800-446-8848.

Retire Ready, by Individual Software Inc., about $50, is a retirement guide and planner that addresses the health, financial, and lifestyle issues of retirees through a solutions-oriented approach. Call 800-822-3522.

No one software is perfect for everyone. The right choice depends on such factors as the depth of your planning needs and your comfort level with your computer.

• • • • • • • • •

Where to Find It: Asset Location Inventory

Name__________________________________ Date ____________
Employer ____
Social Security No. ____

Location of Records

A. Residence ____
Address

B. Safe deposit box ____
Number, Bank, Address

C. Office ____
Address

D. ____

E. ____

F. ____

Indicate code letter (A, B, C, etc.) from above at left of item below

ITEM	NOTES
____Will (original)	______________________________________
____Will (copy)	______________________________________
____Powers of attorney	______________________________________
____Burial instructions	______________________________________

____Cemetery plot deed ________________________________
____Special bequests ________________________________
____Trust agreements ________________________________
____Life insurance, group ________________________________
____Life insurance, individual ________________________________
____Other death benefits ________________________________
____Health insurance policy ________________________________
____Home owner's insurance policy________________________________
____Car insurance policies ________________________________
____Employment contracts________________________________
____Partnership agreements ________________________________
____List of checking and savings accounts________________________________
____Bank statements, canceled checks ________________________________
____Certificates of deposit ________________________________
____Checkbooks________________________________
____Savings passbooks________________________________
____Record of investments ________________________________
____Brokerage account records________________________________
____Stock, bond, and mutual fund certificates ________________________________
____Corporate retirement plans ________________________________
____Keogh and IRAs ________________________________
____Annuity contracts ________________________________
____Stock option and stock purchase plans________________________________
____Tax returns ________________________________
____Titles and deeds to real estate ________________________________
____Title insurance ________________________________
____Rental property records ________________________________
____Notes, loan agreements, and mortgages________________________________
____List of stored and loaned valuables ________________________________
____Auto ownership records ________________________________
____Birth certificates________________________________
____Citizenship papers ________________________________
____Military discharge papers ________________________________
____Marriage certificate ________________________________
____Divorce/separation papers ________________________________
____Safe deposit box key ________________________________

____

____

Index